FLAT PROTAGONISTS

FLAT PROTAGONISTS

A Theory of Novel Character

Marta Figlerowicz

OXFORD
UNIVERSITY PRESS

OXFORD
UNIVERSITY PRESS

Oxford University Press is a department of the University of Oxford. It furthers
the University's objective of excellence in research, scholarship, and education
by publishing worldwide. Oxford is a registered trade mark of Oxford University
Press in the UK and certain other countries.

Published in the United States of America by Oxford University Press
198 Madison Avenue, New York, NY 10016, United States of America.

Library of Congress Cataloging-in-Publication Data
Names: Figlerowicz, Marta author.
Title: Flat protagonists : a theory of novel character / Marta Figlerowicz.
Description: Oxford ; New York : Oxford University Press, 2016. |
Includes bibliographical references.
Identifiers: LCCN 2016018976 (print) | LCCN 2016039589 (ebook) |
ISBN 9780190496760 (cloth) | ISBN 9780190496777 (updf)
Subjects: LCSH: Fiction—History and criticism. |
Characters and characteristics in literature.
Classification: LCC PN3411 .F55 2016 (print) | LCC PN3411 (ebook) |
DDC 808.3/97—dc23
LC record available at https://lccn.loc.gov/2016018976

1 3 5 7 9 8 6 4 2
Printed by Sheridan Books, Inc., United States of America

A version of chapter 1 initially appeared as "'Frightful Spectacles of a Mangled King':
Aphra Behn's *Oroonoko* and Narration Through Theater," *New Literary History* 39.2:
321–334; Copyright (c) 2008 New Literary History, The University of Virginia.

An early draft of chapter 2 initially appeared as "Rester femme, devenir personne:
l'externalisation dans les *Lettres de Mistriss Henley*," *Dix-huitième siècle* 42 (2011):
673–686. I thank both journals for their permission to reprint revised versions
of these essays.

To my sister Matylda

CONTENTS

ACKNOWLEDGMENTS

This book has benefited from the advice and support of many mentors and colleagues who responded to successive drafts of it over the years. Elaine Scarry first gave me the confidence to pursue these ideas, and Dorothy Hale pushed me to sharpen them considerably beyond what I could have imagined. Their mentorship and friendship have been a great and unexpected gift. Brendan O'Neill at Oxford University Press shepherded this manuscript toward publication with a patience and commitment for which I feel continued gratitude. Michael M. Weinstein, Ayesha Ramachandran, and my anonymous readers at Oxford University Press gave me amazing advice when I most needed it. Matylda Figlerowicz, Catherine Gallagher, Len Gutkin, Zachary Manfredi, and Daniel Williams read large portions of this book and offered much valuable feedback. Other colleagues and teachers who generously commented on this work include C. F. S. Creasy, James Engell, Philip Fisher, Jennifer Hudin, Christie McDonald, Jennifer Pranolo, John Searle, Janet Sorensen, Grace Tiao, and Katie Trumpener. I thank them all for their insights, challenges, and counterarguments. I also thank the students whom I taught at Yale in spring 2015—particularly Kyra Morris, Vaclav

Pinos, and Alec Pollak—for teaching me a great deal about Marcel Proust that I did not know before.

I thank my audiences at conferences and seminars at which I presented sections of this argument. These audiences include members of the Berkeley Social Ontology Group, the American Society for Eighteenth-Century Studies, the International Society for the Study of Narrative, the Departments of Comparative Literature and of English at Harvard, Yale, and UC Berkeley, and the Harvard Society of Fellows. Finally, I am grateful to the editors of *New Literary History* and *Dix-huitième siècle* both for their revision suggestions and for their permission to reprint here versions of articles I published with them.

Flat Protagonists stems from a series of essays I wrote at Harvard between 2006 and 2009. I continued to revise these essays, gradually turning them into a book manuscript, until the spring of 2016. I spent these intervening years at the University of California, Berkeley, Yale University, and the Harvard Society of Fellows. All three are vibrant intellectual communities whose rigor and intensity of engagement continue to astound me. Being a part of each of these communities has been life-changing, and they remain a constant source of inspiration for me. My particular thanks go to the editorial board of *Qui Parle: A Journal of the Humanities and Social Sciences*, which I feel extraordinarily lucky to have edited.

I thank Harvard College for the generous financial aid policy that allowed me to get a Harvard B.A. at no cost to my family or to myself—an expense we could not have otherwise afforded. I am also grateful for two Harvard College Undergraduate Research grants that I received, respectively, in 2007 and 2008, and which supported me as I developed the earliest versions of this project. I was able to continue my research at Berkeley thanks to a Mellon-Berkeley Fellowship for Graduate Studies (2009–2013), a Michele McNellis Fellowship for Graduate Studies (2009–2011), and a Dean's Normative Time Fellowship (2012–2013). Awards from the Harvard Society of

Fellows (2013–2016) and the Morse and Hilles Funds at Yale University (2015–2016) enabled me to prepare the final version of this manuscript for publication.

Finally, I could not properly convey my gratitude to the people whose love and friendship were present in my life while this project was taking shape. I thank my dear friends Simon, James, Sanders, Christopher, Daniel, Len, Scott, Padma, Ryan, Jill, Gaby, Chris and Michaela, Tim and Marijeta, Jackie and Alan, my parents Marek and Magdalena, and my sister Matylda. My partner Michael M. Weinstein is my most astute and constant interlocutor, and he knows he has all my love.

FLAT PROTAGONISTS

Introduction

In Marcel Proust's *In Search of Lost Time*, Charles Swann dramatically asks himself why his lover Odette has not yet written to him. Is she angry? Does she want to make him jealous? Swann wonders in long, arcane sentences that meander through an extensive catalogue of what Proust's narrator would call "all possible joys and sorrows."[1] Then—"as a matter of fact," the narrator counters abruptly, "she had not even given him a thought."[2]

Proust's juxtaposition of impassioned rumination and imagined disregard raises an important question for the novel as a genre. Can a represented world make present to its reader not only the breadth and depth of a character's relationships, but also the resurging indifference that, as Proust suggests, inevitably dilutes them? *Flat Protagonists* examines novels that represent the difficulty with which their protagonists attract and maintain other people's attention. These texts include Proust's *Search* as well as works by Thomas Hardy, Isabelle de Charrière, Aphra Behn, and Françoise de Graffigny. A novel, as these authors ironically suggest, has hardly

---

1. Marcel Proust, *In Search of Lost Time*, trans. C.K. Scott Moncrieff and Terence Kilmartin (New York: Modern Library, 1992), I.117. Translation modified. In the original, Proust phrases this as "tous les malheurs et tous les bonheurs possibles." *A la recherche du temps perdu* (Paris: Folio, 1992), I.84.
2. Proust, *In Search of Lost Time*, I.419. "C'est qu'elle n'avait même pas pensé à lui." Proust, *A la recherche du temps perdu*, I.290.

enough time and space to convey the oceanic placidity of the hours, days, months, and years that most of the planet spends without much conscious concern for any particular person's sensations and actions. Nor can a novel easily show how few and slender are the ties of care and attentiveness that bind each of us to people we care about and who care about us.

In such representations of their characters' mutual indifference, these novels aim for more than mere cynicism. Indeed, the works I examine are all deeply interested in processes of interpersonal awareness. They explore the experience of being, and understanding oneself as, the object of other people's attention. To be cared for by others, these novels suggest, is to be forced to recognize how many alternative, equally compelling objects of attention exist around oneself. It is also to discover how finite, in time and in space, are the resources with which one can respond to any outward act of admiration or concern.

All of these works, I argue, embrace a unique device to represent this sense of personal finitude: the *flat protagonist*. Flat protagonists are characters whose represented self-expression and ties to others contract and simplify over the course of a novel. The way they are depicted tends asymptotically toward what E.M. Forster describes as "flat" character construction. These protagonists come ever closer to seeming, as Forster puts it, to be "constructed around a single idea or quality" of limited sophistication and interest.[3] Their behaviors are increasingly stereotypical and predictable, and their means of responsiveness and expression progressively diminish, until other characters no longer even contradict, but simply disregard, what they say. At the same time, flat protagonists are also, against those odds,

---

3. By contrast, a round character, as described by Forster, "is capable of surprising in a convincing way. . . . It has the incalculability of life about it—life within the pages of a book." E.M. Forster, *Aspects of the Novel* (London: Mariner Books, 1956), 67.

protagonists: they are consistently framed as major characters, and no other represented person usurps this central place.

Alex Woloch defines character as "the intersection of an implied human personality—that is, as Dostoevsky says, 'infinitely' complex—with the definitively circumscribed form of a narrative."[4] The novels I examine invert this dynamic: they represent characters who, given their limited capacities, seem to have been given too much narrative space. Rather than wonder how much attention a narrative can maximally accord to a given character, these novels highlight how little a single character might be able to express even when accorded plentiful narrative attention. These novels' representations of such protagonists are haunted by the sense of a receding outer world that is ever more disconnected from the stories they tell, a world in which forgetting about these stories would be manifestly easy. To make this point, *Flat Protagonists* repeatedly reverses the mimetic assumptions with which critics approach the works of fiction I examine. I describe as "flat protagonists" many characters whom, for years, critics have unquestioningly perceived as deep—including the narrator of *In Search of Lost Time*.

The novels to which I draw attention are, arguably, outliers within their genre. In formal terms, they are expressions of an intense metatextual doubt about how much a novel can communicate through the representation of nothing more than a small group of fictional bodies and minds.[5] On an immediate level, I present these

---

4. Alex Woloch, *The One vs. the Many: Minor Characters and the Space of the Protagonist in the Novel* (Princeton, NJ: Princeton University Press, 2003), 13.

5. In this regard, my project dovetails with recent work done in cognitive literary studies, by critics such as Elaine Auyoung or Lisa Zunshine. I share with these critics the belief that readers' reported experiences of perceiving fictional worlds as rich and complete are not directly indicative of these represented worlds' objective qualities. Instead, they are subjective readerly experiences by whose occasional plausibility we ought to be puzzled. See, for example, Elaine Auyoung, "The Sense of Something More in Art and Experience," *Style* 44, no. 4 (2010): 547–565 or Lisa Zunshine, *Why We Read Fiction: Theory of Mind and the Novel* (Columbus: Ohio State University Press, 2006). Some older work done in this vein includes

particular works and their formal choices as exceptions to what realist novels typically take for granted and seek to achieve. To tie them
together, this project traverses several centuries, ranging from the
dawn of (proto-)psychological realism in the late seventeenth century to its zenith in the writings of Marcel Proust.

Even as I describe these novels as exceptions, I argue that they are
important to a broader understanding of their genre. They illustrate
critical insights that can come out of what is usually construed as the
novel's weakness: its incapacity to truly—though it aspires or pre-
tends to do so—represent the full span of real life. By drawing attention to the limitations of their characters as objects of other people's
interest, and to the narrow circumferences of their represented social
groups and communities, the novels I examine set in place a form
of "flat realism" whose aim is to reduce our expectations about how
much any particular person's self-expression interests or affects anybody else.[6] They suggest that the necessary finitude of a novel and of
its characters can ground a mode of critical reflection on human particularity as the experience of entertaining only a limited and inconsistent set of interpersonal relationships. These relationships seem

Richard Gerrig, *Experiencing Narrative Worlds: On the Psychological Activities of Reading*
(New Haven, CT: Yale University Press, 1993); Roman Ingarden, *Cognition of the Literary
Work of Art*, trans. Ruth Ann Crowley and Kenneth R. Olson (Evanston, IL: Northwestern
University Press, 1973); Wolfgang Iser, *The Act of Reading: A Theory of Aesthetic Response*
(Baltimore: Johns Hopkins University Press, 1978); Ruth Ronen, "Completing the
Incompleteness of Fictional Entities," *Poetics Today* 9 (1988): 497–514.

6. The novels I examine could, in this sense, be seen as predecessors and distant cousins of the
French *nouveau roman*. The *nouveau roman* critiques the constructedness, and not the finitude, of subjectivity; otherwise these two modes of critique, and their preoccupation with
conventional novels as means of upholding a false notion of personhood, are quite similar.
See, for example, Alain Robbe-Grillet, *For a New Novel*, trans. Richard Howard (Evanston,
IL: Northwestern University Press, 1992) and his novels such as *Projet pour une révolution
à New York* (Paris: Editions de minuit, 1970) and *La Jalousie* (Paris: Editions de minuit,
1957); Nathalie Sarraute, *L'ère du soupçon* (Paris: Gallimard, 1956) and novels such as *Vous
les entendez?* (Paris: Gallimard, 1972) or *L'Usage de la parole* (Paris: Gallimard, 1980). See
also Jean-Paul Sartre, "The Anti-Novel of Nathalie Sarraute," trans. Beth Brombert, *Yale
French Studies* 16 (1955): 40–44.

extremely partial and narrow when one compares them, as these novels do, to the diversity and breadth of one's surrounding social networks.

Throughout this project, I take for granted the notion that the novel can be treated not merely as a symptom of, but as a critical engagement with, the social and material conditions of the real world. I argue that this is the case not only *despite*, but indeed *because* of the fact that novels and their characters are, very obviously, never complete or fully adequate representations of reality. I show that novels can decenter our forms of self-regard by suggestively depicting just how little the expression of a single mind and body might amount to, and how little it reveals about anything except this person herself. By highlighting the flatness of their major characters, novels can undercut the ease with which we might come to treat our first-person experience as a sufficient measure of the vastness of the world around us. They can unsettle the facility with which we might take the sense of centeredness that comes with inhabiting a particular human body and mind, as proof of our being the center or at least the self-sufficient condensation of a social or material world much larger than our immediate selves.

Flat Protagonists thus aims to overturn—or at least make us see anew—the old adage about the dangers of believing that novel characters provide reliable models for what our lives can or ought to be like. To act as if you were living in a novel: that attitude has been said to doom many people, as well as many novel characters, most famously, of course, Gustave Flaubert's Madame Bovary.[7] But what is usually meant by this cautionary warning is that to think of your life as a novel is to view it as somehow charmed into harmony and importance; it is to think of yourself as the center of a world whose principles and fate your singular life suffices to illuminate. By the light

7. Miguel de Cervantes' Don Quixote would be another example.

of the novels I examine, one can think of this process of imagining one's life as a novel, and oneself as a novel protagonist, very differently. To picture yourself as a character, these novels suggest, is to imagine your existence as something in which other people might be interested only cursorily, or as a pastime, or maybe not at all. It is to recognize your accounts of yourself as something many people might be potentially able to reach for, but never get around to doing so. It is to think about how frequently, and not unjustifiably, so many people merely shelve away the stories you tell them without turning them into master-tropes through which their own lives will be completely re-described. This mental exercise in limiting one's sense of oneself as the object of other people's interest is what *Flat Protagonists* seeks to promote.

In arguing this thesis, I certainly do not suggest that flat protagonists dominate most, or even the majority, of novels, especially not in the nineteenth and early twentieth centuries. But *Flat Protagonists* does seek to persuade its readers to see even more conventional novels from a different angle. On the one hand, I hope to draw attention to briefer episodes—that *do* occur in many of them—in which an otherwise round character is temporarily "flattened." *Flat Protagonists* invites its readers to look more closely at fragments such as this aside in *Sentimental Education*, in which Gustave Flaubert describes his protagonist's naïve social anxiety: "Frédéric . . . was determined never to set foot in that house again or have any further dealings with such people. Not realizing society's almost unlimited capacity for indifference, he thought he'd offended them!"[8]—or like the many scenes in Jane Austen's *Emma* in which the heroine comically over- or

---

8. Gustave Flaubert, *A Sentimental Education*, trans. Douglas Parmée (New York: Oxford University Press, 2008), 261. "Frédéric . . . était détérminé à ne jamais revenir dans cette maison, à ne plus fréquenter tous ces gens-là. Il croyait les avoir blessés, ne sachant pas quels larges fonds d'indifférence le monde possède!" Gustave Flaubert, *L'Education sentimentale* (Paris: Folio, 1965), 264.

underestimates her attractiveness to the men who visit her. The novels I examine encourage one to scrutinize such incidents as potentially important components of the psychological and metatextual critiques other narratives undertake. Such episodes in which versions of the *Bildungsroman* suddenly veer into something like naturalism—threatening to not produce any *Bildung* at all, only a statement about human beings' inevitably simple and selfish worldviews and urges—might constitute a much more sophisticated subversion of their represented social worlds, and of the narrative aims of depicting them, than it might seem on a more traditional reading.[9]

I see the flat protagonist both as a partial corrective to critical assessments of what novelistic realism usually consists in, and—more importantly—as a means of mining novels for critical insights that might still be useful in our present day. This aspiration toward, as one might casually put it, "getting over oneself" as the object of other people's attention is related but irreducible to the novelistic ideal of deeply committed empathy foregrounded by many recent critics. The end of the twentieth and the beginning of the twenty-first centuries saw a number of strong accounts of the novel as a powerful and culturally important model of interpersonal awareness. Novels, as these recent critics argue, empower their readers to reflect on their inner lives and find larger meanings within them. By presenting us with a variety of complicated characters—a variety that is arguably much greater than the range of people we might get to know in everyday life—novels also enrich our awareness of, and openness to, others.[10]

9. In this sense, my project is also sympathetic to, but ultimately departs from, the recent turn to "surface reading" first proposed by Sharon Marcus and Stephen Best in their "Surface Reading: An Introduction," *Representations* 108, no. 1 (2009): 1–21. Even as, like Marcus and Best, I am opposed to what they describe as "deep reading," the alternatives I develop to it hinge less on the notion of the surface (which is related to poststructuralist critiques of interiority), and more on concepts such as narrowness, finitude, and indifference.

10. In *Love's Knowledge*, Nussbaum thus argues that novels present us with a standard of acute sensitivity that is higher than the standards we follow in everyday life. "[Henry] James often

Successive chapters of this project engage with various facets of this recent critical trend. I respond to accounts of novels as sites of beauty, of heightened interpersonal sensitivity, of social subversion, or of expressive self-affirmation, invoking critics such as Martha Nussbaum, Judith Butler, Nancy Armstrong, and Elaine Scarry. As I show, flat protagonists point us toward alternatives to many of these scholars' fundamental assumptions about what the primary critical value of novels might consist in.

Most of these recent studies of the novel focus on the perspective of an observer or reader. They are interested in how novels can

stresses this analogy: the work of the moral imagination is in some way like the work of the creative imagination, especially that of the novelist. I want to study this analogy and to see how it is more than analogy: why this conception of moral attention and moral vision finds in novels its most appropriate articulation. More: why, according to this conception, the novel is itself a moral achievement, and the well-lived life is a work of literary art." Armstrong puts a similar point as follows, referring in particular to novels' role in empowering nineteenth-century women: "the writing of female subjectivity opened the magical space in a culture where ordinary work could find its proper gratification and where the very objects that set men against one another in the competitive marketplace served to bind them together in a community of common domestic values" (35). Invoking Enlightenment theories of consent and social contract, Scarry posits that the kind of sensitivity that novels (and for her, literature in general) foster "enables us actively to re-consent each day to the people and places we are ever more deeply committed to. It also makes us open to new commitments." In "The Values of Difficulty," Butler describes Henry James's *Washington Square* as forcing its reader to encounter the radical, unfathomable uniqueness of a represented person who might otherwise have seemed much more readily explicable and predictable. "We are asked," Butler says, "to understand the limits of judgment and to cease judging, paradoxically, in the name of ethics, to cease judging in a way that assumes we already know in advance what there is to be known." The way in which James's narrative focuses intensely on this character, and restricts our introspective access to her inner life, corners the reader into recognizing in her an instance and perhaps also a model of the indeterminacy of other people, prompting us to consider how this indeterminacy might inflect our relationship to others. Martha Nussbaum, *Love's Knowledge* (New York: Oxford University Press, 1992), 148. Elaine Scarry, "Poetry Changed the World," *Boston Review* 37, no. 4 (2012), 70. Judith Butler, "Values of Difficulty," in *Just Being Difficult? Academic Writing in the Public Arena*, ed. Jonathan Culler and Kevin Lamb (Palo Alto, CA: Stanford University Press, 2003), 208; Nancy Armstrong, *Desire and Domestic Fiction* (New York: Oxford University Press, 1987). See also Lawrence Buell's general introduction to the recent turn to ethics, of which several of these critics are a part: Lawrence Buell, "Introduction: In Pursuit of Ethics," *PMLA* 114, no. 1 (1999): 7–19.

complicate our view of the world by making us focus on more kinds of people than we might otherwise have the mind to attend to.[11] The novels I examine adopt the inverse perspective of a person who wants to be the object of other people's attentiveness, and who seeks insight about herself from her environment. These novels highlight the mimetic difficulty of representing, or even acknowledging, how few experiences and concepts a single person holds out toward others compared to the breadth of the surrounding world. The paucity of the attention their protagonists garner is represented not simply as a failing on the part of these characters' surroundings—though it might seem that way at the outset—but as a feature of the multitude of other human beings with whom they coexist, and of the gradual exhaustibility of ways in which these protagonists distinguish themselves from their communities. The more fully and comprehensively we convey ourselves to others, these novels suggest, the more clearly

---

11. This is true even of the most recent wave of criticism in nineteenth-century studies—with which I partly align myself—that begins to call into question the value of novelistically induced sympathy. Despite the nuance with which these recent critics refine our understanding of the kind of readerly sympathy or empathy we should champion, their work nevertheless takes as a given the centrality of these observer-based questions to the study of the novel. See, for example, Audrey Jaffe, *Scenes of Sympathy: Identity and Representation in Victorian Fiction* (Ithaca, NY: Cornell University Press, 2000); Suzy Anger, *Victorian Interpretation* (Ithaca, NY: Cornell University Press, 2005); Adela Pinch, *Thinking about Other People in Nineteenth-Century British Writing* (Cambridge, UK: Cambridge University Press, 2010); Rae Greiner, *Sympathetic Realism in Nineteenth-Century British Fiction* (Baltimore, MD: Johns Hopkins University Press, 2012); Rachel Ablow, *The Marriage of Minds: Reading Sympathy in the Victorian Marriage Plot* (Stanford, CA: Stanford University Press, 2007) and "Tortured Sympathies: Victorian Literature and the Ticking Time-Bomb Scenario," *ELH* 80, no. 4 (Winter 2013): 1145–1171; Rachel Hollander, "Novel Ethics: Alterity and Form in Jacob's Room," *Twentieth-Century Literature* 53 (2007): 40–66 and "Daniel Deronda and the Ethics of Alterity," *Literature, Interpretation, Theory* 16 (2005): 75–99. Among these critics, the one to whom my views are arguably closest is Aaron Matz, whose *Satire in the Age of Realism* argues that the moral zenith (and ultimate demise) of the Victorian realist novel came from its abandonment of sympathy in favor of a mocking view of human beings' follies and errors. Aaron Matz, *Satire in the Age of Realism* (Cambridge, UK: Cambridge University Press, 2010).

this act of expression is circumscribed, in its range and insights, by the limits of our singular existence.

Following versions of this mode of reasoning, the novels I examine do not simply imply that their characters are easily and justifiably discardable. Instead, they suggest that there is something naïve about assuming that a person's perceived difficulty and interest will always keep increasing, in the eyes of others, the longer and more intently they attend to him—and that the best knowledge to be gotten about oneself and others comes from such extended mutual contemplation. Being attended to by others, these works insinuate, eventually forces one to recognize that there are limits to how much one's body and mind can offer for such scrutiny. When she is being obscured and marginalized, a person might rightly seem, in Woloch's words, "engulfed" by the surrounding world and "explosive[ly]" ready to be put in the limelight.[12] But once under this limelight, we only have so many lines to deliver—and soon the notion that there was something infinitely difficult and complex about us starts to seem like a distant fantasy that masked the more articulable particularity of what we *did* want, and have now finally managed, to convey.

To make this point, the term "flat protagonists" purposefully conjoins, in a paradox, two aspects of novelistic character construction that are usually thought of as incompatible. The characters I examine draw attention to themselves by being somehow simpler, less influential, and more restricted in their self-expression than they themselves, or the novels' implied readers, would have assumed or expected. In this regard, they tend toward Forster's definition of flatness: as each novel progresses, these characters become increasingly like the cardboard-cutout minor figures that populate the margins of novels by Charles Dickens or William Thackeray.

---

12. See Woloch, *The One vs. the Many*, 24.

At the same time, flat protagonists are also characters to whose representation these novels devote the majority of their narrative space. Despite their increasing flatness, these characters hardly need to fight for this narrative exposure. They are also major characters in the further, related sense that their representation changes significantly in the course of the novel. This change is marked, and surprising, even though it is the inverse of the kinds of changes to which we might be accustomed. For instance, Thomas Hardy's novels take considerable time to develop the notion that Tess and Jude might be simplistic and unreliable as rebellious social agents; in Aphra Behn's *Oroonoko*, the eponymous African prince gradually becomes unable to gather his community's attention around himself.

The notion of the flat character is conventionally associated with stereotyped thinking. By contrast, in the novels I examine, flat protagonists are put in the service of a provocatively immoderate, granular sense of commitment to material and social reality. Rather than suggest that their characters embody typical social qualities and conditions, these novels create the vertiginous impression that the people they represent are only a handful among millions into whose distinct, distant lives they give us little or no access. These novels try to recreate the experience of being a single person amid a mass of others: a person whose life story could not possibly stand in for, or even interest, all the people around her.

These novels thus at once fulfill a certain ideal of representation, and rebel against what Catherine Gallagher has described as an essential quality of the novel: "the insistence that the human referent of the text was a generalization about and not an extratextual, embodied instance of a 'species.'"[13] They question what kind of "generalization"

---

13. Catherine Gallagher, "The Rise of Fictionality," in *The Novel*, edited by Franco Moretti, vol. 1 (Princeton, NJ: Princeton University Press, 2006), 342. See also Elizabeth Fowler, *Literary Character: The Human Figure in Early English Writing* (Ithaca, NY: Cornell University Press, 2003).

one could plausibly claim to enclose within the representation of a single human mind and body. They also ask what conventional novels, which convert characters into condensed metonymies of something larger than a single person, elude about our minds and bodies as "embodied instance[s]" existing in vast social networks.

To put this point even more strongly, the novels I examine protest against—and show us ways in which their whole genre could protest against—a quality that most critics, starting with Ian Watt, treat as definitive of the novel: its commitment to individualism.[14] No one, most critics implicitly assume, expects the novel to continually insist on *all* the difficulties posed by *all* the social distances that could potentially affect its characters. A novel's incompleteness, in the sense of always needing to omit or to condense some aspects of the social networks it claims to represent, is merely a truism. As Thomas Pavel puts it, novels are "worlds where a highly structured central area is surrounded by increasingly dark, fuzzy spaces"; their intense concern for and attentiveness to a small set of characters is inevitably fringed with a shrugging of shoulders about anything else.[15] One reason why the novel is easily forgiven this narrowness of focus is because of the

14. Woloch describes the novel's focus on what he claims are always *"too many people"* as so ambitious that it is formally "destabilizing." "Remember that your first duty is to be as complete as possible," says Henry James in *The Art of Fiction*, and what he means by "complete" has to do both with the depth and with the range of incompatible perspectives a novelist should be able to depict. In "Discourse in the Novel," Mikhail Bakhtin famously argues that the novel seeks to accommodate characters and discourses "of all kinds and degrees of otherness." Georg Lukacs defines the novel as the representation of a world in which "distance ... is extended to the point where it cannot be overcome." As D.A. Miller puts it, "though the form projects itself as a kind of home, what is housed in this home, as its contents, is not merely or even mainly comfortable domestic quarters, but also the social-institutional world at large." Henry James, *The Art of Fiction and Other Essays* (New York: Oxford University Press, 1948), 23. D.A. Miller, *The Novel and the Police* (Berkeley: University of California Press, 1988), 84. Woloch, *The One vs. the Many*, 13. Mikhail Bakhtin, *The Dialogic Imagination* (Austin: University of Texas Press, 1982), 275. Georg Lukacs, *The Theory of the Novel*, trans. Anna Bostock (Cambridge, MA: MIT Press, 1971), 59.

15. Thomas G. Pavel, *Fictional Worlds* (Cambridge, MA: Harvard University Press, 1986), 95. Extrapolating from this point, Pavel defends novels by suggesting that all of the worlds we live in are incomplete in this sense. "The distinction between [fictional and non-fictional

heightened detail with which it allows us to appreciate the complexity and importance of individual human beings. It is a major aim of the novel to not only represent great social networks, but also validate the perspectives cast upon them by particular people, helping us see that these people's individual fates within social networks, and their relationships to these networks, might in themselves—and not just in their statistical aggregate—be worthy of scrutiny. In Wayne Booth's words, "*Hamlet* is not fair to Claudius. . . . But who cares? The novelist who chooses to tell this story cannot at the same time tell that story; in centering our interest, sympathy, or affection on one character, he inevitably excludes from our interest, sympathy, and affection some other character."[16]

semantics], he argues, appears to be one of degree rather than nature" (53). "Our everyday worlds host such impossible entities as individual psyches, desires, dreams, and symbols. Consistent worlds originate in a strong idealization, and our commitment to coherence is less warranted than it appears" (50).

16. Wayne Booth, *The Rhetoric of Fiction* (Chicago: Chicago University Press, 1961), 79. Quoted in Woloch, *The One vs. the Many*, 40. See also, for example, passages such as this one from Franco Moretti: "Only by curbing its intrinsically boundless dynamism, only by agreeing to betray to a certain extent its very essence, only thus, it seems, can modernity be *represented*." Franco Moretti, *The Way of the World* (New York: Verso, 2000), 6, or Christopher Prendegast, "The text is to world what microcosm is to macrocosm, a system of interrelated parts whose internal relations yield a model of the set of relations organizing the wider totality of the world beyond. The difficulty with this influential view lies with what the argument from the notion of totality takes for granted: the principle which allows for the unproblematic passage from microcosm to macrocosm, the criteria by which the writer decides, and which enable the reader to accept, that one set of selections and combinations is representative, where another is merely random or arbitrary. In these terms, the success of the mimetic project depends absolutely on the validity of a set of unquestioned prior choices determining the relative value of both its inclusions and exclusions." Christopher Prendegast, *The Order of Mimesis* (Cambridge, UK: Cambridge University Press, 1986), 26. Mikhail Bakhtin describes this principle as follows: "The large epic form (the large epic), including the novel as well, should provide an integrated picture of the world and life, it should reflect the *entire* world and *all* of life. In the novel, the entire world and all of life are given in the cross section of the *integrity of the epoch*. The events depicted in the novel should somehow *substitute* for the total life of the epoch. In their capacity to represent the real-life whole lies their artistic essentiality. Novels differ enormously in their degrees of this essentiality and, consequently, in their artistic significance. These novels depend above all on their realistic penetration into this real-life integrity of the world, from which the formalized essentiality shaped in the novelistic whole is extracted." Mikhail Bakhtin, "The

I offer the works I examine, and their arguably extreme forms of metatextual reflection, as a model for how our accounts of the novel could move away from such an emphasis on this genre's value as an affirmation of the complexity and depth of first-person experience. These works challenge the notion that their genre does us a service, in our understanding of the world and of ourselves, by putting a few represented people in the limelight as substitutes of many other objects of attention. Striving to portray their protagonists, with increasing insistence, from what Pavel might call the "fuzzy spaces" beyond these protagonists' immediate circumferences of attention, these novels gesture toward an unrealized fictional world much larger than the one they represent, a world within which the words and gestures they represent would be completely insignificant.[17] Their insistence on the artifice and the smallness of the environments they represent is, paradoxically, an affirmation of their genre's critical potential. These novels stress their narrowness of focus, and the relative flatness of their protagonists—which otherwise might seem to be a regrettable constraint—as a major component of what makes them powerfully subversive of our understanding of our surroundings and ourselves.

Bildungsroman and Its Significance in the History of Realism," in *Speech Genres and Other Late Essays*, trans. Vern McGee (Austin: University of Texas Press, 1986), 43.

Other critics point out that novels create merely aesthetic, thin illusions of such absolute completeness—and are quite satisfied with them. As Roland Barthes famously puts it, the mark of realism—a novel's "reality effect"—consists in introducing descriptions of details that seem extraneous to its immediate mimetic purpose, details that end up being represented simply, unnervingly, because they *can* be, thereby suggesting a kind of plentitude that metonymically approximates what we take the plentitude of the real world to be like. It is, Barthes says, "as if the referent's exactitude, superior or indifferent to any other function, governed and alone justified its description" (145). "All this shows," he continues, "that the 'real' is supposed to be self-sufficient, that it is strong enough to belie any notion of 'function,' that its 'speech-act' has no need to be integrated into a structure and that the *having-been-there* of things is a sufficient principle of speech" (147). Roland Barthes, "The Reality Effect," in *The Rustle of Language*, trans. Richard Howard (Berkeley: University of California Press, 1989).
17. Pavel, *Fictional Worlds*, 95.

In formal terms, *Flat Protagonists* frequently builds on the questions and methods formulated by Woloch in *The One vs. the Many*.[18] Woloch's account of what he calls "character-spaces" hinges on the notion that every character a novel represents could potentially be a protagonist. Characters, he argues, are always implicitly richer and more complicated than a novel has room to show us. "In this perspective," he says, "the implied person behind any character is never directly reflected in the literary text but only partially inflected: each individual portrait has a radically contingent position within the story as a whole; our sense of the human figure (as implied person) is inseparable from the space that he or she occupies within the narrative totality."[19]

I am compelled by Woloch's idea of examining novels as represented worlds whose formal constraints structure their means of depicting personhood. At the same time, within this framework, the question I pursue is the inverse of Woloch's. The novels I examine do not share Woloch's trust that their characters could easily, complexly expand to fill any narrative space available to them. Indeed, these novels frequently insist that, when given such space, their characters occupy it in much less rich and compelling ways than one might have expected.

Flat Protagonists spans a significant range of novel history, from the late seventeenth until the early twentieth century. Across this

---

18. Woloch's argument hinges on the notion of the "character-space." Woloch defines the "character-space" of a novel as the range and scope of attention this novel is able to give to its characters as a group, and to each of these represented people individually. By molding this space, an author distributes attention among her characters. This distribution process is, for Woloch, in itself a major component of the social commentary in which a novel engages.

19. Woloch, *The One vs. the Many*, 13. As a result, Woloch argues, minor characters often seem to be flattened or "engulfed" by their narratives in a way that is visibly forced and constraining. For Woloch, novels thereby expose the arbitrariness of choosing one protagonist over another. They show us that "there is no such thing as an innocent protagonist in the novel; or, at least, that such a virtue is purchased, like any modern innocence, only through a partial negation of history" (320).

period, notions of what constitutes a character or turns this character into a protagonist change significantly. To do justice to these differences, each chapter centers around a different quality or process through which novel protagonists can be defined: nobility, writing, social rebelliousness, and introspection. On a basic level, these successive chapters all address versions of the same question about the limits to how much can persuasively be conveyed through the representation of a single mind and body. Each of these chapters also touches on a slightly different aspect of character construction, which corresponds to the main emphases of the literary period on which it focuses. I take the concepts of "The Prince," "The Writer," "The Misfit," and "The Solipsist," after which successive chapters of this project are named, as entry points into the various dimensions of "flatness" that each novel I examine attributes to its protagonists, and the kinds of realism or proto-realism with which they engage.

The first chapter, "The Prince," examines Aphra Behn's *Oroonoko* (1688) in the context of the initial rise of the novel amid conflicting discourses of empiricism and romance. I begin with this early narrative to show that the forms of character construction I trace throughout this book accompany the emergent novel from the outset. These narrative strategies outline and respond to a set of concerns about the difficulty of making a single person's thoughts and feelings seem present and intelligible in the wider world beyond her. My reading of *Oroonoko* builds on past critics' descriptions of it as a transitional text that does not follow any single formal or ideological aim: as a novel or proto-novel that straddles fascinations with aristocratic romances and empiricism, with England's rise as a capitalist and colonial power and the breakdown of its old social hierarchies and systems of value. On that basis, this chapter complicates Martha Nussbaum's accounts of the novel as a means of expanding what she calls our "circles of concern" as human beings. *Oroonoko* depicts its protagonist as a potential model for larger patterns of social behavior. He is a person whose words and actions seem to embody and to synthesize many ideals that the societies he lives in problematically lack. But Behn's narrator also underlines the inconsistency with which Oroonoko is acknowledged as a prominent member of his represented communities, as well as the smallness of these communities as testing grounds for his personal qualities. Rather than, as in Nussbaum's examples, use her narrative to expand the ranges of such communities to which her protagonist's life might seem important, Behn makes a point of emphasizing that there is nothing about Oroonoko's social status or personal presence that can guarantee a consistent and receptive audience for his self-expression. Instead, Oroonoko's words and gestures are easily trivialized or distorted by the partial responses they incite in those around him. Behn's narrative strategies insistently highlight these limits to how well a single person's self-expression can convey and uphold the ideals in which he believes. Behn also shows how fragile her protagonist is within these constraints. To understand his plight, Behn suggests, requires one not to extol its generalizability, but to accept how difficult it is for this particular represented person to model any of the general values and virtues he supposedly ought to sustain.

The second chapter, "The Writer," discusses Françoise de Graffigny's *Letters from a Peruvian Woman* (1747) and Isabelle de Charrière's *Letters of Mistress Henley* (1784). They are both epistolary novels. I examine them to show that the forms of character construction this project explores emerge even within this sub-genre that has conventionally been associated with relentlessly deep representations of subjectivity. Responding to Nancy Armstrong's *Desire and Domestic Fiction*, I show that Graffigny and Charrière at once follow and subvert their period's fascination with letters as means of affirming the larger significance of even very small and domestic interactions and events. Rather than—as in Armstrong's account—use letters to produce generalized versions of their protagonists' first-person experience,

these two epistolary novelists treat the physical smallness of these letters as a metonymy of their protagonists' similarly limited scopes of
material presence and experience. Charrière's and Graffigny's novels
depict the effortful process by which their characters try to convey
their thoughts and feelings to others or to relate their material circumstances to broader social conditions. Graffigny's protagonist is a
Peruvian princess who struggles, and fails, to maintain her ties to her
fiancé after they are separated and abducted to Europe on the morning
of their wedding day. Charrière's narrator recounts her futile attempts
to incorporate her cosmopolite upbringing into the traditional country mansion where she and her husband move after their marriage. At
the end of both novels, these protagonists look to their letters as measures not—as they were at first—of their ambitious hopes of being
heard and understood, but of their frailty and finitude as beings who
expect such attention from others. Both novelists gradually come to
represent their protagonists' gestures of withdrawal as paradoxical
forms of self-awareness. They depicts such withdrawals as precondi-
tions of becoming aware of, and taking control of, the limited means
a person has of expressing herself within the much larger and richer
social system to which she belongs.

The third chapter, "The Misfit," examines two novels by Thomas
Hardy, *Tess of the D'Urbervilles* (1891) and *Jude the Obscure* (1895).
Both novels engage with the nineteenth-century notion of novel
protagonists as individuals who are at odds with their society. Tess
is a woman whose loss of virginity sets her in tension with the feminine ideals to which men want to hold her. Jude is a countryside
stonemason who tries to incorporate into his life a range of cultural
knowledge to which his society does not otherwise grant him access.
Rather than just affirm the subversive value of Tess's and Jude's
social maladjustment, Hardy's narratives examine the narrow limits
of these characters' awareness of themselves and others. They focus
on how difficult it is for these protagonists to recognize the broader

social norms against which they struggle, or to articulate any viable alternatives to them. Hardy's narrators make Tess's and Jude's belief that their lives fruitfully engage with these social norms seem vulnerably self-aggrandizing. The words and gestures to which their minds and bodies give rise are much simpler and smaller than the abstractions through which they try to understand themselves. I engage with Judith Butler's notion of performativity and what she calls "giving an account of oneself" to show that Tess and Jude do not even have available to them a responsive "other" who could either affirm or deny their acts of rebellion. Both protagonists are blind not only to the simplicity, but also to the relative invisibility, of their self-expression. I see these narrative choices not simply as a means of mocking these characters, but as a way of highlighting a dimension of the difficulties of social rebellion that critical theory does not usually take into account: one that stems from what Hardy depicts as the inalienable contingency of contexts in which a person's alienation might become visible and pertinent to others.

In the last chapter, "The Solipsist," I examine Marcel Proust's *In Search of Lost Time* (1913–1927) in the context of the modernist novel's preoccupation with representing consciousness. I take Proust's novel as a final and perhaps most counterintuitive example of a work that has been misread because its forms of character construction have tended to be interpreted simply as instances of deeply introspective writing. Proust's famously ambitious aesthetic philosophy hinges on explorations not just of the capacities but also of the limits to any person's affective and sensory receptivity and expressiveness. Proust is also even more emphatic than these other novelists about the value of representing, and coming to terms with, the vastness of the social indifference amid which anyone's acts of self-expression take place. Contrasting Proust's representations of his narrator against Elaine Scarry's notion of literature as a means of creating and sharing experiences of beauty, I show that Proust does not just validate his narrator's sensitivity, but stresses how contingent are the moments when this sensitivity temporarily becomes meaningful and important to someone else.

Like Hardy, Proust explores what it means to see his protagonist's efforts at making sense of his world as at least partly dependent on simplification, forgetfulness, and narrowness of vision. Like Behn, Graffigny, and Charrière, Proust also asks how one should represent a person to whom society does not necessarily look for insights about itself, and to whose notions of order it does not readily attend. After he gives up on his initial hope of making his acts of self-expression more relevant or visible to others, Proust's narrator seeks to come to terms with, and picture to himself, how much less others care about his thoughts and feelings than he himself does. The difficulty of this task is represented both as a comic measure of this narrator's insistent self-regard, and as a serious challenge to an understanding of the novel as a genre that claims to validate the potential importance and meaningfulness of any person's immediate experience of her world.

We have never been as complex, or as deep, as the realist novel would have us believe. Indeed, the relentlessness with which most novels pursue this fantasy of our infinite interest should have clued us in to this realization long ago. In my conclusion, I review ways in which this insight, as pursued by the novels I examine, can paradoxically open up ways of reading novels more open-mindedly and perhaps even more generously. *Flat Protagonists* rebels against the long-established critical tradition of associating the interest and richness of novels with the complexity of their characters, whether this complexity is construed as radical alterity, sophisticated self-awareness, or psychological depth. By following this countercurrent to the novel's insistent faith in its protagonists' significance—and highlighting the ontological and ethical doubts it raises—*Flat Protagonists* reconsiders the history of the novel as a genre as well as its present-day critical uses.

1

The Prince

Aphra Behn's *Oroonoko*

"My Lord," explains Aphra Behn in her preface to *Oroonoko*, addressing her patron Lord Maitland:

> a picture drawer, when he intends to make a good picture, essays the face in many ways, and in many lights, before he begins, that he may choose from the several turns of it which is most agreeable and gives it the best grace; and if there be a scar, an ungrateful mole, or any little defect, they leave it out; and yet make the picture extremely like. But he who has the good fortune to draw a face that is exactly charming in all its parts and features, what colors or agreements can be added to make it finer?[1]

Behn's flattery seems simple: Lord Maitland is so handsome that any painter would easily convey his charm. But in the context of the novel that follows, this question of charm and of its self-sufficiency is not an innocent one. Though Behn begins *Oroonoko* by praising an individual who seems born to be surrounded by admirers, her narrative

---

1. Aphra Behn, *Oroonoko and Other Writings* (New York: Oxford University Press, 2009), 3.

explores what happens when a person's capacity to take up such a central position hits an unexpected limit.

Behn writes *Oroonoko* at a time when, as Michael McKeon puts it in *The Origins of the English Novel*, the novel gradually begins to emerge out of a cluster of competing earlier discourses. These discourses include aristocratic romance, empiricism, and colonial travelogues that combine the empirical with the fantastic. The notion of character that develops amid these conflicting conventions is, as Deidre Lynch persuasively argues, strongly influenced by early modern typologies in which the human body stands in for something larger than itself, such as a vice, a virtue, or a science.[2]

But how much—Behn asks—can a single represented human body actually stand in for? On the one hand, Behn represents her protagonist as a potential exemplar of nobility and virtue. This protagonist, she suggests, is someone from whom many others should want to learn, and whose prominence should be respected. Behn's narrator initially reinforces this impression by depicting Oroonoko through the prism of the romance tradition. Yet Behn also contrasts this aristocratic notion of unquestionable virtue and status against a more empirical understanding of Oroonoko's appeal as fickle and limited in circumference. Her narrator highlights that, exemplary as he might be, Oroonoko is just one human being. Behn's novel tests the limits to how well such a singular mind and body—and, by

2. According to Lynch, writers of the time tend to believe that it is "best to *image* the linguistic grounds of human knowledge and . . . to apprehend the constituents of knowledge through analogies with the human body" (30). The notion of fictionality that eventually develops around this period hinges on understanding characters as fusions of the general and the particular. As Catherine Gallagher puts it, "because a general referent was indicated through a particular, but explicitly nonreferential, fictional individual, the novel could be judged generally true even though all of its particulars are merely imaginary" (342). Deidre Lynch, *The Economy of Character: Novels, Market Culture, and the Business of Inner Meaning* (Chicago and London: University of Chicago Press, 1998); Catherine Gallagher, "The Rise of Fictionality," in *The Novel*, vol. 1, ed. Franco Moretti (Princeton, NJ: Princeton University Press, 2006), 336–363.

extension, a narrative centered around this represented person—can convey anything larger than themselves. Her protagonist discovers how inconsistently and unpredictably his immediate physical presence embodies qualities that others care about. Oroonoko's ability to represent to others any broader concepts and values rapidly comes to seem tragicomically contingent. Other characters hardly respond to his words and gestures if he does not already play a major pragmatic role within their lives.

Oroonoko thus incorporates into its concern with nobility and virtue a parallel attentiveness to the intrinsic limitations of human bodies as carriers of these abstract concepts. It also turns representing the finitude of these bodies into its own mimetic aim. Behn's novel does not yet operate within the framework of distinctions between what Forster—and Lynch and Woloch following him—call flat and round characters.[3] Nevertheless, it poses an early version of a question that the later novels I examine articulate more recognizably in terms of flatness and roundness, or of major and minor character status. Like these later novels, *Oroonoko* explores how central and significant a role its protagonist plays within its represented world. It also asks, with increasing insistence, to what extent this represented person is able to bear the mimetic burdens imposed upon him.[4]

3. See E. M. Forster, *Aspects of the Novel* (London: Mariner Books, 1956), 67; Lynch, *Economy of Character*, 1–22; Alex Woloch, *The One vs. the Many: Minor Characters and the Space of the Protagonist in the Novel* (Princeton, NJ: Princeton University Press, 2003), 12–26.

4. Throughout this chapter I refer to *Oroonoko* as a novel. A long tradition of critical debate of course exists over whether or not this term is generically appropriate. Jane Spencer provides a good discussion of these arguments in *Aphra Behn's Afterlife*. Rachel Carnell also raises this issue in her article on *Oroonoko* as a turn away from tragic conventions. To the extent that all the works I discuss in this volume shift emphasis away from many conventional aims of the novel, *Oroonoko* is perhaps not a novel *stricto sensu*. But by suggesting that the ways in which *Oroonoko* is not a conventional novel resemble ways in which Thomas Hardy's *Tess of the D'Urbervilles* and Marcel Proust's *In Search of Lost Time* are also not conventional novels, I hope to show new reasons why Behn's text should continue to be a point of reference in debates about this genre. Jane Spencer, *Aphra Behn's Afterlife* (New York: Oxford University Press, 2000), 86; Rachel Carnell, "Subverting Tragic Conventions: Aphra Behn's Turn to the Novel," *Studies in the Novel* 31, no. 2 (1999): 133–151.

To flesh out some of these conceptual questions, I set my reading of *Oroonoko* in conversation with the writings of Martha Nussbaum. I engage in particular with Nussbaum's belief that we should value literature as a means of expanding what, in *Political Emotions*, she calls "our 'circle of concern.' "[5] Nussbaum argues that, as human beings, we have a necessarily limited capacity to relate to anything and anyone beyond the scope of our immediate lives. As she puts it, "we may hold that other people have intrinsic value. But the ones who will stir deep emotions in us are the ones to whom we are somehow connected through our imagining of a valuable life."[6] "If distant people and abstract principles are to get a grip on our emotions, therefore," she continues, "these emotions must somehow position them within our circle of concern, creating a sense of 'our' life in which those people and events matter as parts of our 'us,' our own flourishing."[7] By making us care about characters who do not resemble people we know, and making these characters' inner lives seem rich and generalizable, literature helps us undertake such acts of expansion. As Nussbaum puts it, "our experience is, without fiction, too confined and too parochial. Literature extends it, making us reflect and feel about what might otherwise be too distant for feeling."[8]

Behn's novel does not directly contradict Nussbaum's point about the value of literature as a model of heightened sensitivity. But it suggests that the critical value of literature might lie not only in its potential capacity to expand our spheres of sensitivity but also in its ability to highlight the narrowness of these spheres in the first place. Instead of trying to expand the ranges of attention we give to others, Behn's novel draws insight from the experience of being the object of

5. Martha Nussbaum, *Political Emotions: Why Love Matters for Justice* (Cambridge, MA: Harvard University Press, 2013), 11.

6. Nussbaum, *Political Emotions*, 11.

7. Nussbaum, *Political Emotions*, 11.

8. Martha Nussbaum, *Love's Knowledge* (New York: Oxford University Press, 1990), 47.

such acts of attention. Taking for granted that the circles of concern in which we live are intrinsically narrow, Behn exposes as naïve the belief that one's particular mind and body are universalizable enough to transcend them. *Oroonoko* also highlights political and phenomenological reasons why such an awareness of one's finitude might be at least as important to achieve as the broad interpersonal responsiveness Nussbaum describes.

Oroonoko follows several dramatic life events that befall the African prince Oroonoko, grandson of the ruler of his state. While still in his home country, Oroonoko secretly marries the princess Imoinda. His grandfather steals her away and also marries her in front of his whole court, in a way that makes Oroonoko and Imoinda unable to reveal or to consistently act on their prior mutual promises. Oroonoko and Imoinda's feelings for each other are eventually discovered and Imoinda is sold into slavery. The lovers reunite in Surinam, where Oroonoko is abducted and sold by a slave merchant. The man who buys Oroonoko from this merchant treats him respectfully but keeps him under close watch. Fearing that he might otherwise never regain his freedom, Oroonoko attempts to start a slave rebellion. The slaves, his former subjects, flee from their first battle and leave their leader to be whipped by the white governor. After the whipping Oroonoko runs away into a forest, kills the pregnant Imoinda and her unborn child, and disembowels himself. He is finally tortured to death by the governor's henchmen.

When scholarly interest in *Oroonoko* was first revived in the 1980s, most critics read it as a conservative text: as an attempt to restore harmony and coherence to a society whose self-perception is confused and chaotic.[9] Recent criticism on *Oroonoko* treats it, more

9. See, for example, Michael McKeon, *The Origins of the English Novel, 1600–1740* (Baltimore, MD: Johns Hopkins University Press, 1987), 250–251. Moira Ferguson, "Oroonoko: Birth of a Paradigm," *NLH* 23, no. 2 (1992): 344; Eliot Visconsi, "A Degenerate Race: English Barbarism in Aphra Behn's *Oroonoko* and *The Widow Ranter*," *ELH* 69, no. 3 (2002): 673–701;

open-endedly, as the depiction of a society in crisis. For Corrinne Harol, Behn's pessimism about the reliability of social structures is so profound that Behn construes any form of action as necessarily violent and futile. The only proper way to react to the social world she represents is through passive, obedient suffering.[10] Blakey Vermeule goes even further to claim that the brutally deposed and humiliated Oroonoko stands for the recently decapitated Charles II.[11]

Without engaging with Vermeule's specific historical claim, I agree with her in a broad sense that *Oroonoko* explores the fickleness of what might seem like unquestionable rank or prominence. Behn's novel explores not only its protagonist's potential as a model of noble behavior, but also the limits of his appeal to others. *Oroonoko* continues what Ros Ballaster has described as Behn's lifelong fascination with "would-be kings" and royal pretenders.[12] It interrogates the possibility of viewing social prominence not as a birthright but as a fragile and temporary achievement. The way in which Behn's

Susan B. Iwanishniw, "Behn's Novel Investment in *Oroonoko*: Kingship, Slavery and Tobacco in English Colonialism," *South Atlantic Review* 63, no. 2 (1998): 80; Catherine Gallagher, "Introduction: Cultural and Historical Background," in *Oroonoko; or, The Royal Slave*, by Aphra Behn, ed. Catherine Gallagher (Boston, MA: Bedford, 2000), 4; Catherine Gallagher, "*Oroonoko*'s Blackness," *Aphra Behn Studies*, ed. Janet Todd (New York: Cambridge University Press, 1996), 235–258.

10. "[*Oroonoko*] makes a pragmatic, if not a religious, case for passive obedience negatively, by repeatedly showing the consequences of active disobedience as well as the immorality of most action." Corrinne Harol, "The Passion of Oroonoko: Passive Obedience, The Royal Slave, and Aphra Behn's Baroque Realism," *ELH* 79, no. 2 (2012): 448. See also Adam Sills, "Surveying 'The Map of Slavery' in Aphra Behn's *Oroonoko*," *Journal of Narrative Theory* 36, no. 3 (2006): 319–320; Albert J. Rivero, "Aphra Behn's *Oroonoko* and the 'Blank Spaces' of Colonial Fictions," *Studies in English Literature 1500–1900* 39, no. 3 (1999): 443–462; Richard Frohock, "Violence and Awe: The Foundations of Government in Aphra Behn's New World Settings," *Eighteenth-Century Fiction* 8, no. 4 (1996): 437–452; Daniel Gustafson, "Cultural Memory and the Royalist Political Aesthetic in Aphra Behn's Later Works," *Restoration: Studies in English Literary Culture, 1660–1700* 36, no. 2 (2012): 1–22.

11. Blakey Vermeule, *Why Do We Care about Literary Characters?* (Baltimore, MD: Johns Hopkins University Press, 2011), 58.

12. Ros Ballaster, "Fiction Feigning Femininity: False Counts and Pageant Kings in Aphra Behn's Popish Plot Writings," in *Aphra Behn Studies*, ed. Janet Todd (New York: Cambridge University Press, 1996), 58.

narrator depicts Oroonoko's qualities fuses the romance conventions on which his behavior is implicitly modeled with an empirical emphasis on sensory evidence and proof. The capaciousness of the communities that appreciate him is not taken for granted. Instead, it is continually tested and re-tested against the bounds of the world Behn represents—a represented world that is itself, as Behn goes on to suggest, quite incomplete and small. Behn shows that there is nothing inherent in her protagonist's sophistication or charm that would prevent others from ignoring him. She asks whether the marks that Oroonoko's self-expression leaves within this fictional world can ever seem rich and resonant enough to be held up as models of social or political virtue. This reflexivity allows Behn to turn her novel into a tool of thinking about the extent of any single person's ability to affect a broader social world through his immediate experiences and choices.

As Spengemann has rightly observed, Behn's narrator hardly ever interacts with Oroonoko alone, or claims to be his confidante.[13] Instead, Behn emphasizes that each of her narrator's encounters with Oroonoko occurs in the immediate physical presence of other European or indigenous observers. Everything that Oroonoko does is confirmed by at least one other witness besides the narrator herself: "I neither thought it convenient to keep him much out of our view, nor did the country, who feared him; .... if he did [go further away, he was] to be accompanied by some that should be rather in appearance attendants than spies."[14] Although Oroonoko is presented as adamantly truthful, even his own accounts of his early life are corroborated by a merchant who witnessed Oroonoko's conflict with his grandfather. "From his own mouth [I] learned what

13. William C. Spengemann, "The Earliest American Novel: Aphra Behn's *Oroonoko*," *Nineteenth-Century Fiction* 38, no. 4 (1984): 392–393.
14. Behn, *Oroonoko*, 46.

I have related," the narrator reiterates, "which was confirmed by his Frenchman, who was set on shore to seek his fortunes; and of whom they could not make a slave, because a Christian."[15] These strategies provide what McKeon rightly describes as a background of empirical reliability typical for this period's travel narratives: "the credibility of a travel account is enhanced by the confirmation of other travelers."[16] They also have the further effect of drawing increasing attention to the changing numbers of people to whom the course of Oroonoko's life seems important or memorable. They start to turn these shifting levels and kinds of attentiveness into an independent object of narrative scrutiny.

At first, it seems that Oroonoko's central presence in Behn's novel is merely reaffirmed and reinforced by recurrent empirical confirmations of how easily an entire community's eyes come to rest upon him. These affirmations appear to instate Oroonoko as what Nussbaum calls a literary model of perfected human behavior.[17] Behn's narrator claims that Oroonoko's impact on others is so powerful that he often needs to hide from them: "When he found his habit made him liable, as he thought, to be gazed at the more, he begged Trefry to give him something more befitting a slave, which he did, and took off his robes. Nevertheless, he shone through all, and his osenbrigs (a sort

15. Behn, *Oroonoko*, 44.
16. McKeon, *Origins of the English Novel*, 108.
17. In the fictional works Nussbaum singles out for praise, "we have a perfectionist view that insists that not all human lives are equally complete, equally flourishing—even when moral development itself is concerned—and that this is so, in great part, because the central human capabilities have, for their development, material and educational necessary conditions that are not, as things are in most actual societies, available to all" (*Love's Knowledge*, 201). Literature, Nussbaum argues, sets before its readers a standard of attentiveness that is much higher than what most of us might follow in real life. "It is the demand that we not rest content, as social beings, with half-baked abstract discourse and crude perceptions, with what James elsewhere calls 'the rule of the cheap and easy'; but that, in public and in private, we create our lives with one another with as much subtlety, responsiveness, delicacy, and imagination as are involved in the creation of a work of literary art, dismantling our anger, fostering our gentleness" (*Love's Knowledge*, 216–217).

of brown Holland suit he had on) could not conceal the graces of his looks and mien."[18] When other characters do see him, they often share the narrator's interest in Oroonoko spontaneously, and in large numbers. "He was adored as the wonder of all that world, and the darling of the soldiers," the narrator says about Oroonoko's past life in Africa.[19] Oroonoko's former slaves and war prisoners render him homage upon first seeing him in Surinam: "The Negroes all having left work," says the narrator ". . . they all came forth to behold him, and found he was that prince who had, at several times, sold most of 'em to these parts; and, from a veneration they pay to great men, especially if they know 'em, and from the surprise and awe they all had at the sight of him, they all fell at his feet, . . . [and] paid him even divine homage."[20]

In this last quotation, the narrator's mention that Oroonoko previously sold his admirers into slavery is an ironic reminder of the ruthlessness of the slave trade. But on a more immediate level, these displays of how easily Oroonoko awes others establish him as someone whose fate could be exemplary and enriching: someone whom others might want to follow or look up to. Behn suggests that he could easily become prominent in each of the communities he is forced to join, and potentially also in the most refined social circles that Behn's Western readers might know about. "He had nothing of barbarity in his nature," she declares elsewhere, "but in all points addressed himself as if his education had been in some European court."[21]

Many critics assume that these early emphases on Oroonoko's striking presence are intended to stress that he is a worthy model of conduct even though his admiring spectators eventually abandon

18. Behn, *Oroonoko*, 39.
19. Behn, *Oroonoko*, 10.
20. Behn, *Oroonoko*, 40.
21. Behn, *Oroonoko*, 11.

him. Dickson thus argues that, even though Oroonoko cannot survive within the community in which he has found himself, such scenes of homage express a hope that the courtly ideals he represents might, in the long run, attract a more consistent following.[22] McKeon puts a similar point as follows: "Oroonoko is also able to represent the condition of the new man, who, passively transported from the Old World to the New, shows that he embodies the best principles of progressive ideology more successfully than most of his fellow moderns."[23] But Behn does not merely assert that Oroonoko's qualities are valuable models for his society. She forges a narrative space in which it also becomes possible to acknowledge reasons why one particular body and mind might not suffice to carry such social models very far, or to present them consistently and adequately to others.

In the course of her novel, Behn contrasts scenes where Oroonoko seems unquestionably moving to others, against episodes where his intentions and desires are ignored or dismissed. She also casts a critical eye on the moment-by-moment resonance of Oroonoko's words and actions. Chi-ming Yang has observed that Behn often compares Oroonoko's charismatic appeal to the beauty of Chinese and Japanese luxury items that are a novelty in England around that time. These comparisons make his presence seem, in Yang's terms, "luxurious, ancient, yet thoroughly commodified."[24] Oroonoko is powerful but also potentially trivial. Indeed, the high ideals he embodies are readily dismissed if he cannot find adequate space for their expression.

The story of Oroonoko's life does not have a consistently grand, public arc. Instead, it is composed of a series of transitions in and out

22. Vernon Guy Dickson, "Truth, Wonder, and Exemplarity in Aphra Behn's *Oroonoko*," *Studies in English Literature 1500–1900* 47, no. 3 (2007): 573–594.
23. McKeon, *Origins of the English Novel*, 251.
24. Chi-ming Yang, "Asia Out of Place: The Aesthetics of Incorruptibility in Behn's *Oroonoko*," *Eighteenth-Century Studies* 42, no. 2 (2009): 237.

of the limelight, in and out of the tragic, heightened visibility for which he initially seems singularly destined. Even though Oroonoko's life consistently seems momentous to Oroonoko himself, Behn shows how inconstantly the various communities around him share this view. This series of inflations and deflations begins while Oroonoko is still in Africa. Rivero has argued that "the world of Oroonoko's royal court is bloody and treacherous, as Behn understands all 'real' worlds to be, yet it is a world in which, despite the machinations of evildoers, such noble virtues as loyalty, honesty, and true love are unequivocally prized and held up for admiration."[25] Still, the novel's opening section is striking not only in how much the members of the king's court claim to admire Oroonoko, but also in how narrowly this admiration is constrained by a set of fragile conditions and contexts. His romantic exploits matter little to his community once they come into conflict with the king's interests. The king himself exerts power over Oroonoko by acting as if the latter's desires and claims could simply be ignored or overlooked. He takes Imoinda away from Oroonoko by pretending not to know that she is already his wife. When the king marries Imoinda, Oroonoko is powerless to do anything more than arrange secret meetings with her through a servant. Once the king grows suspicious of them, Imoinda and Oroonoko do not have enough social power to declare their love openly without being killed. Indeed, the king occasionally taunts them by reasserting how little such a declaration would matter to him. "She therefore said a thousand things to appease the raging of his flame," the narrator recounts, "and to prepare him to hear who it was with calmness, but before she spoke he imagined who she meant, but would not seem to do so, but commanded her to lay aside her mantle and suffer herself to receive his caresses; or, by his gods, he swore that happy man whom she was going to name should die, though it were even Oroonoko

25. Rivero, "Aphra Behn's *Oroonoko*," 452–453.

himself."[26] Rather than be rejected, Oroonoko's and Imoinda's love is merely cast aside. The king shows his greater prominence by emphasizing how easily he can reduce their bond to a mere hypothetical hyperbole. Oroonoko is a person whose conflict with the king does not even merit a confrontation, and whose love for Imoinda does not need to be discussed as a social fact.

As she dramatizes the unexpectedly tight circumference of the contexts where Oroonoko's love is acknowledged and admired, Behn also shows how much its shrinking stage constrains the way his love can be expressed and described to others. When the king nearly catches the two lovers together, Imoinda saves herself by pretending that Oroonoko tried to rape her: "She fell on her face at his feet, bedewing the floor with her tears, and imploring his pardon for a fault which he had not with her will committed, as Onahal, who was also prostrate with her, could testify: that, unknown to her, he had broke into her apartment and ravished her."[27]

It is striking both how readily Imoinda and Oroonoko resort to such misrepresentations of each other, and how easily Behn's narrator accepts these less than flattering accounts of their relationship. The way Behn describes these events does not even suggest that the lovers draw from them any of the moral lessons about respect and dignity that a romance character might acquire, with remorse, after betraying her lover in similar fashion. Rather than praise the independent value of Oroonoko's passion, Behn shows how trivial this love affair can seem if the spaces in which it can be openly valued are reduced even slightly. She represents such forms of distorted, constrained self-expression as intrinsic aspects of the ambiguous condition their relationship has in their community. These are not indignities Imoinda

26. Behn, *Oroonoko*, 16.
27. Behn, *Oroonoko*, 27.

and Oroonoko could and should strive to prevent, but tonal shifts neither of them can do much about.

This emphasis on the narrow, parochial contexts of Oroonoko's self-expression is also reinforced, even in this early fragment, by the narrator's suggestions that the court in which Oroonoko lives is itself a network of petty tensions and resentments:

> This Onahal, as I said, was one of the cast-mistresses of the old king, and it was these (now past their beauty) that were made guardians or governants to the new and the young ones and whose business it was to teach them all those wanton arts of love with which they prevailed and charmed heretofore in their turn, and who now treated the triumphing happy ones with all the severity, as to liberty and freedom, that was possible, in revenge of those honors they robbed them of.[28]

The young and beautiful women at the center of the intrigues Behn follows are tended to by others whose high point of royal favor has passed. These older women's jealousy circumscribes the freedom the younger ones are given to enjoy the love and admiration of their suitors. The older women's pettiness is also the new expression their self-love finds once their own beauty has faded. Between these reminders of the small-mindedness they might fall into when they are no longer beautiful, and of the disregard with which they are met at present, the lovers Behn depicts are surrounded by signs of how easily the love that is precious to them might find expressions that will make it much less admirable. In a way that becomes ever more explicit as the novel progresses, these actual or potential dismissals of Oroonoko's feelings, relationships, or actions are interpreted by the narrator not directly as Oroonoko's moral failings, but as indications of how few

28. Behn, *Oroonoko*, 21.

are the contexts in which his qualities express themselves resoundingly and clearly.

Critics often emphasize the differences between this first part of Oroonoko's story and the narrative of his stay in Surinam.[29] Despite these differences, it is striking how insistently the patterns of restricted, distorted admiration and easy indifference established in early parts of Behn's novel are repeated in its second section. Oroonoko's fate in Surinam is not so much a change from as a confirmation of the inconsistent ranges and kinds of influence that he experiences from the start. In this sense, rather than—as critics have suggested—representing either a critique of or a fall from the first society Oroonoko inhabits, these later parts of Behn's novel continue its initial exploration of the difficulty Oroonoko experiences in giving his life the tone and grandeur it deserves.

As I show earlier, the second section of the novel is rife with moments when Oroonoko's whole community is suddenly stunned by his appearance and pays him homage. Yet Oroonoko's words and gestures are just as often treated as if they had no importance at all. Rather than argue with what he says, others just disregard his statements. The admiration that, at first, he seems to garner

---

29. Laura Rosenthal articulates these differences most extensively. She highlights the relatively greater historical accuracy of Behn's account of Surinam and argues that the two parts of the novel are also disparate in their style and generic influences. For Ramesh Mallipeddi and Jacqueline Pearson, much of *Oroonoko*'s potential as a critique of slavery comes from the contrast it stages between Oroonoko's social position in Africa and the constraints he suffers as a slave. As Mallipeddi puts it, "As an honorable prince, Oroonoko is in full possession of his royal person. But under slavery, in the wake of his extirpation from Coramantien, he is alienated not only from all claims of birth and lineage, but also most immediately from his own body." Laura J. Rosenthal, "*Oroonoko*: Reception, Ideology, and Narrative Strategy," in *The Cambridge Companion to Aphra Behn*, ed. Derek Hughes and Janet Todd (New York: Cambridge University Press, 2005), 152. Jacqueline Pearson, "Slave Princes and Lady Monsters: Gender and Ethnic Difference in the Work of Aphra Behn," in *Aphra Behn Studies*, ed. Janet Todd (New York: Cambridge University Press, 1996), 219–234; Ramesh Mallipeddi, "Spectacle, Spectatorship, and Sympathy in Aphra Behn's *Oroonoko*," *Eighteenth-Century Studies* 45, no. 4 (2012): 476.

everywhere, all of a sudden finds a humblingly immediate limit point. Once on board the slave ship, Oroonoko swears solemn oaths of obedience that he expects will be honored by its captain, as coming from a nobly born person: "Let him know I swear by my honor, which to violate would not only render me contemptible and despised by all brave and honest men, and so give myself perpetual pain, but it would be eternally offending and diseasing all mankind, harming, betraying, circumventing, and outraging all men."[30] Without even responding to this speech, the captain of the ship binds him just like the other slaves whom he has captured. Later in the novel, Oroonoko promises the narrator and Trefry, both of them ostensibly well disposed toward him, that he will not run away from the plantation. "Before I parted that day with him I got, with much ado, a promise from him to rest yet a little longer with patience, and wait the coming of the lord governor, who was every day expected on our shore. He assured me he would, and this promise he desired me to know was given perfectly in complaisance to me, in whom he had an entire confidence."[31] Despite this promise, and unbeknownst to himself, Oroonoko is nevertheless put under close watch.

Alongside such suggestions that the attention given to Oroonoko is surprisingly limited, Behn also highlights the smallness of the represented world in which his appeal is tested. Oroonoko expresses himself in contexts that—even if they are entirely pliant to his wishes—condense his prominence into something much smaller and pettier than the grand ideals to which he aspires. Even though his self-expression does occasionally become noted and admired by others, it only ever seems relevant to small groups of people and for brief periods of time.

30. Behn, *Oroonoko*, 35.
31. Behn, *Oroonoko*, 46.

As Behn's narrative progresses, these contextual distortions
of Oroonoko's self-expression grow more frequent. The way in
which Oroonoko is described frequently changes depending on
the expectations and backgrounds of the other characters with
whom he engages. Behn does not comment on these changes, nor
does she try to piece together Oroonoko's identity from among
the various conventions into which his interlocutors insert him.
Instead, she focuses on these conventions' incompatibility with
each other, and on the idiosyncrasies of each range of expression
his feelings and actions are given. Thus, when Oroonoko leads an
army into battle, Behn's style is dramatic and her portrayal of him
seems grandly heroic. When he attempts to start a slave rebellion,
both his initial enthusiasm and his later anger are represented as
animal-like and incomprehensibly frightening. When, on rare
occasions, our perspective on Oroonoko is narrowed down to his
direct interactions with the narrator, his actions take on an allegorical meaning laden with the narrator's retroactive knowledge of
his fate. This allows Behn's narrator to read into whatever he does
foreshadowings of his future life: most self-evidently, the pierced,
scarred heart of the tiger he kills becomes a prophecy of his painful
death.[32] By contrast, whenever Oroonoko is shown in the company
of the narrator's friends, his actions descend to the level of parlor
talk and popular anecdote. In their presence, he resembles merely
a favored servant of the narrator, bringing her tiger cubs and helping her look for animals in the surrounding waters. In one such episode, Oroonoko—to whom the narrator's friends half-mockingly
and only half-admiringly refer as "Caesar"—searches the water for
an electric eel. "Caesar," the narrator says, "used to laugh at this,
and believed it impossible a man could lose his force at the touch

32. See Susan Andrade, "White Skin, Black Masks: Colonialism and the Sexual Politics of
   Oroonoko," *Cultural Critique* 27 (1994): 192.

of a fish, and could not understand that philosophy, that a cold quality should be of that nature. However, he had a great curiosity to try whether it would have the same effect on him it had on others, and often tried, but in vain."[33] Soon after this boast, the eel's electric shock paralyzes Oroonoko and he nearly drowns. To suggest, as Dickson does, that in feats of bravery such as his fights with eels and tigers, "Oroonoko repeatedly outshines all other patterns within the text, emphasizing honor and royal order as well as absolute moral truth and character,"[34] is to overlook the attention Behn draws to these episodes not only as proofs of his courage but also as evidence of the provinciality and seclusion within which this courage is made manifest. The narrator and her friends call Oroonoko "Caesar" while also keeping him enslaved and only taking him on minor local escapades. Such scenes stress not only Oroonoko's eagerness to express his high ideals, but also the scarcity of objects upon which he can exercise this eagerness, as well as these objects' limited visibility and importance to anyone. Behn represents such changes in her protagonist's momentary kinds and degrees of immediate prominence as, apparently, an inherent part of his condition. As Elizabeth Young puts it, Behn thus depicts Oroonoko's irreducibility to any single social status—and the multiplicity of the more or less trivial roles he could potentially be fitted into— not as an individualist value he ought to defend, but as the source of his constraints and frustrations.[35] Rather than try to integrate these allegorical and romantic, serious and vaguely comic scenes into a coherent whole, Behn lets them stand apart from each other in a way that continues to highlight how incompatible these different visions are, and how little sense they collectively give us of

33. Behn, *Oroonoko*, 51.
34. Dickson, "Truth, Wonder, and Exemplarity," 584.
35. Elizabeth V. Young, "Aphra Behn, Gender, and Pastoral," *Studies in English Literature, 1500–1900* 33, no. 3 (1993): 531.

Oroonoko or of the breadth and convincingness of the ideals he is supposed to embody.

In Nussbaum's terms, *Oroonoko* might, superficially, seem to be merely a nightmarish version of the insensitivity that Nussbaum hopes novels might combat. Rather than model how our "circle of concern" as observers can be expanded, *Oroonoko* persists in making its represented observers seem narrow-minded and easily distractible. But instead of merely refusing the ideals of perfectibility and self-awareness Nussbaum praises, Behn's novel examines these ideals from the perspective of a person trying to come to terms with how limited and contingent is his capacity to focus other people's attention on himself. To the extent that Behn's novel can be seen as a critical challenge, the challenge it poses is not to our preconceptions about what we should focus on, but to the conclusions we might draw from, and the expectations we might have about, being attended to by others.

In the following passage, Behn's narrator self-consciously comments on the many senses of enclosure and constraint with which her narrative is carefully hedged:

> [Oroonoko's] misfortune was to fall in an obscure world, that afforded only a female pen to celebrate his fame; though I doubt not but it had lived from others' endeavors, if the Dutch, who, immediately after his time, took that country, had not killed, banished and dispersed all those that were capable of giving the world this great man's life much better than I have done.[36]

In fragments such as these, as in earlier comments about Oroonoko's petty observers at his grandfather's court, Oroonoko seems to be cheated out of his potential grandeur by the lack of a community in

36. Behn, *Oroonoko*, 40.

which he could prove its full range and dimensions. There is a sense in which, as Holmesland puts it, Behn represents Oroonoko's lofty ideals of honor as attempts at some higher and more transcendent form of morality.[37] Yet passages such as this one also highlight that Oroonoko is a particular body and mind whose impact can only be measured by the contingent ways in which he affects the few objects and people around him. Behn does not just affirm the abstract value of what Oroonoko stands for. She also stresses the vulnerability and oddity of trying to embody these ideals as a single person not fully in control of the environment in which he finds himself.

This gap between the admiration Oroonoko's qualities might potentially deserve, and the degree to which the course of his life does them justice, is also showcased by the narrator's statements that a person other than herself and her immediate circle might find Oroonoko's fate boring. What we as readers are told about him is already filtered through the narrator's self-consciousness about how little attention a story like his can most likely claim. "I shall omit, for brevity's sake," she says, "a thousand little accidents of his life, which, however pleasant to us, where history was scarce, and adventures very rare, yet might prove tedious and heavy to my reader in a world where he finds diversions for every minute new and strange."[38]

This statement and the one just quoted might seem contradictory. Behn's narrator suggests that Oroonoko's life is not yet being given enough attention. Yet she also needs to prevent herself from lingering with his story more than is appropriate. Recognizing that Behn represents her protagonist as a person with unfulfillably great aspirations makes these statements seem not only complementary,

37. Oddvar Holmesland, "Aphra Behn's *Oroonoko*: Cultural Dialectics and the Novel," *ELH* 68, no. 1 (2001): 73.
38. Behn, *Oroonoko*, 5.

but strikingly perceptive of the political and formal problem Behn's narrative foregrounds. By stressing the smallness of the environment in which her narrator is able to follow Oroonoko, as well as the limits of his capacity to center even this small environment around himself, Behn highlights how much of the impact of the story she tells hinges not merely on the abstract value of her protagonist's qualities, but on the success with which—moment by moment—this represented person and his environment are able to express them. Within this represented world it is striking both how large a following Behn's protagonist can attract, and how easily one nevertheless reaches the limits of this single person's impact. *Oroonoko* highlights how many characters its protagonist's life marks, as well as how difficult it is to shape the various kinds of influence he has into coherent proofs of his value as the model of a moral abstraction. This fragment and the one quoted above are, of course, backhanded feminist gestures. Behn draws attention not only to Oroonoko's lack of consistent resonance within his community, or within the novel's potential readership, but also to the limited respect both groups might accord to a woman's writing. She stresses the short attention span her society might have, in particular, for "a female pen."[39]

Oroonoko's death and dismemberment are the culmination of these narrative explorations of his limited, unreliable impact as a leader or ideal for the characters around him. On the one hand, the climax of Behn's narrative is marked by the dramatically increasing numbers of characters who attend to Oroonoko and even try to share

---

39. For more extended feminist readings of this and other passages, see Jacqueline Pearson, "Gender and Narrative in the Fiction of Aphra Behn," *The Review of English Studies* 42, no. 165 (1991): 40–56; Janet Todd, "Who is Silvia? What is She? Feminine Identity in Aphra Behn's *Love-Letters between a Nobleman and his Sister*," in *Aphra Behn Studies*, ed. Janet Todd (New York: Cambridge University Press, 1996), 199–218; and Joanna Lipking, "Confusing Matters: Searching the Backgrounds of *Oroonoko*," in *Aphra Behn Studies*, ed. Janet Todd (New York: Cambridge University Press, 1996), 259–281.

his fate. Oroonoko's struggle against the colonizers triggers both a collective uprising and a collective humiliation: Oroonoko leads his tribe into rebellion and, when he is defeated, the entire tribe is forced to whip him publicly. In the course of the story's gory finale, no fewer than forty people look for Oroonoko after he has murdered his wife. These people are then overwhelmed by the rotting body of Imoinda: "A party, of about forty, went that way he took; among whom was Tuscan, who was perfectly reconciled to Byam. They had not gone far into the wood, but they smelt an unusual smell, as of a dead body . . . so that they concluded that they should find him dead, or someone that was so."[40] The rebellion also causes mass panic among the narrator's entourage, who flee from Oroonoko and his followers in fear of incurring harm: "When the news was brought on Monday morning, that Caesar had betaken himself to the woods, and carried with him all the Negroes, we were possessed with extreme fear which no persuasions could dissipate . . . his apprehension made all the females of us fly down the river, to be secured."[41]

Behn zeroes in on one group after another whom Oroonoko's feelings affect or with whom they resonate. The threat he poses is amplified not by a moving description of his anger, but by the effect this anger has on ever new groups of people whom it touches or threatens. Indeed, in this passage the scope of the protagonist's rage is so great that he drives away the very people who later recount his life to the novel's implied reader. In this emphasis on the way Oroonoko impacts others, even the narrator's bodily weaknesses become useful in stressing the force of her narrative. Behn underscores the horrific sight and stench of Oroonoko's wounded body by stating that the narrator did not find its sight and odor physically

40. Behn, *Oroonoko*, 69.
41. Behn, *Oroonoko*, 64.

bearable: "His discourse was sad; and the earthly smell about him so strong, that I was persuaded to leave the place for some time, (being myself but sickly, and very apt to fall into fits of dangerous illness upon any extraordinary melancholy)."[42] These references to the narrator's body might have additional sexual connotations (as a number of critics have suggested).[43] Still, seen within the broader framework of this novel, such evocations have the more basic narrative purpose of adding to the general aura of high tragedy that at first temporarily surrounds Oroonoko's death. They show that the event she and her friends are witnessing is overpowering even in an immediate physical sense.

On the other hand, in parallel with these strong statements of how moving and admirable Oroonoko's presence can be, Behn stages a cascade of deflations in which the contexts and the consequences of these pronouncements of Oroonoko's grandeur are dramatically curtailed. As the narrator describes it, Oroonoko resorts to violence because the local community fails to "divert" him from thinking about the many dangers his captivity threatens to pose to him and his family: "It was thus for some time we diverted him, but now Imoinda began to show she was with child, and did nothing but sigh and weep for the captivity of her lord, herself and the infant yet unborn, and believed, if it were so hard to gain the liberty of two, 'twould be more difficult to get that for three."[44] By so abruptly juxtaposing Imoinda's despair against the narrator's casual politeness, Behn draws attention not merely to their divergent modes of reasoning, but also to these attitudes' mutual isolation. Rather than—as in sentimental literature—suggest that these characters' feelings are

42. Behn, *Oroonoko*, 71.
43. See, for instance, Susan Andrade's "White Skin, Black Masks," or Moira Ferguson's "Oroonoko: Birth of a Paradigm."
44. Behn, *Oroonoko*, 57.

instantly transmissible, Behn emphasizes how powerless her novel's central couple is to make its worry resonate even with a purportedly intimate audience.

After he starts to share Imoinda's concerns, Oroonoko seeks to make his anger at his captivity known to the other members of his tribe who are enslaved in Surinam. More overtly and more consistently than ever before, he expresses the grandeur of his personal ambitions. He wants his personal suffering to be a model and guide for the suffering of his people. He also wants others to recognize the violence to which he resorts as an act of political protest. Oroonoko delivers an impassioned speech against slavery, and compares himself and his assembled army to Hannibal and his soldiers: "he spoke of the impassable woods and rivers, and convinced 'em, the more danger, the more glory. He told them that he had heard of one Hannibal, a great captain, had cut his way through mountains of solid rocks, and should a few shrubs oppose them, which they could fire before 'em?"[45]

Like Imoinda's fears, these comparisons are dramatic but anticlimactic. Oroonoko's army is nowhere near as large and as redoubtable as Hannibal's; it has no great empire to overthrow, and no great mountains to scale. Instead, Oroonoko and the small number of poorly armed, already frightened men by his side are facing a provincial governor. Only a few lines later, Oroonoko's army abandons him after the slaves' wives beg them to put down their arms to escape punishment. His speech proves powerless to center even its immediate audience around him as their leader, even for just one day. After Oroonoko's soldiers flee from their imminent battle, the colonizers promise that he will not be punished if he surrenders. Once he is recaptured—in

45. Behn, *Oroonoko*, 59.

what is by now a predictable gesture of easy dismissal—they bind and whip him instantly:

> They were no sooner arrived at the place where all the slaves receive their punishments of whipping, but they laid hands on Caesar and Tuscan, faint with heat and toil, and, surprising them, bound them to two several stakes, and whipped them in a most deplorable and inhumane manner, rending the very flesh from their bones, especially Caesar, who was not perceived to make any moan, or to alter his face, only to roll his eyes on the faithless governor, and those he believed guilty, with fierceness and indignation; and to complete his rage, he saw every one of those slaves who, but a few days before, adored him as something more than mortal, now had a whip to give him some lashes, while he strove not to break his fetters, though if he had, it were impossible. But he pronounced a woe and revenge from his eyes that darted fire, that 'twas at once both aweful and terrible to behold.[46]

Oroonoko's former army now become witnesses and accessories to his humiliation. The crowd gazes at his whipped body even as he tries his utmost to not let his defeat become more visible than it already is. Spengemann describes these final bouts of violence as signs of Oroonoko's definitive isolation from the community in which he tried to assert a bolder and more idealistic set of values.[47] But perhaps most striking about these last sections of the novel is the ease with which these acts of violence keep rapidly changing their meaning, tone, and apparent social scope. This fragment quickly evolves from an attempted epic battle to a description of familial quarrels and petty provincial politics. The temporary ranges of influence Oroonoko holds change at a moment's notice. Behn's transitions between them

46. Behn, *Oroonoko*, 63.
47. Spengemann, "Earliest American Novel," 404.

highlight how much the meaning and weight of his story depend on such shifting kinds and scopes of resonance.

These oscillations between grand and trivial expressions of Oroonoko's anger and suffering culminate when, in a dramatic final gesture of despair, he takes his pregnant wife into the forest and kills her and their unborn child. At first, his disappearance moves his community to nothing more than a bustling, gossipy sense of concern: "In all this time you may believe we were in no little affliction for Caesar and his wife; some were of opinion he was escaped never to return, others thought some accident had happened to him."[48] When the colonizers do finally find his family's bodies and begin to mourn them, Oroonoko rips out his bowels in an attempt at suicide. "At that, he ripped up his own belly; and took his bowels and pulled 'em out, with what strength he could; while some, on their knees imploring, besought him to hold his hand."[49] He then begins to throw pieces of his body at his pursuers: "'Look ye, ye faithless crew,' said he, ''Tis not life I seek, nor am I afraid of dying,' and at that word cut a piece of flesh from his own throat and threw it at 'em, 'yet still I would live if I could till I had perfected my revenge.'"[50]

Rivero and Charlotte Sussman point out that it is possible to read these acts of self-mutilation as attempts to reenact the horror of Imoinda's and her child's death.[51] As Gustafson and Rivero have also suggested, the very excess of these final moments of violence could represent the extreme degree to which Oroonoko is misunderstood in this environment.[52] But again, Oroonoko's wounds are perhaps most striking in how easily his onlookers are able to marvel at these

48. Behn, *Oroonoko*, 69.
49. Behn, *Oroonoko*, 70.
50. Behn, *Oroonoko*, 70.
51. Rivero, "Aphra Behn's *Oroonoko*," 457; Charlotte Sussman, "The Other Problem with Women: Reproduction and Slave Culture in Aphra Behn's *Oroonoko*," in *Rereading Aphra Behn: History, Theory, and Criticism*, ed. Heidi Hutner (Charlottesville: University Press of Virginia, 1993), 212–233.
52. Rivero, "Aphra Behn's *Oroonoko*," 457; Gustafson, "Cultural Memory," 10.

mutilations without articulating any deep or precise conclusions about them. Oroonoko's attempts at communicating his anger and despair to others in this most physical manner registers as pathetic. He cannot possibly be able to throw these body parts very far, especially compared to the grand scope of his prior ambitions, and the literalness of this gesture is deeply vulnerable. As they behold this tragic self-display, Oroonoko's onlookers do not even treat his self-mutilation as the mark of an epistemic limit to their understanding of him. Whatever rich meanings his gestures might have been intended to express remain unprobed. The spectacle of his near-death provokes merely superficial comments about his lost virile beauty: "We ran all to see him, and, if, before we thought him so beautiful a sight, he was now so altered that his face was like a death's head blacked over, nothing but teeth and eyeholes."[53] Soon after, when his friends carelessly leave him alone with his doctors, the governor once again submits Oroonoko to a whipping and has his body quartered. The governor then uses Oroonoko's fragmented body parts as warnings against future attempts at rebellion. In a way that seems at once sympathetic and—again—anticlimactic, other colonizers actively arrest this circulation process, refusing to see Oroonoko's body or to show it to others. "They cut Caesar in quarters," says the narrator, "and sent them to several of the chief plantations: one quarter was sent to colonel Martin, who refused it; and swore, . . . he could govern his Negroes without terrifying and grieving them with the frightful spectacles of a mangled king."[54]

This ending does suggest that Oroonoko's story might keep circulating outward. New communities might be confronted not merely with echoes of this story, but with direct empirical proof of Oroonoko's existence.[55] At the same time, these final descriptions of

53. Behn, *Oroonoko*, 71.
54. Behn, *Oroonoko*, 72–73.
55. A similar point was made by Robert B. Chibka in his "Truth, Falsehood, and Fiction in *Oroonoko*," revised from "Oh! Do Not Fear a Woman's Invention: Truth, Falsehood, and

Oroonoko's body also confirm the doubts and hesitations voiced by Behn in the self-reflexive comments I quote earlier: even at its most "mangled" and most vividly evocative, Oroonoko's body can still easily be removed from social visibility and circulation. The fragility, partiality, and disfigurement of Oroonoko's body parts embody the similarly precarious distortedness of the means by which and contexts in which his qualities find expression moment by moment. By anchoring her ending ever more firmly to Oroonoko's body, Behn makes this body seem impossible to transcend in pursuit of larger and more universal values. In her insistence that the value of Oroonoko's story needs to be derived from and measured by this story's immediate physical details, she construes this attachment to its particulars both as her narrative's power and as its limitation.

To emphasize Behn's doubts about how grand and broad an ideal her protagonist can embody is not to suggest that this novel is apolitical. But it is to propose that Behn turns *Oroonoko* into an exploration not merely of its protagonist's virtues, but also of the larger difficulty of using a single person's life to comment on how an entire community does or ought to perceive itself. She stresses how little content can be conveyed through such a single person's life—however laudable it is—and how few other people such a particular life affects.

Nussbaum argues that literature "speaks about us, about our lives and choices and emotions, about our social existence and the totality of our connections. . . . [I]t searches for patterns of possibility— of choice, and circumstance, and the interaction between choice and circumstance—that turn up in human lives with such a persistence that they must be regarded as our possibilities."[56] My reading of *Oroonoko* highlights that Nussbaum's understanding of these

Fiction in Aphra Behn's *Oroonoko*," *Texas Studies in Literature and Language* 30, no. 4 (1988): 510–537, reprinted in *Oroonoko: A Norton Critical Edition*, 223–224.
56. Nussbaum, *Love's Knowledge*, 171.

"patterns of possibility" is only partial, and perhaps excessively optimistic. In focusing on what Nussbaum would call the "circles of concern" of the communities she represents, Behn stresses the experience of being an occasional, inconsistent focus of circumscribed acts of attentiveness. She underlines the uncontrolled shifts in the tone and apparent significance of a person's actions that come from falling in and out of the scopes of other people's concern—shifts that, as she suggests, one can at best only acknowledge and accommodate.

Behn's final image of Oroonoko's fragmented corpse circulating across South America provides an apt bridge into the notion of character addressed in the following chapter. The protagonists of the two novels this next chapter examines—by Françoise de Graffigny and Isabelle de Charrière—never face fates as gruesome as Oroonoko's, but they stake out their claims to social significance by inserting themselves into analogous processes of circulation. They do so by pouring their thoughts and feelings into writing.

2

The Writer

Françoise de Graffigny's *Letters from a Peruvian Woman* and Isabelle de Charrière's *Letters of Mistress Henley*

"Aza, my dear Aza! Like a morning mist the cries of your tender Zilia rise up and have dissipated before reaching you," writes the protagonist of Françoise de Graffigny's *Letters from a Peruvian Woman*.[1] She is composing a letter to her fiancé Aza, from whom she has been separated by white invaders of her native country. Zilia describes her voice as frail and easily perishable. Drafting this missive is her best attempt at traversing the distance that separates her from her fiancé.

The eighteenth century is often seen as a breakthrough period in the development of Western European individualism. Around this time, notions of personhood also become more closely and pervasively wedded than they were before to the process of writing about oneself. Nancy Armstrong describes this cultural development in *Desire and Domestic Fiction*. She claims that novels are not merely the effect of, but a major influence on, this period's changing ideas about writing and subjectivity. They model the process by which writing can help one discover the unique qualities of one's experience—and

---

1. "Mon cher Aza! les cris de ta tendre Zilia, tels qu'une vapeur du matin, s'exhalent et sont dissipés avant d'arriver jusqu'à toi" (17). Françoise de Graffigny, *Letters from a Peruvian Woman*, trans. David Kornacker (New York: MLA, 1993), 17. Françoise de Graffigny, *Lettres d'une Péruvienne* (New York: MLA, 1992).

generalize from this experience to call into question prevailing social conventions. In her analysis of Samuel Richardson's *Pamela*, Armstrong describes how Pamela's body is gradually transmuted into written language. This act of translation empowers Pamela: by pouring her life into her letters, she compels Mr. B. to recognize and respect her moral principles. "Richardson stages a scene of rape that transforms an erotic and permeable body into a self-enclosed body of words. Mr. B.'s repeated failures suggest that Pamela cannot be raped because she is nothing but words."[2] Circulated throughout Pamela's community, her letters move this entire community to admire her. As Armstrong puts it, Pamela's writing eventually "addressed millions that came to understand themselves as basically the same kind of individual."[3] These letters allow Pamela (and *Pamela*) to tie her plight to recognizable moral rules and principles. They also enable her to gain control over what happens to her body and how others describe it.[4]

---

2. Amanda Armstrong, *Desire and Domestic Fiction* (New York: Oxford University Press, 1987), 116.

3. Armstrong, *Desire and Domestic Fiction*, 115. In *Publics and Counterpublics*, Michael Warner puts a similar point as follows: "This form of address is tightly knit up with a social imaginary: any character trait I depict typifies a whole social stratum. Individual readers who participate in this discourse learn to place themselves, as characterized types, in a world of urbane social knowledge, while also ethically detaching themselves from the particular interests that typify them." Michael Warner, *Publics and Counterpublics* (New York: Zone Books, 2005), 105.

4. For Armstrong, the way in which the early novel identifies personhood with the written word persists unto this day. Armstrong emphasizes that this conjunction of personhood with writing and, by consequence, with a self-reflexive, self-affirming individualism is endemic to the novel as a genre: "New varieties of novel cannot help taking up the project of universalizing the individual subject. That, simply put, is what novels do." Armstrong sees this persistent legacy of the novel as both a weakness and a significant strength. On the one hand, the novel thus necessarily buys into the way in which "modern culture" in general—including our contemporary culture—"depends on the form of power that works through language—and particularly the printed word—to constitute subjectivity." As a genre, it is unable to transcend the discursive means by which our identities, and our belief in their uniqueness, are conventionally forged and maintained. At the same time, within this framework, the novel thereby helps its readers perceive themselves as having some amount of subversive agency within

Like Pamela and the other novel characters described by Armstrong, the protagonists of Graffigny's *Letters from a Peruvian Woman* and Isabelle de Charrière's *Letters of Mistress Henley* work toward new forms of personal and social self-awareness by writing about themselves. The writing process, which in both novels is thematized through personal correspondence, serves these protagonists as a means of reflecting upon their individual desires. The protagonists of both novels also use letters to try to enhance the degrees of agency they have for pursuing their wishes or beliefs.

At the same time, a significant difference separates Graffigny's and Charrière's protagonists from the characters singled out by Armstrong. For Armstrong, to write about oneself is to increase the ranges and kinds of influence one has over how one is perceived and treated. For Graffigny and Charrière, writing is a means of recognizing and examining the limits of one's impact on others. The letter, and the small piece of paper on which it is written, become metonymic of these characters' narrowly circumscribed bodies and minds. The composition and circulation of letters makes Charrière's and

their social contexts. It models, for its readers, a way of using writing to protest against, and potentially alter, the norms by which one is conventionally perceived and judged. Nancy Armstrong, *How Novels Think: The Limits of British Individualism from 1719–1900* (New York: Columbia University Press, 2005), 10; Armstrong, *Desire and Domestic Fiction*, 25.

Lynch similarly argues that the culture, and more particularly the fiction, of eighteenth-century Western Europe are preoccupied with the notion that human beings could be treated as, or translated into, texts. "According to the understanding of linguistic behavior that prevailed at the opening of the century," she shows, "discourse was embodied—at ease with its immersion in a print culture in which language necessarily assumes visible, corporeal form. At the same time, the body was discursive, a telltale transcript of the identity it housed" (30). Lynch illustrates the novel's commitment to this notion by pointing to the very word *character* (in English, at least), as the semantic fusion of the terms *trait* or *stroke* and *person*. In French (the language that is more relevant here), the parallel pun is less obvious, but similarly meaningful: *personnage* can mean both *person* and *persona* or mask, both a constructed identity and the person hidden behind it. Deidre Lynch, *The Economy of Character: Novels, Market Culture, and the Business of Inner Meaning* (Chicago and London: University of Chicago Press, 1998), 38–42.

Graffigny's protagonists aware of how little control they have over anything except small segments of their environments. It also forces them to realize how few people they might be able to convince of the generalizability and insightfulness of their experiences.

The counterintuitive, flattening ways in which Graffigny and Charrière tie their character construction to writing stem from their novels' focus on the experience of being responded to as an author. Writing about oneself, both novelists suggest, lets one perceive one's life as potentially very significant and generalizable. It leads one to recognize how many of one's immediate perceptions and observations might serve as models or examples for others. But to actually *send* these letters, and follow the responses they incite in their environments, compels one to admit that many parts of these environments are not at all affected by these letters' circulation. It forces one to see this process of self-expression as only one social force among many others whose impact easily becomes forgotten or lost. Graffigny and Charrière construct their protagonists in a way that focuses not only on these protagonists' potentially convincing claims to universality, but also on the multitude of people whom these protagonists try to persuade about such claims. Both authors set the forms of seemingly generalizable self-understanding created by writing about oneself in tension with the vastness of the physical and social world within which these attempts at generality would need to be defended. In the process, they turn the novel, and character construction in particular, into a means of reflecting about the difficulty of enacting the kind of self-affirming individualism Armstrong describes. They dismiss the notion that writing allows one to discover and secure the broader value of one's thoughts and feelings, as a fantasy whose grandiosity is inevitably curbed in actual life.

Graffigny and Charrière are of course, as francophone writers (and as, respectively, French and Dutch nationals), part of a novelistic tradition whose arc differs from the concurrent development of the

English novel. As Stephanie Hilger puts it—following Joan DeJean—"Whereas in the English tradition, the early nineteenth century represents both the height of the novel and of women's writing, in the French context this is not the case because a female literary tradition can be located earlier: French women's writing . . . came very quickly and fully into its own, so that we can speak of a veritable tradition of French women's writing as early as the 1660s."[5] The eighteenth-century French novel builds on the seventeenth-century tradition of letter writing and on aristocratic proto-novels by authors such as Madame de Lafayette. It also emerges in dialogue with utopian and dystopian philosophical narratives by writers such as Denis Diderot or Voltaire. As I juxtapose Charrière's and Graffigny's works against Aphra Behn's and, in my next chapter, against Thomas Hardy's, I do not argue that these authors directly influence each other, or that they all react to analogous social conditions. Instead, I highlight the formal concerns they share about how much the figure of a novel's protagonist can reliably convey.

Letters from a Peruvian Woman is Graffigny's most famous novel; prior to its publication, Graffigny also enjoyed much success as a playwright. Critics have tended to interpret this text as a wide-ranging form of social commentary. They have also described it as deeply invested in personal writing.[6] With these other scholars, I stress

5. Stephanie Hilger, "Comment peut-on être Péruvienne? Françoise de Graffigny, a Strategic *Femme de Lettres*," *College Literature* 32, no. 2 (2005): 63; Joan DeJean, *Tender Geographies: Women and the Origin of the Novel in France* (New York: Columbia University Press, 1991), 7.

6. Heidi Bostic describes this novel as a form of instruction in how a woman living in French society can wrest command of language and of reason as efficient tools of her self-expression. Nancy Miller and Janet Whatley consider ways in which this novel diagnoses the misogyny of French society. For Janie Vanpée, the *Letters* also explore larger questions of cultural and linguistic displacement and exile. On a more biographical level, English Showalter focuses on the breadth of reading to which this novel testifies. It shows Graffigny to be intimately connected to, and versed in, a variety of contemporaneous and prior traditions of writing. Heidi Bostic, "Graffigny's Self, Graffigny's Friend: Intimate Sharing in the Correspondence 1750–52," *Studies in Eighteenth Century Culture* 42, no. 1 (2013): 215–236. Nancy K. Miller,

ways in which Graffigny's novel explores its protagonist's capacity to use writing in order to inhabit an engaged, critical position within her community, carving out within this community some space of autonomy and potential influence. But my reading of the *Letters* also highlights Graffigny's skepticism about the empowering potential of putting one's thoughts on paper. This skepticism, when it has previously been remarked on, has been read simply as the reactionary stance of a privileged aristocrat.[7] Putting a more positive spin on these critiques, I take Graffigny's novel as an exploration of how difficult it is for a single person to critique larger social norms—however inadequate these norms might be—through the prism of her immediate experience and self-expression.

Graffigny's protagonist and narrator Zilia initially writes her letters with a belief in the importance and universality of her personal experience. At the beginning of the novel, Zilia is engaged to an Incan prince named Aza. She believes she is destined to marry him by popular acclaim and divine decree; they are also in love with each other. The public and the private, the cosmic and the human, merge in her early letters into a totalizing, harmonious picture of her central place

"Men's Reading, Women's Writing: Gender and the Rise of the Novel," *Yale French Studies* 75 (1988): 40–55; Janet Whatley, "The Eighteenth-Century Canon: Works Lost and Found," *French Review* 61 (1988): 414–420. Janie Vanpée, "From Graffigny's *Lettres d'une Péruvienne* to Leila Sebbar's and Nancy Huston's *Lettres parisiennes*: Figuring Cultural Displacement," *Dalhousie French Studies* 61 (2002): 137. English Showalter, "Mme de Graffigny, Reader of Fiction," *Eighteenth-Century Fiction* 13, no. 2–3 (2001): 475.

7. Jack Undank describes this novel as the work of an inherently overprivileged person, a work that can be enjoyed as entertainment but not as serious political or philosophical critique because of its "lingering and aristocratic obtuseness." Erin Isikoff argues—specifically against Nancy Miller's more generous reading—that Graffigny's novel teaches women not to rebel but to accommodate themselves. It leads them not toward genuine self-knowledge but into a safe, solipsistic illusion of self-transparency. Jack Undank, "Graffigny's Room of Her Own," *French Forum* 13, no. 3 (1988): 298. Erin Isikoff, "The Temple, the Château, and the Female Space: Nancy Miller's Overreading of Graffigny's *Lettres d'une Péruvienne*," *Dalhousie French Studies* 33 (1995): 15–26.

in this world. She claims that Aza's love for her expresses the Sun's own love: "I thought that the Sun was showing me his will through you and that he was choosing me to be his elite spouse."[8] Her affection for Aza fuses—and can potentially replace—the love of a whole nation. "You will be more of a king," she says "ruling over my soul than you are doubting the affection of a countless people."[9] The letters she writes about their love will preserve it not only at present, but for generations to come: "I hastened to knot [my *quipus*] in the hope that with their help I might immortalize the story of our love and happiness."[10]

After Zilia is kidnapped and taken away to France, her vision of herself as the center of this world is shattered. At first, she still expresses confidence that all the new places and people she sees must be subordinate to her fiancé as the embodiment of the Sun god. "Certainly I am being conducted to this land I have been made to see. Obviously it is part of your dominion since the Sun sheds its beneficent rays upon it."[11] But Zilia also begins to notice, and is troubled by, two forms of cultural shock: a sense of disconnectedness and of disempowerment. Both experiences undermine the self-sufficiency and generality of her self-expression. Deprived of the cultural tropes into which she was born, she now needs to consciously find and reinforce some new connections between her experiences and the people and environments around her.

---

8. Graffigny, *Letters from a Peruvian Woman*, 27. "Je crus que le Soleil me manifestait sa volonté par ton organe, qu'il me choisissait pour son épouse d'élite" (*Lettres d'une Péruvienne*, 27).

9. Graffigny, *Letters from a Peruvian Woman*, 25. "Tu seras plus roi en régnant sur mon âme, qu'en doutant de l'affection d'un peuple innombrable" (*Lettres d'une Péruvienne*, 24).

10. Graffigny, *Letters from a Peruvian Woman*, 19. "Je me hâtai de les nouer, dans l'espérance qu'avec leur secours je rendrais immortelle l'histoire de notre amour et de notre bonheur" (*Lettres d'une Péruvienne*, 19).

11. Graffigny, *Letters from a Peruvian Woman*, 46. "Il est certain que l'on me conduit à cette terre que l'on m'a fait voir; il est évident qu'elle est une portion de ton empire, puisque le Soleil y répand ses rayons bienfaisants" (*Lettres d'une Péruvienne*, 45).

The first cultural shock Zilia undergoes is a sense of disconnectedness. She is stunned by her apparent inability to affect the people and
environments around her by what she says and how she behaves. She
is also struck by how solipsistic and distant others seem to her. As her
letters cannot reach Aza and no one else around her speaks her language, her cries start to seem merely like so much air—evaporating
without affecting anyone.[12] She also begins to suspect that Aza's
seeming presence in the landscapes she sees might be a figment of her
imagination: "I find the thought of you in the least of my inquisitive
desires yet encounter it in none of the objects offering themselves to
my view."[13] Reduced to tears before her French captors, she finds that
even her open displays of distress cannot claim their attention and
care: "Far from being moved by my entreaties, my abductors are not
even touched by my tears; deaf to my language, they understand no
better the cries of my despair."[14] Zilia's intimations of the distance that
separates her from others reach an apex when, upon meeting French
aristocrats—who she supposes will recognize her as an equal—she
finds that her appearance moves them to laughter. "I was displeased,"
she says, "by the general amazement shown at the sight of me. The
excessive laughter that several young girls attempted to keep back and
that started again when they looked upon me stirred in my heart a
feeling so disturbing that I would have taken it for shame had I felt
myself guilty of some offense."[15]

12. "Aza, my dear Aza! Like a morning mist the cries of your tender Zilia rise up and have dissipated before reaching you" (Graffigny, *Letters from a Peruvian Woman*, 17). "Mon cher
Aza! les cris de ta tendre Zilia, tels qu'une vapeur du matin, s'exhalent et sont dissipés avant
d'arriver jusqu'à toi" (*Lettres d'une Péruvienne*, 17).
13. Graffigny, *Letters from a Peruvian Woman*, 62–63. "Je trouve ton idée dans le moindre
de mes désirs curieux, et je ne la rencontre dans aucun des objets qui s'offrent à ma vue"
(*Lettres d'une Péruvienne*, 61).
14. Graffigny, *Letters from a Peruvian Woman*, 18. "Loin d'être touchés de mes plaintes, mes
ravisseurs ne le sont pas même de mes larmes; sourds à mon langage, ils n'entendent pas
mieux les cris de mon désespoir" (*Lettres d'une Péruvienne*, 18).
15. Graffigny, *Letters from a Peruvian Woman*, 53–54. "L'étonnement général que l'on témoigna
à ma vue me déplut; les ris excessifs que plusieurs jeunes filles s'efforçaient d'étouffer et

François Rosset and Madeleine Dobie describe such scenes as breakthrough moments when Zilia recognizes how unique and complex she is.[16] Yet what makes such passages most striking is not the difficulty she poses to others, but the ease with which other people refuse to engage with her unfamiliar behavior. They notice only details of her body and dress that they find amusing, and neglect to draw any broader conclusions from their mutual differences. Graffigny focuses on the shock Zilia causes these represented people as well as on the way this shock is instantly buffered as mere entertainment.

Just as the people around Zilia are unable or unwilling to acknowledge her feelings, she also cannot adequately discern and respond to theirs. Zilia interacts with Captain Déterville for months, and stays with him and his sister Céline, without realizing that he is in love with her. She also shows no sympathy toward Déterville's and Céline's desperate struggle for their inheritance after their dying mother attempts to disown them, recording this struggle only in passing in spite of how centrally her two friends' fates depend on its outcome. The public displays of European culture Zilia witnesses leave her cold. When she is taken to the theater, Zilia describes the actors as enveloped in private joys and sorrows in which she has no part. She notices not the potential universality of their feelings, but these feelings' complete isolation from anything that seems reasonable to her: "Those who represent these personages shout and flail about like madmen. I saw one of them push his fury to the point of killing himself."[17]

---

qui recommençaient lorsqu'elles levaient les yeux sur moi, excitèrent dans mon cœur un sentiment si fâcheux, que je l'aurais pris pour de la honte, si je me fusse sentie coupable de quelque faute (*Lettres d'une Péruvienne*, 52).

16. Madeleine Dobie, "The Subject of Writing: Language, Epistemology, and Identity in the *Lettres d'une Péruvienne*," *The Eighteenth Century* 38, no. 2 (1997): 104; François Rosset, "Les nœuds du langage dans les *Lettres d'une Péruvienne*," *Revue d'Histoire littéraire de la France* 96, no. 6 (1996): 1106–1127.

17. Graffigny, *Letters from a Peruvian Woman*, 76. "Ceux qui les réprésentent crient comme des furieux; j'en ai vu un pousser sa rage jusqu'a se tuer lui-meme." (*Lettres d'une Péruvienne*, 74).

Entering this new society also causes Zilia to feel disempowered. She repeatedly describes her encounters with Europeans as experiences of being violated or invaded. From her forceful abduction, through her voyage on the slave ship, and later on in her attempts to make sense of the conflict-ridden domestic world of Déterville's family, she often notes how much the objects and people around her crowd her in. "I cannot even," she says, "enjoy in peace the novel sort of desert to which my inability to communicate my thoughts has consigned me, for I am surrounded by bothersome objects whose attentive gazes disturb my soul's solitude, constrain my body's postures, and inhibit my very thoughts."[18]

Such experiences of physical constraint—which are often even more dramatic than the scene quoted above—abound throughout the novel. Zilia is violently abducted, locked in small rooms, confined to her bed, forced into unfamiliar clothing and incomprehensible daily habits. In the midst of what she calls a "desert" of mutual indifference, she finds herself surrounded by a multitude of confusing stimuli. These objects whose purposes she does not know restrict her sense of who she is and what she can do. Graffigny embeds this sense of violation and helplessness even in scenes of what—on the part of the characters who surround Zilia—appear to be attempts not to hurt but to help her. In this early episode, she is forcibly subjected to her abductors' care after she falls ill while they are at sea: "In addition to a countless number of petty refusals," Zilia recounts, "they deny me, dearest Aza, the very nourishments necessary to sustain life, the very freedom to choose the place where I wish to be. By means of a form of violence they hold me in this bed, now grown intolerable to me."[19]

18. Graffigny, *Letters from a Peruvian Woman*, 38. "Je ne puis même jouir paisiblement de la nouvelle espèce de désert où me réduit l'impuissance de communiquer mes pensées. Entourée d'objets importuns, leurs regards attentifs troublent la solitude de mon âme, contraignent les attitudes de mon corps, et portent la gêne jusque dans mes pensées" (*Lettres d'une Péruvienne*, 37).

19. Graffigny, *Letters from a Peruvian Woman*, 39. "Sans compter un nombre infini de petites contradictions, ils me refusent, mon cher Aza, jusqu'aux aliments nécessaires au soutien de

Scenes such as these make it seem that the problem Zilia is facing is not just cultural distance but the bewildered disempowerment with which she experiences these new people and settings. Even others' attempts at kindness leave no room for her to express herself within this new environment.

As she seeks to regain a sense of control over herself and her surroundings, Zilia turns to writing. In the absence of her beloved Aza, Zilia comes to identify with her letters to him ever more strongly. She trusts that, once these letters finally reach him, they will reaffirm their mutual love even in her bodily absence. Zilia also begins to treat these letters as means by which her sense of alienation could be generalized into a critical commentary about the society in which she has found herself. Writing them leads her to hope that, perhaps, her particular plight could be instructive to many other people, allowing her to regain some of her former regal status by becoming an intellectual model for others. In the course of this transition, Zilia's attitude toward her letters resembles those that Armstrong attributes to many other eighteenth-century novels and novel heroines. Armstrong describes how, for Jane Austen, writing is "a form of power in its own right, which could displace the material body of the subject and the value of those objects constituting the household."[20] Writing gives Zilia an analogous hope of restoring to her personal experience the values that she was raised to believe in, and which are missing from her current circumstances.

But Graffigny's novel does not go on to simply affirm letters as means of shoring up Zilia's sense of herself. Indeed, the fact that Graffigny associates Zilia's turn to writing with beliefs that she held as a cloistered, lonely adolescent already begins to suggest that her trust

---

la vie, jusqu'à la liberté de choisir la place où je veux être: ils me retiennent par une espèce de violence dans ce lit, qui m'est devenu insupportable" (*Lettres d'une Péruvienne*, 38).

20. Armstrong, *Desire and Domestic Fiction*, 156.

in these letters will become an object of critique. Writing letters to Aza does allow Zilia to gain a kind of awareness that she badly needed within this new setting. Yet the awareness Zilia acquires concerns not the broad significance of her thoughts and feelings, but the ease with which these thoughts and feelings can be disregarded by others, and the narrow circumferences of the environments over which she can claim mastery. Instead of undoing the sense of marginality and disempowerment produced by her culture shock, writing eventually helps her develop a sense of herself that acknowledges these experiences of confusion and indifference as intrinsic parts of her existence among other people.

The *Letters* build up toward this recognition slowly, by setting up and then repeating a version of the crisis Zilia experiences at the start of the novel. The first parts of the *Letters* are punctuated by Zilia's complaints that the messages she writes to Aza will never reach him, and that she is running out of the writing materials she brought with her from Peru. After Zilia learns to read and write in French, she has at her disposal a wealth of pen and paper. Déterville locates Aza in Spain and Zilia's letters to him begin to be delivered. She is also able to start corresponding with other people. As this correspondence brings ever closer the time when she and Aza will finally be reunited, it restores to her the confidence she lost at the start of this narrative. The letters she writes grow in scope and ambition. Rather than merely recount her immediate confusions and confirm her continued love for Aza, Zilia begins to voice wide-ranging opinions about French society. She generalizes her culture shock into statements about why the new society in which she finds herself is inferior to the one she left behind. "Were the shows of zeal and attentiveness with which they dress up the least social duties here natural," she says, "these people would have to have more goodness and humanity in their hearts than do ours. Is this conceivable, my dear Aza?" "Had they as much serenity in their souls as on their faces," Zilia continues, "were the penchant of joy that I notice in all their actions sincere, would they choose for their amusement spectacles such as the one I was made to see?"[21]

In this passage, Zilia reframes her sense of cultural disconnectedness as a statement about the superficiality of French society. She redescribes her inability to reach the people who surround her, as a reflection of how shallow and false their society is in general. Graffigny's novel eventually undermines many of these critical claims as signs of Zilia's excessive trust in how accurately and extensively her experience of this society illuminates its condition. These grand forms of social critique disappear toward the end of the novel, when Zilia's sense of how large a world she can (and wants to) be concerned with is again recalibrated. But in the middle sections of the *Letters* such passages mark a high point of the confidence Zilia gains from discovering that her missives reach other people across expanses that she would previously have found unbridgeable. This capacity to convey her thoughts and feelings in writing gives her hope and apparent proof that her thoughts and feelings, intimate as they are, can illuminate and change a larger world beyond herself.

Zilia's letters also record and reinforce the progress she makes in wresting control of her immediate physical surroundings. As Zilia finds new friends in French society, she moves from the crowds of people and objects that first surround her on the slave ship, to the private cabin and then the family mansion of Déterville himself. Within these much more stable and controlled material settings, she

---

21. Graffigny, *Letters from a Peruvian Woman*, 75–76. "Si les démonstrations de zèle et d'empressement, dont on décore ici les moindres devoirs de la société, étaient naturelles, il faudrait, mon cher Aza, que ces peuples eûssent dans le cœur plus de bonté, plus d'humanité que les nôtres: cela se peut-il penser? S'ils avaient autant de sérénité dans l'âme que sur le visage, si le penchant à la joie, que je remarque dans toutes leurs actions, était sincère, choisiraient-ils pour leurs amusements des spectacles tels que celui que l'on m'a fait voir?" (*Lettres d'une Péruvienne*, 73).

gradually makes her wishes intelligible to the people around her. At first, her attempts at expressing herself to others are painfully modest. Thus, when Zilia first makes friends with her French maid, she takes comfort merely in the fact that the maid patiently sits beside her without understanding what Zilia is saying: "I told her my troubles as if she could understand me. I asked her a thousand questions as if she could answer them."[22] But gradually Zilia begins to reconstruct around herself an ever wider and more reliable space of social expression. She finds within this world many people and objects who reflect back to her the person she believes herself to be.[23] Her royal status is confirmed and reinstated by the respect shown to her by Déterville and his sister, as well as by the readiness with which they put themselves at her beck and call. Meanwhile, her beauty finds affirmation in how many of the men she meets at Déterville's house are drawn to her: "He uttered several words that I know from having heard Déterville say them a thousand times: 'How beautiful she is! What lovely eyes! . . .' Another man replied, 'What grace! The figure of a nymph! . . .' Apart from the women, who said nothing, everyone kept repeating more or less the same words."[24]

Zilia's happiness about these many forms of recognition and validation reaches its apex when Déterville restores to her the Peruvian treasures stolen by her abductors, and builds her a house in which

22. Graffigny, *Letters from a Peruvian Woman*, 66. "Je lui contais mes chagrins, comme si elle eût pu m'entendre; je lui faisais mille questions, comme si elle eût pu y répondre" (*Lettres d'une Péruvienne*, 65).

23. Graffigny's novel here shares much with the dramatic externalizations of Behn's *Oroonoko*. Zilia expresses herself not simply by pouring her feelings outward—as Stephanie Hilger has suggested—but by assembling herself from gradually collected objects and persons whose material reality appears to confirm her feelings and steady her social position. Hilger, "Comment peut-on être Péruvienne?," 77–78.

24. Graffigny, *Letters from a Peruvian Woman*, 54–55. "Il lui dit plusieurs paroles que je sais pour les avoir entendu prononcer mille fois à Déterville: *Qu'elle est belle! les beaux yeux! . . .* Un autre homme lui répondit: *Des grâces, une taille de nymphe!* Hors les femmes, qui ne dirent rien, tous répétèrent à peu près les mêmes mots" (*Lettres d'une Péruvienne*, 53).

these treasures can be permanently displayed. Zilia feels "drunk" with
joy to behold this house when Déterville and Céline first lead her into
it: "A confused feeling composed of sadness and joy, pleasure and
regret filled my whole heart. I prostrated myself before these sacred
remnants of our religion and our Altars, covered them with respectful
kisses, bathed them with my tears. I could not tear myself away from
them and had forgotten Céline's very presence."[25] In this house, she is
once again able to perform the rituals from which she was removed by
her capture. She can make her lived environment expressive of beliefs
she temporarily lost hope of making intelligible at all. Zilia at first also
hopes that Aza will move into this house with her, and that they will
get married there in a delayed enactment of the wedding with whose
disruption the novel started. As Roulston rightly puts it, "Zilia bor-
rows the markers of male cultural dominance and domesticates them,
reducing them to the parameters of her own home."[26] Julia Simon
adds that this home seems all the more "authentic" as an expression
of her thoughts and feelings because it is built out of remnants of the
actual buildings in which she grew up.[27] It becomes a site at which
the material and social world by which she is surrounded is forced to
bend around her feelings and beliefs. From a helpless person expressing confusion at events that bewildered and restrained her, she has
become someone who forges her own relationships within this new
society as well as between this new society and the one from which
she was abducted. Her self-expression begins to create new forms of

25. Graffigny, *Letters from a Peruvian Woman*, 116. "Un sentiment confus, mêlé de tristesse et
de joie, de plaisir et de regret, remplit tout mon cœur. Je me prosternai devant ces restes
sacrés de notre culte et de nos Autels; je les couvris de respectueux baisers, je les arrosai de
mes larmes; je ne pouvais m'en arracher, j'avais oublié jusqu'à la présence de Céline" (*Lettres
d'une Péruvienne*, 112).
26. Christine Roulston, "Seeing the Other in Mme de Graffigny's *Lettres d'une Péruvienne*,"
Eighteenth-Century Fiction 9, no. 3 (1997): 324.
27. Julia Simon, "On Collecting Culture in Graffigny: The Construction of an 'Authentic'
Péruvienne," *The Eighteenth Century* 44, no. 1 (2003): 25–44.

connection among these different communities and cultures, and to offer what seem to be generalizable insights into them. Armstrong describes letter-writing as a means of creating a synergic relationship between a woman's enclosure within a household, and her desire to intervene into her society by setting a moral example for others. "The writing of female subjectivity," she says, "opened the magical space in a culture where . . . the very objects that set men against one another in the competitive marketplace serve to bind them together in a community of common domestic values."[28] A similar transformation seems to take place in Graffigny's novel. Thanks to the shareable sense of self Zilia develops through her letters, there seems to be no contradiction between the peace she finds in this reduced version of her Peruvian palace, and her hope of regaining a sense of connectedness similar to that which she enjoyed in her homeland.

The ending of the novel shatters this optimism. When Zilia and Aza are finally reunited, she realizes that he fell in love with another woman while he was being held captive in Spain. She received no responses to the letters she sent him not merely because, at first, these letters could not reach him, but also because he has stopped caring for her. "No longer is it the loss of my freedom, my rank, or my homeland that I regret, no longer the anxieties of an innocent tenderness that wring tears from me; rather, it is good faith betrayed and love scorned that rend my soul. Aza is unfaithful!"[29] As Zilia also finds out during her last exchange with Aza, the characters who have been taking care of her—including Déterville—have long known about Aza's infidelity. Zilia's domestic comforts were supposed to distract her from finding out about this betrayal sooner.

---

28. Armstrong, *Desire and Domestic Fiction*, 95.
29. Graffigny, *Letters from a Peruvian Woman*, 164. "Ce n'est plus la perte de ma liberté, de mon rang, de ma patrie que je regrette; ce ne sont plus les inquiétudes d'une tendresse innocente qui m'arrachent des pleurs; c'est la bonne foi violée, c'est l'amour méprisé, qui déchirent mon âme. Aza est infidèle!" (*Lettres d'une Péruvienne*, 159).

Ostensibly, this denouement might recall the final pages of Montesquieu's *Persian Letters*, whose influence on Graffigny's *Letters* has often been noted. In Montesquieu's epistolary novel, a man travels from Persia to Western Europe and begins to receive increasingly dramatic letters from his harem. Finally, as the last letter he receives informs him, the harem falls into disarray and one of his wives murders another out of jealousy. As in the *Persian Letters*, Graffigny's protagonist discovers that, after going to Europe, she can no longer retreat back into her previous life. But in Montesquieu's novel, the Persian traveler's harem falls into chaos because of how important a role this traveler played within it. His position in his community is so significant that even a brief absence dismantles it entirely. By contrast, Zilia's prior life falls apart because, as it turns out, she was never quite as important to her loved ones as she had assumed. The letters she persistently sent to Aza were not enough to perpetuate his affection.

Early on in the novel, Zilia finds comfort in the power writing gives her to imagine that she and Aza are physically present to each other: "These knots strike my senses and seem to lend greater reality to my thoughts. The kind of likeness I imagine they bear to words gives me an illusion that tricks my pain, for I believe myself to be speaking to you, telling you that I love you."[30] Given the resolution of this love affair, Zilia's optimism about the power of writing sounds not only assertive but also misguided about the actual capacity a letter has to affect, let alone to stand in for, a living, breathing person. As Christine Roulston puts it, Zilia reveals herself to have "a stage with no audience."[31] The house in which

---

30. Graffigny, *Letters from a Peruvian Woman*, 37. "Ces nœuds qui frappent mes sens, semblent donner plus de réalité à mes pensées; la sorte de ressemblance que je m'imagine qu'ils ont avec les paroles, me fait une illusion qui trompe ma douleur: je crois te parler, te dire que je t'aime" (*Lettres d'une Péruvienne*, 36).

31. Christine Roulston, "No Simple Correspondence: Mme de Graffigny as 'Epistolière' and as Epistolary Novelist," *L'Esprit Créateur* 40, no. 4 (2000): 33. J. David Macey further

she lives also begins to seem less like an embodied synthesis of her complex social connections, and more like a refuge within which she can forget about the great distances that separate her from other people and from her old life.

Surprising as it is, this anticlimax is not nearly as unconventional as the final resolution that follows. After she and Aza part ways, Zilia continues her correspondence, now addressing it to Déterville. She remains in her house even though the love it was supposed to celebrate has failed entirely. She also once again refuses to marry Déterville. Instead, she invites him to join her at this house once he accepts that she and he will always remain nothing more than friends—and she will otherwise devote her life to reflection and writing.

In these final letters to Déterville, Zilia claims to have discovered happiness by "economizing" her spiritual resources, and focusing merely on her own physical existence:

> The pleasure of being—a forgotten pleasure not even known to so many blind humans—that thought so sweet, that happiness so pure, "I am, I live, I exist," could bring happiness all by itself if one remembered it, if one enjoyed it, if one treasured it as befits its worth.
>
> Come, Déterville, come learn from me to economize the resources of our souls and the benefits of nature.[32]

observes that this stage is made of scraps and fragments of a culture those who give her this house do not quite understand, and thus "unintentionally emphasizes her spiritual and cultural isolation." J. David Macey Jr., "Eden Revisited: Re-visions of the Garden in Astell's *Serious Proposal,* Scott's *Millenium Hall,* and Graffigny's *Lettres d'une Péruvienne,*" *Eighteenth-Century Fiction* 9, no. 2 (1997): 179.

32. Graffigny, *Letters from a Peruvian Woman,* 173. "Le plaisir d'être; ce plaisir oublié, ignoré même de tant d'aveugles humains; cette pensée si douce, ce bonheur si pur, *je suis, je vis, j'existe,* pourrait seul rendre heureux, si l'on s'en souvenait, si l'on en jouissait, si l'on en connaissait le prix. Venez, Déterville, venez apprendre de moi à économiser les ressources de notre âme, et les bienfaits de la nature" (*Lettres d'une Péruvienne,* 168).

On the one hand, these last passages echo the intellectual ambitions Zilia expresses around the middle of the novel. Zilia treats her letters not merely as a means of communication, but also as a medium of self-discovery. But Zilia's aims are now markedly different. Writing about herself allows her to accept that her relationships are indirect and limited in intimacy or mutual impact. Indeed, these letters help her stress such distance as a necessary component of who she is and what she wants from life. The insistence with which Zilia invites Déterville to stay with her reinforces how poor a substitute these letters are, in the end, for the immediate presence of another person.

These final statements highlight the independence of Graffigny's protagonist and of the small world that she gathers around herself. The person at the center of this novel is not merely a mirror of social relations, but a center of gravity around whom a new set of ties among people and objects can arise. But Graffigny also emphasizes that the environment to which Zilia retreats is small and incomplete. Her sense of personal freedom depends as much on her ability to expand the initially non-existent range of her self-expression, as on her willingness to contract the scope of her cares around the limits of what, as she discovers, her mind and body can move others to do.

In "The Fiction of Bourgeois Morality and the Paradox of Individualism," Armstrong shows that the rising novel emphasizes its ability to bind its protagonist to a broad network of social relations: making it seem as if all these social relations were somehow at stake, or at least in play, in the way that this protagonist tries to forge for herself some acceptable way of life. "Literary history," argues Armstrong, "has indeed smiled on fiction that sets a protagonist in opposition to the prevailing field of social possibilities in a relationship that achieves synthesis when two conditions are met":

(1) the protagonist acquires a position commensurate with his or her worth, and (2) the entire field of possible human

identities changes to provide such a place for that individual.
To be a novel, the sheer preponderance of examples suggest, a
narrative must strive to produce this outcome, no matter how
difficult that may turn out to be. As a result, we tend to recognize a narrative as a novel when it evaluates both a protagonist
and the field of possibilities in which he or she acquires a social
identity on the basis of whether they further or frustrate such
a synthesis.[33]

Graffigny is apparently aware of these aspirations of her genre, but
she persistently mocks them. Her *Letters* stress that this seemingly
"realist" aspiration of fiction is, perhaps, one of the most unreal fantasies it fosters: a fantasy of transforming the particulars of one's life
into a trove of knowledge for many other people, or of discovering
that one's life poses a general challenge to one's surrounding social
network. The diminishment of Graffigny's protagonist turns her
narrative and the writing process that it thematizes into a means of
discovering the disconcerting finitude of the insights that any single mind and body can offer to its broader surroundings, or of the
attentiveness with which one can expect one's self-expression to be
received by others.

Compared to Graffigny's *Letters of a Peruvian Woman*, Charrière's
Letters of Mistress Henley is much more negative in tone. This nega-
tivity can be traced back to the inherently vulnerable position from
which Charrière's protagonist begins her narrative. Zilia starts out
as a member of a royal family whose social importance is embodied in masses of communal wealth and attention. Toward the end of
the novel, even though the physical and social territory over which

33. Nancy Armstrong, "The Fiction of Bourgeois Morality and the Paradox of Individualism,"
in *The Novel*, ed. Franco Moretti (Princeton, NJ: Princeton University Press, 2006), 2:349.

she regains control is much smaller, it is nevertheless represented as unequivocally hers. By contrast, Charrière's protagonist-narrator Mistress Henley has no personal possessions that she can call her own. The futility of her attempts to empower herself by writing letters is likened by Charrière to the futility of her efforts to inscribe her husband's household with her own beliefs and values. As she tries, much like Pamela, to write her way out of disempowerment and subjugation, Mistress Henley finds that her letters are even paltrier than the couches and paintings over whose arrangements she fights with her husband. Within this framework, Charrière's skepticism about the range of Mistress Henley's self-expression frequently verges on satire. Marie-Paule Laden writes that "Charrière tells us that we attach too much importance to the moral significance of fiction. . . . All that fiction does is make us lose touch with reality."[34] Indeed, to the extent that the *Letters* offer their reader potential real-world insights, these insights consist in expositions of the relative insignificance of the lines of ink and bits of paper out of which Charrière's protagonist hopes to construct a powerful image of herself. The fact that these small pieces of paper eventually turn out to be the only physical entities over which she can claim possession becomes a marker of her social and familial insignificance. Writing, Charrière suggests, cannot substitute for the material comfort and sense of control that allows

34. "On attache trop d'importance," writes Laden, "à l'impact des fictions sur la morale, nous dit Charrière. . . . Les fictions nous font tout simplement perdre le contact avec le réel." Marie-Paule Laden, "*Trois femmes*: Isabelle de Charrière et la réappropriation," *French Forum* 28, no. 3 (2003): 34. See also Claire Jaquier, "Le damier, la harpe, la robe salie: médiations et symboles du désir dans l'œuvre Romanesque d'Isabelle de Charrière," in *Une Européenne: Isabelle de Charrière en son siècle*, ed. Doris Jakobec and Jean-Daniel Candaux (Neuchâtel: Editions Gilles Attinger, 1994), 177; Jean Starobinski, "Belle en ses miroirs," *Conférence prononcée le 15 juin 1990 à Genève lors de la rencontre de l'Association Belle de Zuylen—Isabelle de Charrière et de l'Association Suisse des Amis de Madame de Charrière* (conference pamphlet), 6–7.

Mistress Henley's husband to frequently disregard her missives altogether.

The Letters of Mistress Henley is presented as a series of letters written by Mistress Henley to her unnamed "dear friend." Mistress Henley is a young British woman orphaned in her childhood and raised by kind relatives. After rejecting many matches, she marries a wealthy widower with a daughter. As described by Yves Citton, Mistress Henley's is a tragedy of failed emotional communion.[35] Mistress Henley is mired by her inability to move her husband or to compel him to make himself vulnerable to her. In the novel's final lines, she suggests that she will either die of misery in a matter of months or entirely lose her personality, becoming the husband's passive, obedient shadow.

In her letters, Mistress Henley frequently describes the ways in which she and her husband negotiate their household's rules. These rules are always potentially bound up with much more than this couple's immediate preferences. The man whom Mistress Henley has married, and into whose house she moves at the beginning of the novel, is a widower with a daughter. He lives in a family mansion whose walls and furnishings were slowly acquired by many prior generations. Mistress Henley's relationship to this house, and her actions within it, exist in the constant presence of these more and less distant predecessors. Any painting she moves, or any dress she wears, appear to have the potential to create a relation of harmony or discord between her and the many other people who used to live here—people whom her husband still remembers and of whose lineages and opinions he often informs her.

35. Yves Citton, "L'économie du bon ménage: Chagrins domestiques et soucis éthiques autour d'Isabelle de Charrière," in *Romancières des XVIIIe et XIXe siècles*, ed. Catherine Mariette and Damien Zanone (Grenoble, forthcoming).

Mistress Henley's ambition, as she enters this house, is to engage with these former generations as their equal. She tries to inscribe her values into these objects in much the same way as she writes them down in her letters. She also seeks to turn both these objects and her letters into means of generalizing her marriage problems into a broader set of social issues. Making explicit her trust in these connections between domestic self-expression, correspondence, and more public forms of rhetoric, her letters are overtly framed in the novel's opening pages as a response to the very popular *Le Mari Sentimental*—a then-recent epistolary narrative of unhappy marital life told from the husband's rather than the wife's perspective. Charrière's protagonist wants her narrative to serve as a counterweight to the description of marital life provided by this other text. Since, as is stated in the novel's full title (*Letters of Mistress Henley, Published by Her Friend*), the letters are published not by Mistress Henley herself, but by the friend to whom she sends them, Charrière makes it seem as if the impact they could have were already to some extent present before us. These letters have already moved, and seemed important to, at least one other person.

But Charrière also consistently undermines her protagonist's optimism about how richly and expansively she might be able to express herself. Her novel stages a gradually increasing dissonance between the persistence with which Mistress Henley records her feelings and thoughts in her letters, and the ease with which these feelings and thoughts are disregarded or erased whenever she tries to convey them more directly. Her husband's strong sense that he, rather than his wife, is the owner of everything around him—including his wife's body— effectively prevents him from perceiving her as someone who could persuasively challenge his views. Rather than affirm these letters and other gestures by which Mistress Henley tries to endow the objects around her with broader meanings, Charrière depicts them as comically paltry attempts to counter Mister Henley's easy dominance over this household. Instead of making this protagonist seem self-aware and insightful, these acts of writing serve to remind the reader of how much more Mistress Henley should worry about her immediate wants and needs than about their potential generalizations—and of how much more her capacity to influence anyone depends on her range of control over particular domestic surroundings, than her trust in the abstract superiority of her principles leads her to believe.

As in Graffigny's novel, this shift in focus is achieved through Charrière's emphasis on her protagonist not as the agent, but as the object of attention. Instead of highlighting how much Mistress Henley discovers and conveys about herself, the *Letters* emphasize this protagonist's nearly non-existent capacity to compel others to attend to her self-expression, especially when most of the objects through which she tries to express herself are not her own. In the process, Charrière does not simply defend this protagonist as a misunderstood, complex being. Indeed, she continues to highlight how greatly Mistress Henley overestimates the potential interpersonal significance of the actions and contexts through which she expresses herself. A major reason why this protagonist eventually falls into despair, Charrière's novel implies, is because she notices far too late that what she approached as an abstract conflict of conventions and beliefs is, much more pragmatically, a local struggle for control over the spouses' shared immediate material territory—a struggle that, in her husband's eyes, she has lost from the start. Mistress Henley's capacity to shape her surroundings around her own values depends much more directly on her access to and control over these immediate, prosaic settings than on her ability to prove her husband wrong in a conceptual sense: and these two modes of relating to the world are not mutually equivalent or even synergic. Like the protagonists of the earlier novels I examine, Mistress Henley is belatedly confronted with the humiliating finitude of what her concerns and capacities appear to have amounted to in the eyes of others. She realizes that writing about her domestic life cannot change anything about the conditions that continue to make this life so difficult to bear.

Despite being frequently—and not incorrectly—described as a philosophical writer, Charrière does not present her characters as reliable social critics or as embodiments of moral ideals.[36] Like most of Charrière's major characters, Mistress Henley is also by no means a forceful or confident narrator. The protagonist of the *Letters* is at pains to articulate her views forcefully even in small domestic disputes. She rarely names her feelings and desires with much precision, and often regrets having expressed them at all. "I have too much obeyed my impetuosity of temperament," Mistress Henley tells her reader

36. See, for example, Gina Fisch, "Charrière's Untimely Realism: Aesthetic Representation and Literary Pedagogy in *Lettres de Lausanne* and *La Princesse de Clèves*," *MLN* 119, no. 5 (2004): 1058–1082. Such strong philosophical and political readings, still present in contemporary research on Charrière, were first sparked by a seminal set of feminist studies written in the eighties by Susan Lanser, Marie-Paul Laden, Monique Moser-Verrey, and Jenene Allison. Susan Lanser, "Courting Death: *Roman, romantisme,* and *Mistriss Henley*'s Narrative Practices," *Eighteenth Century Life* 13, no. 1 (1989): 49–59; Marie-Paul Laden, "'Quel aimable et cruel petit livre': Mme de Charrière's *Mistriss Henley*," *French Forum* (1986): 289–299; Monique Moser-Verrey, "Isabelle de Charrière en quête d'une meilleure entente," *Stanford French Review* 11, no. 1 (1987): 63–76; Jenene J. Allison, *Revealing Difference: The Fiction of Isabelle de Charrière* (Newark: University of Delaware Press, 1995), 81; 81–106. Quoted from Alison, *Revealing Difference,* 3. See also Kathleen M. Jaeger, *Male and Female Roles in the Eighteenth Century: The Challenge to Replacement and Displacement in the Novels of Isabelle de Charrière* (New York: Peter Lang, 1994), 24. More recently, Michel Gilot and several other critics have argued that Charrière's fiction traces and ultimately accomplishes a quest for a distinctive, and politically powerful, feminine voice. Michel Gilot, "La voix d'Isabelle de Charrière," in *Une Européenne: Isabelle de Charrière en son siècle,* ed. Doris Jakobec and Jean-Daniel Candaux (Neuchâtel: Editions Gilles Attinger, 1994), 25–36. See also Emma Rooksby, "Moral Theory in the Fiction of Isabelle de Charrière: The Case of *Three Women*," *Hypatia* 20, no. 1 (2005): 7; Gina Fisch, "Charrière's Untimely Realism," 1081; Pierre H. Dubois, "Le scepticisme d'Isabelle de Charrière," in *Une Européenne: Isabelle de Charrière en son siècle,* ed. Doris Jakobec and Jean-Daniel Candaux (Neuchâtel: Editions Gilles Attinger, 1994), 42–43. Paul J. Smith thus notes that the moral or ethical systems Charrière's characters defend tend to be schematic and disconnected, more reminiscent of fables than of rigorous philosophical thought. Paul J. Smith, "Madame de Charrière lectrice de La Fontaine," in *Une Européenne: Isabelle de Charrière en son siècle,* ed. Doris Jakobec and Jean-Daniel Candaux (Neuchâtel: Editions Gilles Attinger, 1994), 49–63.

immediately after one of her more assertive moments.[37] "I trust you were aware, day before yesterday, of my shame at my extravagant outburst," she tells her husband after another conflict.[38]

Charrière's novel takes place almost entirely within the confines of the Henleys' mansion. In this house, the narrator struggles to find expression for her urban tastes, as well as for her frustration at no longer being able to follow these tastes as much as she would like. Charrière's narrator anticlimactically finds that she cannot center this domestic world around her thoughts and feelings, or even compel others to acknowledge them. Her attempts at self-expression are readily reframed by her husband as a series of passing whims or mistakes that he easily corrects.

The narration of the *Letters* is structured as a series of episodic interactions with physical objects or with people other than the protagonist and her husband. In each such episode this object or third person, rather than one of the spouses, is the focus of both characters' attention. These external referents function as means by which Charrière's protagonist seeks to make her thoughts and feelings visible to her husband and tie these thoughts and feelings back to some larger network of conventions and beliefs. This narrative strategy highlights—as do *Oroonoko* and the *Letters of a Peruvian Woman*— that even the most abstract content these characters try to convey to each other has to have some material canvas on which to express and unfold itself. To an extent that is even more pronounced than in these two prior novels, Charrière's narrative also shows how easily these purportedly context-independent abstractions fade from view as soon as their immediate material expressions prove unreliable. Deidre

37. Isabelle de Charrière, *Letters of Mistress Henley, Published by Her Friend*, trans. Philip Stewart and Jean Vache (New York: MLA, 1993), 26; "J'ai trop suivi l'impétuosité de mon humeur," *Lettres de Mistriss Henley, publiées par son amie* (New York: MLA, 1993), 27.
38. Charrière, *Letters of Mistress Henley*, 32. "Vous avez vu, j'espère, avant-hier combien j'étais honteuse de mon extravagante vivacité" (*Lettres de Mistriss Henley*, 34).

Lynch argues that "deep" character construction initially emerges in the eighteenth century—at the time of Charrière's writing—around the notion that some characters deserve to be read, and reread, repeatedly.[39] Charrière subverts this affirmation of rereading—and reduces her protagonist to a kind of flatness—by reminding her readers of how narrowly circumscribed an object—merely a piece of paper— her novel asks them to examine with such great attention, and of how little such an object can do to buttress a particular person's importance if it is called into doubt by other means.

The first few sections of *Mistress Henley* record several of its protagonist's unsuccessful attempts to add to or to alter her surrounding material world in order to express her feelings and values to her husband. These early episodes highlight Mistress Henley's dependence on her immediate domestic environment for any sense of resonance and importance her feelings and thoughts might have. Her continual attempts to inscribe the objects around her with broad claims about herself are easily counterbalanced or simply ignored by her husband, who knows this house much better and has much more control over it than she does.

The narrator thus tries to show her love of Mr. Henley, and to share her cosmopolite ideals with him, by dressing up his child from his first marriage: "I bedecked the child in finery I had brought her from London, and presented her to her father, for whom I hoped it would be an agreeable surprise."[40] Mr. Henley is not impressed by this

---

39. "Austen identifies to her readers the proper means of and motives for literary experience when she demonstrates that the truth of a letter is situated beneath or beyond the face of the page and when she demonstrates that character cannot be known at first sight. [In *Pride and Prejudice*], the scenes of 'reperusal' establish Elizabeth's development and the character depth while they present her close reading as an impetus to revision" (Lynch, *Economy of Character*, 131).

40. Charrière, *Letters of Mistress Henley*, 10. "Je parai l'enfant des parures que j'avais apportées pour elle de Londres, et je la présentai à son père, que je comptais surprendre agréablement" (*Lettres de Mistriss Henley*, 11).

attempted show of taste and feeling: " 'Your intentions are lovely,' he said, 'but that is a taste I would not wish to inculcate in her; I would fear that such pretty shoes would prevent her from running about freely; artificial flowers contrast unpleasantly with the simplicity of the countryside.' "[41]

Mr. Henley does not say that he objects to his wife's cosmopolite upbringing, or that he prefers to it his local countryside customs. Instead, he restricts his judgments to his child's immediate appearance. The new shoes "prevent her from running about freely." They are also jarring in their current environment, and throw their potentially harmonious everyday existence out of tune. Jaquier has described Charrière's work as "crowded with objects" that she uses to express various nuances of her characters' feelings and social position. "L'oeuvre de Mme de Charrière est tout encombrée d'objets qui ont . . . cette fonction de symboles migratoires: insignifiants à première vue, ils parcourent le texte tel un signifiant neutre, telle une carte blanche qui vient brouiller les règles du sens, dans le roman" [Charrière's works are all filled with objects that function as such migrating symbols: insignificant at first, they traverse her texts as seeming blank signifiers or blank slates around which received conventions of meaning are suspended].[42] The above scene offers a good example of such attempts at subverting a staid local convention by means of a material object charged with alternative values. Yet contrary to what Jaquier suggests, Mistress Henley's uses of material objects also emphasize how difficult it is for her to intelligibly inscribe such objects with any compelling broader meanings. Further, they stress the narrowness of the physical territory over which Charrière's

41. Charrière, *Letters of Mistress Henley*, 11. " 'Votre intention est charmante,' me dit-il, 'mais c'est un goût que je ne voudrais pas lui inspirer; je craindrais que ces souliers si jolis ne l'empêchassent de courir à son aise; des fleurs artificielles contrastent désagréablement avec la simplicité de la campagne' " (*Lettres de Mistriss Henley*, 11).
42. Jaquier, "Le damier, la harpe, la robe salie," 183.

narrator is fighting in the first place. By channeling a potential conflict between urban and provincial values through nothing more
than a pair of children's shoes, Charrière makes her protagonist's
confidence in these shoes' capacity to change her husband's tastes,
or even to express her urbanity to him, seem vulnerably naïve. These
ephemeral, small objects could never outlast or outweigh the fields
and courtyards whose form and significance Mistress Henley is trying to change. Mr. Henley's daughter in fact wears out these shoes
within a few days.

Several pages later, Mistress Henley rebels against her husband
by rearranging furniture in the house: "He had told me I was the mistress; I had the armchairs taken to the parlor, the settee to a storage
room. I ordered a lackey to take down the portrait of the first Mrs.
Henley, which was opposite my bed."[43] Mr. Henley responds by push-
ing these changes even further: "Mr. Henley, having returned from
the hunt, had the surprise of finding his wife's portrait in the dining
room." "He came up to my room without a word," Mistress Henley
continues, "and wrote to London for the finest India wallpaper, the
most elegant armchairs and brocaded muslin for the curtains."[44]

Cecil P. Courtney argues that Charrière's characters often succeed in adapting to their local environments by accepting that the
values they cherish can only be expressed and followed in some very
limited sphere: "le thème principal de chaque diptyque de cette oeuvre est le même: la disproportion qui existe entre l'idéal et le réel et la
recherche d'un art de vivre qui, dans l'oeuvre de la maturité d'Isabelle

43. Charrière, *Letters of Mistress Henley*, 15. "Il m'avait dit que j'étais la maîtresse; j'ai fait porter
les fauteuils dans le salon, le canapé dans un garde-meuble. J'ai ordonné à un laquais de
dépendre le portrait de la première Madame Henley, qui était en face de mon lit" (*Lettres
de Mistriss Henley*, 15).

44. Charrière, *Letters of Mistress Henley*, 15. "M. Henley, revenu de la chasse, vit avec surprise le
portrait de sa femme dans la salle à manger. Il monta dans ma chambre sans me rien dire,
et écrivit à Londres pour qu'on m'envoyât le plus beau papier des Indes, les chaises les plus
élégantes et de la mousseline brodée pour les rideaux" (*Lettres de Mistriss Henley*, 16).

de Charrière, prendra la forme d'une via media très proche de la maxime de Candide: 'Il faut cultiver notre jardin'" [The main theme of each part of her work is the same: the disproportion between the real and the ideal and the search for a way of life that, for the mature Isabelle de Charrière, takes the form of a middle path very close to Candide's maxim: "Each needs to tend to his garden"].[45] But such a reading underestimates the irony that undergirds Mistress Henley's successive discoveries of how pettily circumscribed the sphere of her quarrels effectively is. By listing the various objects her protagonist rearranges—and highlighting the ease with which her husband can rearrange them again, or buy an entirely new set—Charrière fragments what her protagonist apparently intends to be a general statement about her values into a series of local, individually insignificant gestures that overstate the broader meanings of these objects and her capacity to lay claim to them.

To appreciate the ironic edge of these narrative strategies, it is useful to compare them to the ending of another short novel by Charrière, called *The Nobleman*. The protagonist of *The Nobleman*—who, from the start, is much more shrewd and independent than Mistress Henley—is a young woman named Julie who wants to marry a man of whose birth and status her parents disapprove. Julie eventually decides to elope with her lover, but finds that she cannot easily traverse the moat around her parents' centuries-old castle. To make this crossing, she goes back into her family's chambers and carries out of them a stack of ancestral portraits. She throws these portraits face-up into the moat and makes her way out of the mansion by jumping from one portrait onto another, turning these paintings into a makeshift bridge: "Grandpa was thrown into the mud, and he, not

45. Cecil P. Courtney, "Bovarysme et réalisme dans la correspondance de Belle de Zuylen," in *Isabelle de Charrière (Belle de Zuylen): De la correspondance au roman épistolaire*, ed. Yvette Went-Daoust (Amsterdam and Atlanta, GA: CRIN, 1995), 22.

being sufficient, was followed by a second, and then a third. Julie had never thought her ancestors could be so useful."[46]

The medium of representation Charrière mocks here is painting, not writing, but the point of her mockery is similar. Even as many writers of her period—the writers Armstrong discusses—emphasize the ties that aesthetic representation can forge across many human bodies and experiences, Charrière insists on reminding her readers of the paltry physical means by which these ties supposedly come into being. A painting, she suggests in *The Nobleman*, is ultimately just a piece of wood, pigment, and canvas. As a physical object, it is powerless to prevent Julie from throwing it into the water to use it for a purpose directly opposed to the ideals this portrait is supposed to embody. Indeed, it is only by reimagining these portentous entities as portable pieces of wood that Julie is finally able to take control over her life.

In *The Nobleman*, Julie makes these realizations about her family's paintings almost instantly. A great part of the agility with which she is able to follow her desires comes from her readiness to privilege the material usefulness of any given object over its historical or conceptual significance. In the *Letters*, Mistress Henley is increasingly disempowered by her inability to make such realizations. Her attempts to present her immediate actions and surroundings as metonymies of more general values and beliefs continually blind her to the precarious, narrowly circumscribed physicality of her presence in this social world, and of the means by which she tries to signal her disagreements with it.

One such moment of dramatic disempowerment comes when, rather than generalizing herself into a model of urban connoisseurship at a local ball, Mistress Henley finds herself reduced to a local

46. Isabelle de Charrière, *The Nobleman and Other Romances* (New York: Penguin, 2012), 19.

expression of her husband's tastes. During this ball, Mr. Henley criticizes his wife for not dressing as conservatively and simply as he would want her to. Mistress Henley looks around the ballroom, searching for some means of defending herself, and her eyes rest on her extravagantly dressed sister-in-law. "My sister-in-law entered with a hint of rouge; her feathers well outdid mine," Mistress Henley reassures herself. " 'You see!' said I to Mr. Henley. 'She is not my wife,' he replied."[47] Local customs—customs that are not even familial, but apparently just personal—matter much more to her husband than the cosmopolitan fashion to which she tries to introduce him. Her dress and mien, however well she believes them to follow the fashions of her day, cannot convey to Mister Henley any of her supposed sophistication and superiority. Indeed, rather than seeing her as the carrier of more general urban tastes with which he might agree or disagree, her husband perceives her merely as a component of the self-image that he wants to present to others—which, as he imperiously suggests with his possessive "my," Mistress Henley has no right to change.

On one level, the letters Mistress Henley writes about these interactions are a form of resistance against such dismissals and erasures. Mistress Henley's letters record the marks she tries to make within her husband's house and give these marks an alternative, potentially more lasting, medium of expression. These letters also travel outward, to settings different from the one in which she is so easily ignored. Yet Charrière also constantly reminds her reader that the putative broader effects of these letters are effectively irrelevant to the fate of the woman at the center of her novel. By the time Mistress Henley

47. Charrière, *Letters of Mistress Henley*, 29. "Ma belle-soeur est entrée avec un doit de rouge; c'était bien d'autres plumes que les miennes!
" 'Voyez!' ai-je dit à M. Henley.
" 'Elle n'est pas ma femme,' a-t-il répondu" (*Lettres de Mistriss Henley*, 30).

writes each of her letters, the interactions she describes have always already been undone by her husband's responses—and writing about them can in itself do nothing to prevent these constant erasures. The person to whom she addresses these letters apparently cares about her enough to publish them, but is unable to change their author's condition.

The futility of Mistress Henley's letters as means of expanding the fragile scope of her self-expression is made explicit even in the novel's opening sequence. As the *Letters* begin Mistress Henley has just read *Le Mari Sentimental*. She is moved by how much her own feelings—and even their external referents—resemble those of that other novel's protagonist: "In reading alone the story of the portrait, the furniture switched around, poor Hector, I painfully remembered a portrait, a piece of furniture, a dog."[48] She sees in the narrative she is reading a clear depiction of her own disempowerment and frustration. Monsieur Bompré, the henpecked husband represented in *Le Mari Sentimental*, seems to her like a male equivalent of herself. Mistress Henley is then shocked to realize that her husband does not at all share or even recognize the affective associations that these depicted objects so self-evidently embody for her. Instead, when she reads this novel out loud to him, he treats it as an opportunity to imagine himself as his wife's victim: "In reading all that to my husband," she says, "instead of his feeling such differences even more than I, as I had fondly imagined in undertaking the reading, or not at all feeling this sort of resemblance, I saw him sometimes smile, sometimes sigh; he muttered a few words, petted his dog, and looked up where the portrait used to be. My dear friend, they will all think of

---

48. Charrière, *Letters of Mistress Henley*, 3. "En lisant seule l'histoire du portrait, les meubles changés, le pauvre Hector, je me suis souvenue douloureusement d'un portrait, d'un meuble, d'un chien" (*Lettres de Mistriss Henley*, 3–4).

themselves as being like Mr. Bompré, and will be surprised at how patiently they have borne life."[49]

This opening depicts domestic objects—both immediately present and represented ones—as embodiments of individuals' thoughts and feelings. The links that Mistress Henley and her husband draw between the pieces of furniture before them and the fictional ones they read about implicitly express the hope that writing about such domestic material entities might be a means of sharing social insights across great social distances. But rather than affirm such resonances, Charrière stresses that her two characters' interpretations of their reading are mutually hermetic. Though both spouses immediately forge connections between the objects this other novel describes and the ones among which they live, their respective versions of these connections are starkly, comically incompatible, in a way that neither spouse confronts the other one about and that the husband does not even notice. Instead of, as Guillemette Samson has argued, making the letters of which her novel is composed seem more forceful and generalizable by analogy, Charrière emphasizes how difficult it is to turn the objects such letters describe, or even the letters themselves, into clear mediators or syntheses of any stable moral and political content.[50] It seems that any person who reads these letters can imprint them with meanings and emotional charges of her own. In a way that is retroactively deeply ironic—given how much of what Mistress Henley struggles for is control over similar entities—Charrière suggests that writing about the objects one cares about might effectively

---

49. Charrière, *Letters of Mistress Henley*, 4. "Quand j'ai lu tout cela à mon mari, au lieu de sentir encore mieux que moi ces différences, comme je m'en étais flattée en commençant la lecture, ou de ne point sentir du tout cette manière de ressemblance, je l'ai vu tantôt sourire, tantôt soupirer: il a dit quelques mots, il a caressé son chien et regardé l'ancienne place du portrait. Ma chère amie, ils se croiront tous des Messieurs Bompré, et seront surpris d'avoir pu supporter si patiemment la vie" (*Lettres de Mistriss Henley*, 4).

50. Guillemette Samson, "De Neuchâtel à la Martinique: espace et mouvement chez Mme de Charrière," *Eighteenth-Century Fiction* 12, no. 1 (1999): 68–69.

be a means of giving them away to any potential reader. Charrière also stresses how easily such different reading experiences coexist with each other without changing the social relations they perpetuate, and without even becoming incitements for an open exchange of opinion. Rather than rise above this domestic material world as a way of abstracting from it some larger principles or ideals, the letter is reduced to yet another object with which a person can entertain herself within her home, without being compelled to change her life around it.

The irony of this opening is echoed, and compounded, in a later passage when the despairing Mistress Henley writes her husband a letter that expresses her affection toward him and her frustration with their miscommunications. In more conventional epistolary novels, such as the ones described by Armstrong, such a written confession would have the effect of deeply moving its reader and of reshaping his moral and political principles. Most famously perhaps, in *Pamela*, reading Pamela's letters gradually leads Mr. B. to ask for her hand in marriage, instead of violently trying to make her his lover. These "tropes of self production," as Armstrong calls them, "shifted the entire struggle for political power from the level of physical force to the level of language."[51] But none of this happens in Charrière's novel. Not only is Mister Henley unaffected by this letter; he barely acknowledges having received it at all.

Moments like these remind one of what Colette Cazenobe describes as Charrière's misanthropic tendencies.[52] Such episodes also cast an ironic light on Valerie Cossy's claim that Charrière is

---

51. Armstrong, *Desire and Domestic Fiction*, 98.

52. As Cazenobe shows, Charrière's refusal to adopt strong political positions frequently takes the form of generalized doubt about the possibility of any large-scale social knowledge or order. Colette Cazenobe, "Les lumières au pouvoir: la 'philosophie' d'Isabelle de Charrière à l'épreuve de la Révolution," in *Une Européenne: Isabelle de Charrière en son siècle*, ed. Doris Jakobec and Jean-Daniel Candaux (Neuchâtel: Editions Gilles Attinger, 1994), 87–121.

much more invested in the experience of connecting to individual readers than in achieving public fame as an author. Cossy believes Charrière to want "une relation entre l'auteur et son lecteur qui soit au plus près du rapport de réciprocité, d'égalité et de complicité qui existe entre deux correspondants" [a relationship between the author and her reader that most closely resembles the reciprocity, equality, and complicity that exists between two correspondents].[53] Within the context of Charrière's novel, the experience of writing letters starts to seem, instead, like a vulnerable form of semi-solipsistic disconnectedness.

The ending of the *Letters* emphasizes this sense of detachment through a series of anticlimaxes in which Mistress Henley's increasingly desperate attempts to change the values upheld in her husband's household fail one after another. These last pages also stress perhaps most overtly that Mr. Henley's power over Mistress Henley comes not from his richer set of connections to a wide social world, but from his capacity to remain independent of anything except his local, self-sufficient means of sustenance.

The first of these crises is sparked by Mistress Henley's encounter with a former suitor. At the beginning of the novel, Mistress Henley chooses Mr. Henley over another, richer man, who she now realizes might have made her happier. At the time, she refused this suitor in part because she felt guilty about how easily he might have given her all the possessions she might ever want. She believed that her marital bond ought to be based on finer feelings and values, rather than on a material exchange of her body for an array of physical wealth. "Forced to purchase happiness by such base means," Charrière has her say with heavy irony, "I would have been happy without shame

---

53. Valerie Cossy, "Isabelle de Charrière, Frances Burney et le métier d'écrivain," in *Une Européenne: Isabelle de Charrière en son siècle*, ed. Doris Jakobec and Jean-Daniel Candaux (Neuchâtel: Editions Gilles Attinger, 1994), 137.

and perhaps even with pleasure; but to give myself of my own choice, in exchange for diamonds, pearls, rugs, perfumes, gold-brocaded muslins, dinners, parties—to this I could not resign myself, and I betrothed myself to Mr. Henley."[54] At a ball toward the end of the novel, she meets this former suitor, Sir Bridgewater, once again. His charming and fashionably dressed wife implies that her husband may have fallen in love with her because she reminded him of Mistress Henley. "Sir John Bridgewater, my husband, who has often spoken to me of you, . . . told me that I look like you."[55] When she describes this encounter to her husband, suggesting that she will invite Sir Bridgewater to their house, Mr. Henley agrees to it with unruffled calm. Mistress Henley is humiliated to realize how utterly unthreatened he is by her past love life and by the opulent lifestyle it might have connected her to. "The injustice of a jealous husband, the excesses of a tyrant," she exclaims, "would be less exasperating than the disinterest and dryness of a sage."[56] Mr. Henley's indifference reminds Mistress Henley that, upon entering his house, she withdrew from the many other social contexts and networks to which she could have belonged—and about which she still fantasizes. Mister Henley's household is recast as a means of making his wife's past love affairs, as well as her past suitor's possibly continuing infatuation with her, effectively irrelevant to their current lives. Not only is this house, over which he holds total sway, cast as a means of obstructing her capacity

54. Charrière, *Letters of Mistress Henley*, 9. "Forcée de devenir heureuse d'une manière vulgaire, je le serais devenue sans honte et peut-être avec plaisir; mais me donner moi-même de mon choix, contre des diamants, des perles, des tapis, des parfums, des mousselines brodées d'or, des soupers, des fêtes, je ne pouvais m'y résoudre, et je promis ma main à M. Henley" (*Lettres de Mistriss Henley*, 9).

55. Charrière, *Letters of Mistress Henley*, 29. "Sir John Bridgewater, mon mari, . . . m'a parlé souvent de vous, m'ayant dit que je vous ressemblais" (*Lettres de Mistriss Henley*, 31).

56. Charrière, *Letters of Mistress Henley*, 31. "Les injustices d'un jaloux, les emportements d'un brutal, seraient moins fâcheux que le flegme et l'aridité d'un sage" (*Lettres de Mistriss Henley*, 33).

to determine her present condition; it is now also represented as a way of making even her past life seem effectively irrelevant.

This disappointment sets Mistress Henley up for the final one described in the last letter she sends to her friend. That final crisis makes her lose her sense of control not only over her past, but also over her future. Mistress Henley becomes pregnant. Rejoicing at the thought of her child's eventual adulthood—in which this child might, she hopes, fulfill some of the dreams she now realizes she will not fulfill in her own life—she expresses a wish for her son or daughter to be successful and beautiful, and to become a member of the royal court. Mr. Henley dismisses this ambition. He would prefer his children to live on in the countryside just as he does, preserving the house he lives in and its local traditions. He also reveals to Mistress Henley that he has just refused a major government post that would have allowed them to move back to London. In a way that continues the novel's suggestions that the Henleys' household is not only old but also provincial, Charrière here perhaps most forcefully represents it as a means of curtailing how much social and cultural history its inhabitants need to care about—now, or in any future generation.

In response to this disappointment, in the last sentences of this last letter Mistress Henley suggests that she will soon either die or reconcile herself to her current life calmly and quietly. "I am but a woman," she says, "I would not take my own life, I would not have the courage; if I become a mother, I hope I will never desire to do so; but grief too kills." All she can hope for now, she claims, is that she will learn to enjoy the narrow scope of the world built and managed by her husband. "In a year, in two years, you will learn, I trust, that I am reasonable and contented, or that I am no more."[57] Rather

---

57. Charrière, *Letters of Mistress Henley*, 42. "Je ne suis qu'une femme, je ne m'ôterai pas la vie, je n'en aurai pas le courage; si je deviens mère, je souhaite de n'en avoir jamais la volonté; mais le chagrin tue aussi. Dans un an, dans deux ans, vous apprendrez, je l'espère, que je suis raisonnable et heureuse, ou que je ne suis plus" (*Lettres de Mistriss Henley*, 45).

than focusing on the larger significance she hoped her plight to have, Charrière's narrator ends by trying to understand, and come to terms with, her own exhaustion with her domestic struggles and what these struggles have revealed about her husband's indifference to her needs and wishes. Writing letters cannot outweigh the sense of constraint and disempowerment she feels within this household; by the end of the novel, these letters have become only one more domestic activity on which Mistress Henley feels she might no longer be able to expend much energy. Without even expressing the hope that her letters might outlive her, she offers their impending absence as a mark of her nearly expired capacity to oppose her husband's customs and standards, and of the bodily and mental fragility that her rapid exhaustion indicates. In the end, not even her own personal experience might be hers to keep, in a way that these letters can do nothing to prevent.

Gina Fisch has suggested that "even though relationships fail in Charrière's novels as well, what they leave in their stead are not stronger, more experienced individuals but persons affected by a lingering awareness of the stakes that form the substance of the relationships themselves."[58] The *Letters* do show how temporarily empowering her characters' enclaves of epistolary self-expression might potentially be. Writing helps her protagonist notice small ways in which she attempts, and is occasionally able, to take control of certain aspects of her life; it also helps her articulate the terms of her domestic struggle, and understand the reasons for her disempowerment within it. Yet Charrière also highlights that the effect of these letters is, in the end, to force Mistress Henley to admit how little her attempts at inscribing her thoughts and feelings into the world around her can represent to anyone but herself, if she has no more direct control over her

---

58. Fisch, "Charrière's Untimely Realism," 1061.

surroundings. They expose the apparent generality and abstraction of her rhetoric as a pretense that fails as soon as such a letter leaves its author's hands.

Graffigny and Charrière, as well as Aphra Behn, place most emphasis on ways in which the wider social and material world resists the small marks that any single person makes within it. In the nineteenth- and twentieth-century texts against which I juxtapose these earlier ones, this emphasis on represented communities' capacity to ignore a person's life is accompanied by an interest in the inherent limitedness of these characters' inner lives. If, in Charrière, Behn, and Graffigny, their protagonists' finitude is most importantly measured by the smallness of their bodies and material possessions, in Marcel Proust and Thomas Hardy this sense of finitude is also marked by the paucity of thoughts, feelings, and gestures that their protagonists are able to produce. These later novels attempt to come to terms with processes of simplification and reduction through which their protagonists make sense of their lives.

As *Flat Protagonists* leaps into the late nineteenth century, it obviously skips over many major works of realism: novels by Charles Dickens and by Honoré de Balzac, by Charlotte Brontë and by William Thackeray, by Stendhal, Gustave Flaubert, and Henry James. As I mention in my introduction, this chronological jump is by no means intended to imply that the few novels I examine are representative of these other ones. I chose the novels studied here for their atypicality and idiosyncrasy. These works alienate their readers from what most other novels usually succeed in achieving, and from the conventional assumptions realist fiction typically follows.

To examine Hardy's and Proust's novels is, surely, to be reminded of smaller ways in which other Victorian and early modernist novels *do* also draw attention to their characters' relative insignificance. In the fragment from *Sentimental Education* quoted in the introduction, Flaubert's narrator briefly makes fun of his protagonist's egotistical conviction that the people he just met at a party—who hardly noticed him at all—have already developed strong negative feelings toward him. In Virginia Woolf's *Mrs. Dalloway*, Peter Walsh guiltily ponders how "for hours at a time (pray God that one might say these things without being overheard!) for hours and days he never thought of [his fiancée] Daisy."[59] The novels I examine suggest that more might be at stake in such asides than the egotism or indifference of the particular characters involved in them. By occasionally invoking a wider world that does not care about the represented people to whose thoughts and feelings they themselves devote much attention, these more traditional novels might be acknowledging, and grappling with, a much more general metatextual tension between the focus and the payoffs of their acts of attention. Even as the novels I examine do not in any way suggest that these asides should be taken as the primary conclusions or aims of their entire genre, they do invite us to scrutinize such seemingly tangential scenes more closely, as potential expressions of a doubt or reflexivity that might deserve the critic's more sustained attention.

At the same time, flat protagonists also make one aware that, most of the time, narrative fiction seeks to underplay or to marginalize such deflationary moments: most other novels quickly leap away from such ironic passages, back into a vision of their characters that is much more affirming of the potential generality and importance of their plights. The works I examine remind one of the rhetorical insistence required to make a character seem central and complex enough to warrant such sustained, intense attention. Put very positively—perhaps too positively—flat protagonists help us appreciate afresh the aesthetic effort that most novels put into constructing a vision of our social world as a space in which any person's narrative

---

59. Virginia Woolf, *Mrs. Dalloway* (London: Harcourt, 1981 [1925]), 79.

could potentially deserve infinite scrutiny. The novels I examine thus also encourage us to see this aura of endless psychological depth as a precarious and questionably "realist" artifice. These novels suggest that, even though the more conventional novelistic mode of character construction might vividly represent the challenges of attending to others, it is a short-sighted way of perceiving oneself as the object of such attention. They also show that this experience of being the object of other people's scrutiny deserves aesthetic mirrors and engagements of its own.

3

The Misfit

Thomas Hardy's *Tess of the D'Urbervilles* and *Jude the Obscure*

Midway through *Tess of the D'Urbervilles*, Tess agrees to marry a pastor's son named Angel. She soon begins to fear that Angel will reject her once he discovers she is not a virgin. Tess builds up the courage to tell him about her past, heartened by Angel's admission that he has had prior sexual relations with other women. But after she tells Angel her story, he looks upon her in horror. "No," he insists, "forgiveness does not apply to [her] case."[1] During their dialogue, the material world around the newlyweds withdraws from them in apparent indifference. "The fender grinned idly, as if it too did not care. The light from the water bottle was merely engaged in a chromatic problem. All material objects around them announced their irresponsibility with terrible iteration."[2]

Angel cannot bear to be around Tess once he knows she has violated the social norms appropriate to her gender. On a most basic level, this passage excoriates a well-known Victorian double standard: why should women remain chaste, Hardy asks, if men hardly ever do so? The way Hardy sets up this critique also reveals a broader principle of his character construction that is not limited to gender

1. Thomas Hardy, *Tess of the D'Urbervilles* (New York: Penguin, 2003), 298.
2. Hardy, *Tess of the D'Urbervilles*, 297.

relations. Angel refuses to change his worldview around Tess's particular plight. But to what extent—Hardy makes his reader wonder by invoking the indifferent material world around Tess and Angel—can a person ever hope her surroundings to be responsive to her particularity? Even while representing Angel's stance as hypocritical, Hardy suggests that Tess lacks a certain protective self-awareness that would allow her to recognize the narrow significance her life might have to others, and the infrequency with which it might affect their staid perspectives.

Tess and many of Hardy's other protagonists perform acts of social rebellion whose partial invisibility or irrelevance to others usually escapes them. The two novels I examine—*Tess of the D'Urbervilles* and *Jude the Obscure*—draw attention to their protagonists' vulnerable, frequently disappointed expectation that their experiences and feelings can influence the world around them.[3] Hardy highlights these disappointments to illustrate the finitude of his protagonists' minds and bodies as means by which a social norm could be contested or remodeled. This finitude makes it hard for them to garner their communities' attention or even to formulate a capacious, rich notion of the conventions they are trying to subvert. In so doing, Hardy does not simply mock his protagonists as naïve or inadequate. Instead, he suggests that their plights illustrate a more fundamental difficulty that any person might encounter when trying to assert the broader social significance of her particular life—and which many other novels obscure in their more conventional insistence that their rebellious protagonists are consistently interesting and provocative.

3. The metatextual self-awareness I find in these two novels does not yet appear in Hardy's earlier works, such as *Far from the Madding Crowd* or *The Return of the Native*. A tonal difference also clearly exists between *Tess* and *Jude* that makes the similarities I note in their character construction even more eerie. Compared to *Tess, Jude the Obscure* is much less overtly dramatic in tone: not only the protagonist himself, but also the plot he is inserted into, are "flat" in a way that Tess's rape, her act of violence, and her execution are not.

The ties that Hardy draws between social norms and personal self-expression are considerably different from those depicted in the novels I discuss in the two preceding chapters. Following in the footsteps of the mature realist novel, Hardy responds to a model of character construction based on a combination of introspective reflection about social conventions, and their repeated outward performance toward others. As Franco Moretti puts it, in the realist novel "personality" becomes a sort of "third dimension, with ever-expanding confines, in which nothing can be declared a priori as entirely insignificant," even as the exact broader significance of each of this person's feelings, thoughts, and gestures remains to be determined. A character's inward experience of her social situation, and the norms of her larger community, are thereby set in constant dialogue with each other.[4] By acting on feelings and thoughts that do not strictly correspond to the conventions by which she is surrounded, a character is able to articulate her difference to herself and to others. She thereby also challenges her society, as well as a novel's implied readers, to interrogate and potentially revise the norms they follow.

What if one did not take for granted that one's acts of rebellion will be noticed by others? To bring out the significance of this question, my analysis of Hardy's characters engages with notions of performativity developed by Judith Butler. The heroes of late nineteenth- and early twentieth-century novels—by Willa Cather, Nella Larsen, or Henry James—provide some of Butler's most prominent examples of what it means to properly attend to and understand a person's particularity. Extrapolating from these novels (among other sources), Butler defines the experience of embodied selfhood as the process of reenacting social norms that a person learns from her environment. Even as the repeated performance of social norms confirms the self's

---

4. Franco Moretti, *The Way of the World: The* Bildungsroman *in European Culture* (New York: Verso, 2000), 44.

subjection to outward pressures, it also gives this self means to reflect on these pressures and to eventually recognize herself as irreducible to them. It turns out, Butler argues, that "bodies never quite comply with the norms by which their materialization is compelled."[5] Instead, "the subject emerges both as the *effect* of a prior power and as the *condition of possibility* for a radically conditioned form of agency."[6] What makes novels valuable to Butler is their capacity to show that a character's experiences and sheer embodied presence can exceed the shared discourses and conventions in which he operates.[7] As she puts it—here discussing Willa Cather—a narrative can thereby show us that to claim knowledge of a person through social norms is to "engage a certain violence" against her.[8] Novels can also represent the ways in which a person's irreducible uniqueness shines through in the performance of what would otherwise be conventional social gestures.

In the process of enacting social conventions, Hardy's protagonists do often feel disconnected from the norms that these conventions stand for. However, unlike in Butler's examples, this does not lead them to discover their inward complexity. Instead, Hardy's protagonists learn that their minds and bodies are too narrowly

5. Judith Butler, *Bodies that Matter* (New York: Routledge, 1993), xii.
6. Judith Butler, *The Psychic Life of Power* (Stanford, CA: Stanford University Press, 1997), 15.
7. Butler argues that individuals undo the hold that social discourse has on them by realizing that their bodies, as well as the immediate contexts in which they follow conventional norms of behavior, are always partial, unpredictable exceptions to these social norms. Moreover, as she puts it, "every effort to refer to materiality takes place through a signifying process which, in its phenomenality, is always already material." Butler, *Bodies that Matter*, 35. In addition, "when the 'I' seeks to give an account of itself, it can start with itself, but it will find that this self is already implicated in a social temporality that exceeds its own capacities for narration; indeed, when the 'I' seeks to give an account of itself, an account that must include the conditions of its own emergence, it must, as a matter of necessity, become a social theorist." Judith Butler, *Giving an Account of Oneself* (New York: Fordham University Press, 2005), 7–8.
8. Butler, *Bodies that Matter*, 101. Other critics who have expressed versions of this idea include Sara Ahmed, in "Willful Parts," *NLH* 42, no. 2 (2011): 231–253, and Amanda Anderson, in "Character and Ideology," *NLH* 42, no. 2 (2011): 209–229.

constrained to convincingly embody or challenge such external standards. As Hardy depicts them, these minds and bodies are pitifully small as canvases onto which broader conventions could be drawn and in which they could be enacted. He represents his protagonists' attempts at amending these norms, or at establishing sustainable alternatives to them, as vulnerable hopes of embodying much larger concepts, and acting on much greater amounts of social knowledge, than a singular mind and body could plausibly be expected to hold.

A further difference between Hardy's character construction and Butler's theoretical framework concerns the status of what Butler refers to as the "other." For Butler, the belief that some other person is always potentially responsive to the account we give of ourselves through words or gestures is part of the necessary grammar of self-expression. As she puts it, "whether or not there is an other who actually receives is beside the point, since the point will be that there is a site where the relation to a possible reception takes form." We cannot help but assume that somebody is always listening to our self-expression, and this assumption reflects the great critical stakes that expressing oneself intrinsically has.[9] Hardy's characters, like the subjects described by Butler, constantly sense around themselves the presence of an other to whom they try to give an account of themselves. Also like Butler's subjects, these characters treat the constant, watchful presence of other people as unquestionable. But Hardy also continues to emphasize that the attention that the outside world bestows on his protagonists is much more sporadic and cursory than Tess and Jude assume it to be.[10] Both characters grossly overestimate

9. Butler goes so far as to claim that it is impossible to conceive of self-expression without simultaneously conceiving of another person responding to it. "If I have lost the conditions of address, if I have no 'you' to address," Butler says, "then I have lost 'myself.'" Butler, *Giving an Account of Oneself*, 32, 67.

10. One could say that Hardy thereby also turns what Butler describes as a near-grammatical psychoanalytic dynamic of self-awareness into a much more contingent and plastic dynamic of rumor and shame. For an account of rumor in Hardy's writing, see Daniel

how readily the surrounding world will take note of them, let alone treat their self-expression as a sustainable challenge to its current standards. To the extent that Jude and Tess do occasionally imprint themselves on other people's memories, it is often in contexts and for reasons that escape them. Rather than claim, as does Butler, that the actual presence or absence of witnesses to our self-expression is irrelevant to our accurate perception of this self-expression as potentially impactful, Hardy thus makes his characters' wishful expectations about how attentively others respond to them into a central object of representation.[11] These expectations, Hardy suggests, belie the much

Williams' "Rumor, Reputation, and Sensation in *Tess of the D'Urbervilles*," *NOVEL: A Forum on Fiction* 46, no. 1 (2013): 93–115. For a broader account of shame and its Aristotelian foundations (to which Hardy, given his classical references, is probably looking back in both novels), see Bernard Williams' *Shame and Necessity* (Berkeley: University of California Press, 1993).

11. My reading of Hardy's novels confirms what many critics have described as his intense awareness of and responsiveness to the nineteenth-century realist tradition of treating novel protagonists—and novels in general—as cruxes and explorations of wider social discourses, material conditions, and systems of knowledge. My argument also partly relies on critics who see Hardy's protagonists as symptoms of his society's growing lack of coherence and of an overarching, uniform sense of itself. But I contest the suggestion—which underlies many of these latter readings—that Hardy represents the crisis his genre is facing simply by refusing to give his characters the psychological and social complexity of earlier realist protagonists. See, for example, Rosemary Summer, *Thomas Hardy: Psychological Novelist* (London: Macmillan, 1981), 3; Raymond Williams, "The Educated Observer and the Passionate Participant," in *Hardy: The Tragic Novels*, ed. R.P. Draper (London: Macmillan, 1975), 94; Richard Beckman, "A Character Typology for Hardy's Novels," *ELH* 30, no. 1 (1963): 73; Forest Pyle, "Demands of History: Narrative Crisis in *Jude the Obscure*," *NLH* 26, no. 2 (1995): 359; Lionel Johnson, *The Art of Thomas Hardy* (New York: Haskell, 1973), 171; Jules David Law, "Sleeping Figures: Hardy, History, and the Gendered Body," *ELH* 65, no. 1 (1998): 223; George Levine, "Thomas Hardy's *The Mayor of Casterbridge*: Reversing the Real," in *Critical Essays on Thomas Hardy: The Novels*, ed. Dale Kramer (Boston: G.K. Hall, 1990), 170; Eve Sorum, "Hardy's Geography of Narrative Empathy," *Studies in the Novel* 43, no. 2 (2011): 179–199; J. Hillis Miller, *Thomas Hardy: Distance and Desire* (Cambridge, MA: Harvard University Press, 1970); William R. Siebenschuh, "Hardy and the Imagery of Place," *Studies in English Literature 1500–1900* 39, no. 4 (1999): 773–789; Ruth Yeazell, "The Lighting Design of Hardy's Novels," *Nineteenth-Century Literature* 64, no. 1 (2009): 59; John Goode, "Hardy and Marxism," in *Critical Essays on Thomas Hardy: The Novels*, ed. Dale Kramer (Boston: G.K. Hall, 1990), 23; Elaine Scarry, "Participial Acts: Working," in *Resisting Representation* (New York: Oxford University Press, 1994), 49–90; Gilles Deleuze and Claire Parnet, *Dialogues*, trans. Hugh Tomlinson and Barbara Habberjam (New York: Columbia University Press, 1987), 39–40.

greater sense of disempowerment and confusion into which a person is propelled when broader social conventions do not apply to her.

Hardy's novels thus offer examples of aspects of social performance, intrinsic even to the limited historical and aesthetic sphere of the novel, that Butler does not take into account. His novels depict the experience of social disconnectedness or rebellion as one, in part, of discovering how difficult it is for any single person to embody social norms and ideals—especially counterintuitive ones—for others. Indeed, Hardy's character construction frequently suggests that the very notion of a social type as something that a single person could embody is a fantasy about knowing what others expect of one's self, and to what aspects of one's behavior they pay attention.

Hardy sets up this mode of character construction by depicting his protagonists' dreams about achieving a cosmic unity with the world around them. Tess's and Jude's reveries presciently register that they are not as harmoniously adjusted to their social surroundings as they might like to be. Both characters fantasize about bearing relations to these outer environments that would somehow be total, seamless, and unquestionable. Their daydreams also express hopes of becoming free from the limits of their minds and bodies altogether: of an existence in which their bodies and minds could somehow be transcended in favor of a miraculously universalized mode of thinking and perceiving. While having breakfast with her fellow milkmaids, Tess rhapsodizes about how thrilling it "is to lie on the grass at night and look straight up at some big bright star; and, by fixing your mind upon it, you will soon find that you are hundreds and hundreds o' miles away from your body, which you don't seem to want at all."[12] In the opening pages of *Jude the Obscure*, Jude feels at one with the birds he is surreptitiously feeding: "they stayed and ate, inky spots on

12. Hardy, *Tess of the D'Urbervilles*, 175.

the nut-brown soil, and Jude enjoyed their appetite. A magic thread of fellow feeling united his own life with theirs. Puny and sorry as those lives were, they much resembled his own."[13]

These passages establish Tess and Jude as characters who are able and willing to blend into another person or even into a whole environment. They also depict both protagonists as beings whose attunement to others might put them in a privileged position to understand the larger principles by which their world is governed, whether in order to adjust themselves to these principles, or to change them. This otherworldly, quasi-mystical quality of Tess's and Jude's bearing draws the attention of other characters, who approach them with idealism and hope. Tess enraptures Angel after he hears her describe the fantasy quoted above. When the husband of Jude's lover Sue explains to someone why he condones Jude's and Sue's relationship, he describes them as follows: "I found from their manner that an extraordinary affinity, or sympathy, entered into their attachments, which somehow took away all flavor of grossness. Their supreme desire is to be together—to share each other's emotions, and fancies, and dreams."[14]

These idealistic hopes of communion and open-ended, expansive connectedness are reminiscent of similar ideals expressed by Mistress Henley or by Zilia, and of the occasional forms of hero worship garnered by Oroonoko. But by comparison to these prior novels, Hardy devotes very little narrative space to nurturing his protagonists' fantasies of sharing in, or expressing, some broader networks of influence or mutual knowledge. Instead, from the beginning, Hardy's novels brim with scenes in which these expressions of hope are undercut. In ways that are even more multifarious and sophisticated than in the writing of the three earlier authors I discuss, Hardy mines both his represented material world, and the conventions he applies to it, for

13. Thomas Hardy, *Jude the Obscure* (New York: Penguin, 2001), 16.
14. Hardy, *Jude the Obscure*, 244.

expositions of the finitude and disconnectedness of his characters' physical and mental presence. He thus comes ever closer to depicting the phenomenology of inhabiting such a finite mind and body, as they register various qualities of their environments and of their own engagements with them.

"Who is this 'you' who demands something of me I cannot give?" asks Butler in one of her essays, describing an assumption that one is being constantly observed and interpellated by others, as an intrinsic condition of self-understanding.[15] This assumption is similarly unquestionable to Tess and Jude, but Hardy's novels undermine this attitude as a means of understanding one's relationships to others. To make this point, Hardy frequently represents Tess and Jude as excessively certain—in ways that seem by turns tragic and comic—that they are personally addressed by every social norm they encounter, and that their minds and bodies can best be understood as these broad norms' embodiments. Tess and Jude treat most of what they see or hear, including walls, cows, fields, and fenders, as if it held a message addressed specifically to them. They also act as if their own lives were adequate, self-sufficient examples of the concepts and conventions about which they learn. The insistence with which they do so soon starts to seem like a sign of their inability to understand how many different people, with varied lives, fates, and capacities, exist among them, and of how uninvolved these other people's thoughts and actions might be in their particular existence.

Upon seeing a random itinerant preacher paint biblical injunctions against adultery on a nearby wall, Tess thus acts personally insulted, as if this preacher, whom she has never seen before, aimed to shame her in particular.[16] When she overhears Angel's family

15. In this passage, Butler is also paraphrasing Jean Laplanche. *Giving an Account of Oneself*, 72.
16. As Jonathan Wike has noted, Hardy often metaphorically compares the landscapes he unfolds to pages of writing in which his characters read out archaeologies and premonitions

describe as a "tramp" someone who would enter their village barefoot, as she just did unbeknownst to them, she decides that they have
spurned her before they are even introduced to each other. Prior to
entering this village, Tess leaves her boots by the side of the road to
hide from her husband's relatives that, since he left her, she has had to
take up farm labor. As she approaches their gate, Tess hears his family
ridicule these boots without seeing her. "Here's a pair of old boots,"
says her brother-in-law Cuthbert Clare. "Thrown away, I suppose, by
some tramp or other." Miss Chant, her husband's cousin, continues:
"Some imposter who wished to come into the town barefoot, perhaps, and so excite our sympathies.... Yes, it must have been, for
they are excellent walking-boots—by no means worn out. What a
wicked thing to do!"[17] After she overhears this dialogue, Tess turns
back and heads home in silence, as if her own, as yet unarticulated
intentions to ask her husband's family for help have been directly and
decisively rejected.[18]

Jude's interpretations of his world are animated by a similar insistence that everything he sees or hears must be addressed to him personally and with full cognizance of his particular condition. Seeing a
beautiful photograph of his cousin Sue rapidly makes Jude feel that
he and Sue are meant to meet and be together. When Jude hears that
any ambitious scholar should go to Christminster, he decides that
Christminster is his personal destiny. "You know what a university
is, and a university degree?" his village schoolteacher Phillotson asks
him. "It is the necessary hallmark of a man who wants to do anything
in teaching. My scheme, or dream, is to be a university graduate, and

of their fates. Jonathan Wike, "The World as Text in Hardy's Fiction," *Nineteenth-Century Literature* 47, no. 4 (1993): 455–471.

17. Hardy, *Tess of the D'Urbervilles*, 300.

18. Alicia Christoff describes this feature of Hardy's character construction in psychoanalytic terms, as a means of depicting Tess's "loneliness"—a loneliness that is always, paradoxi-cally, filled with the imagined or remembered voices and presences of other people. Alicia Christoff, "Alone with Tess," *NOVEL: A Forum on Fiction* 48, no. 1 (2015): 18–44.

then to be ordained. By going to live at Christminster, or near it, I shall be at headquarters, so to speak, and if my scheme is practicable at all, I consider that being on the spot will afford me a better chance of carrying it out than I should have elsewhere."[19] As Matthew Potolsky puts it, Jude immediately turns onto this city the attention of an aesthete. He studies it as a source of beauty and value of which he is personally, necessarily, meant to partake.[20] The bits of information he receives about it gradually coalesce into a fantastic ideal of enlightenment and prosperity in which his career will follow illustrious steps.

Tess's and Jude's apparent belief in the centrality and exemplarity of their experience is punctured not only by the way these two protagonists respond to their surroundings, but also by the way they express themselves to others. To explain their feelings and identities, Hardy's protagonists frequently juxtapose themselves against, or costume themselves as, culturally recognizable figures: writers, philosophers, folk or literary characters.[21] Embodied by these characters, such broader discourses usually seem comically oversimplified or trivialized. Invoking familiar cultural tropes does not ensure that these characters' lives will become compelling to others, or that the relationships to which they refer in these grand terms will last.

In one famous instance of this narrative pattern, Tess takes it upon herself to baptize the extramarital child she has with Alec, and

---

19. Hardy, *Jude the Obscure*, 10.
20. Matthew Potolsky, "Hardy, Shaftesbury, and Aesthetic Education," *SEL Studies in English Literature 1500–1900* 46, no. 4 (2006): 863.
21. As Mary Rimmer points out, most of Hardy's protagonists are also hounded by feelings of provinciality and cultural homelessness, and by fears that they cannot quite fit any of the niches among which they travel. Mary Rimmer, "Hardy, Victorian Culture and Provinciality," in *Palgrave Advances in Thomas Hardy Studies*, ed. Philip Mallett (London: Palgrave, 2004), 151. A similar point is raised by John Goode in *Thomas Hardy* (Oxford: Blackwell, 1988), 1–13, and by Raymond Williams in "The Educated Observed and the Passionate Participant."

names this child after the feelings with which Alec's assault filled her. "Sorrow, I baptize thee in the name of the Father, and of the Son, and of the Holy Ghost," Tess proclaims as her many prepubescent brothers and sisters behold her and little Sorrow in incomprehension.[22] Despite the grandiose agency Tess adopts in front of her young siblings, she is not able to persuade the local parish priest that this baptism was meaningful enough, or that her sadness about this child's passing was exceptional enough, for him to bury Sorrow in hallowed ground. Later on in the novel, Tess's lover Angel transforms himself, in her eyes, into an image of an actual angel playing the harp. As the narrator puts it, claiming to channel Tess's own perspective, "The exaltation which she had described as being producible at will by gazing at a star, came now without any determination of hers; she undulated upon the thin notes of the second-hand harp, and their harmonies passed like breezes through her, bringing tears into her eyes. The floating pollen seemed to be his notes made visible, and the dampness of the garden the weeping of the garden's sensibility."[23]

In this passage, Tess compares Angel's music to the stars from which she gathered transcendental insights in earlier parts of the novel.[24] The scene becomes an eerily direct representation of their courtship: it literalizes Angel's name as well as the qualities Tess attributes to him; it also relates this man, and her love of him, to a higher realm of virtues and abstract values. But these literalizations and parallels are so totalizing that, rather than illuminate or enlarge the novel's plot, they merely stress how naïvely hopeful Tess's notions of Angel currently are. They ironically prepare for the narrative reversal Tess's confession will create a few chapters later, which these

22. Hardy, *Tess of the D'Urbervilles*, 145.
23. Hardy, *Tess of the D'Urbervilles*, 123.
24. For a closer analysis of Hardy's suggestions that Angel is an angel—coupled with his simultaneous connection of Alec with the devil—see Penelope Vigar, *The Novels of Thomas Hardy: Illusion and Reality* (London: Athlone Press, 1974), 182.

broad-stroked enactments of cosmic unity and heavenly joy prove unable to prevent. On some level it seems right to find in such scenes attempts at linking these characters' fates to very large concepts and ideas such as Christian redemption, fears of losing religious faith, or the possibility of treating sexuality and religion as expressive of each other.[25] But to highlight these connections is to note not how richly these larger spheres of reference are represented here, but how reductive is the way in which Tess attempts to find them embodied in her immediate environment. Her forms of momentary, local self-expression are insufficient to unravel these contexts and ideals very complexly or fully, even in order to apply them to her own situation.[26]

In *Jude the Obscure*, Jude's attempts to insert himself into larger cultural tropes produce similar effects of inadvertently comic distortion. At the beginning of the novel, Jude carves into the tree at his village crossroads an arrow pointing toward Christminster with his initials above it, as if his own departure there were as self-evident and important as the city's geographical location. Despite this sense of certainty, he is not able to travel to Christminster for many more years—and once he does so, he does not even pass through these crossroads. When asked what he thinks Christminster might look like, he replies "the heavenly Jerusalem"—comparing the city he longs for to a holy site that any Christian should desire to see.[27] The person to whom Jude speaks in these terms does not even respond to his generalization; rather than convey to his environment the grandeur of his ambition, Jude's comment appears to merely show others that he has never left his small hometown before.[28]

---

25. Oliver Lovesey, "Reconstructing Tess," *Studies in English Literature, 1500–1900* 43, no. 4 (2003): 914.

26. For an extensive account of the presence of allusions in Hardy's fiction, see Marlene Springer, *Hardy's Use of Allusion* (Lawrence: University Press of Kansas, 1983).

27. Hardy, *Jude the Obscure*, 21.

28. Commenting on this tendency, Anna Kornbluh describes Jude's relationship to social norms and laws as so abstract that it becomes "geometric"—in a way that is especially

This pattern of hurried overgeneralization also accompanies Jude's early love life. To seduce him, all that Arabella has to do is throw pig genitals in his direction. Taking that as a sign of her abiding desire, "Jude was lost to all conditions of things in the advent of the fresh and wild pleasure" of being chosen by her.[29] Jude then easily makes the leap from a brief series of sexual encounters with Arabella, which culminate in her suggestion that she might be pregnant, to the belief that he and she need to be officially wed. The narrator describes this commitment with heavy irony. "The two swore," he says, "that every other time of their lives until death took them, they would assuredly believe, feel, and desire precisely as they had believed, felt, and desired during the few preceding weeks."[30]

One might be tempted—as many scholars have been—to see these instances of the naïve hopefulness of Hardy's characters as a sign that his novels are just not psychologically sophisticated. For many of Hardy's critics—among them Henry James, who famously referred to him as "good little Thomas Hardy"—his reluctance to focus his novels on complex and deeply self-aware characters makes him a lesser novelist than the great British realists whom he superseded.[31] Even those who praise Hardy's work rarely disagree with this baseline assessment of his character construction as apparently unconcerned to uncover complicated ways in which these represented people relate to the world around them. Half a century later, J. Hillis Miller thus notes Hardy's "distaste for introspection." As he explains, "nowhere in Hardy's writings is there a description of an

meaningful given how much the rise of non-Euclidean geometry is just then shaking Hardy's society's understanding of the knowability and accessibility of time and space. See Anna Kornbluh, "Obscure Forms: The Letter, the Law, and the Line in Hardy's Social Geometry," *NOVEL: A Forum on Fiction* 48, no. 1 (2015): 1–17.

29. Hardy, *Jude the Obscure*, 44.
30. Hardy, *Jude the Obscure*, 61.
31. Henry James, *The Letters of Henry James*, ed. Percy Lubbock (New York: Scribner, 1920), 1:190.

originating act in which the mind separates itself from everything but itself. His self-awareness and that of his characters are always inextricably involved in their awareness of the world."[32]

I propose that these readings gloss over the knowing irony with which Hardy depicts his characters' constant, illusory sense of being commented on and watched by others, and their attempts to respond to these supposed external gazes with an appropriate grandeur and generality of self-expression. The point of Hardy's character construction, I argue, is not merely to represent "simple" people, but to highlight, in dramatically exaggerated form, how disempowering it is to measure the finite particularity of one's mind and body against the social norms that this body might not, all by itself, be able to embody or to challenge. Tess's and Jude's disconnectedness, as Hardy depicts it, is not merely a personal failing on their part, but a condition of their unsuccessful attempts to show others the kinds of alternative social conventions through which they want their lives to be seen.

As both novels progress, Tess's and Jude's failures of awareness are represented as increasingly inevitable and structural. Rather than show these characters gradually transcending their physical and intellectual sense of constraint through some form of *Bildung*, Hardy depicts the failures of one possible means after another through which they seek to escape these constraints: abstract learning, physical sensation, or the instructive presence of other people. He also begins to suggest that his protagonists' limitations are shared, and could potentially be matched, by those of the other people among whom they live.

Tess's and Jude's attempts to more meaningfully relate their lives to broader social norms are undercut, first, by the ways they try to obtain new pieces of social knowledge from others. Tess and Jude only introduce abstractions into their thinking through (usually

32. Miller, *Thomas Hardy: Distance and Desire*, 3.

imperfect) rote memorization. The thinness of their engagements with new concepts serves as a hallmark both of the grandeur of their ambitions, and of the very limited bodily, mental, and temporal resources through which these characters could begin to fulfill them.

In a way that both discomfits and amuses Tess's seducer Alec when they meet again after several years, Tess turns out to have memorized Angel's arguments against religion without understanding them. When she reiterates them to Alec, he is surprised both by how perfectly Tess has internalized Angel's language, and by how little sense she can make of it. "She reflected; and with her acute memory for the letter of Angel Clare's remarks, even when she did not comprehend their spirit, she recalled a merciless polemical syllogism."[33] Hardy makes the earnestness with which Tess pursues these imitations seem futile: Tess cannot appreciate what it would be like to actually become, rather than merely try to sound like, the kind of intellectual she admires.

To get to Christminster, Jude learns by heart long passages of Greek and Latin. Much later in the novel, after his hope of getting a degree is gone, he repeats one of these passages at a bar in order to prove to the other men there that he did try to better himself. "[Jude] stood up and began rhetorically, without hesitation: *Credo in unum Deum, Patrem omnipotentem, Factorem coeli et terrae, visibilium omnium et invisibilium.*"[34] Coming late in the novel, after Jude's many efforts at educating himself, the fact that he can only attempt to impress others by repeating the Nicene Creed—one of the most elementary bits of church Latin—is deeply anticlimactic. The lists of books that Jude has previously been shown reading prepared the reader for a much more wide-ranging display of erudition; what is remarkable about this scene is not only how much Jude has

33. Hardy, *Tess of the D'Urbervilles*, 400.
34. Hardy, *Jude the Obscure*, 128.

attempted to absorb, but also how pitifully little, it turns out, he was able to retain.

In the midst of these protagonists' attempts at abstraction, Hardy also draws attention to the physical particularity of their bodies. He highlights the narrow empirical limits of the space their bodies occupy and the resonance they have moment by moment. In his famously vivid descriptions of the landscapes around his characters, Hardy frequently stresses—as he does in the passage quoted in the opening of this chapter—that his protagonists' environments seem indifferent to them. He depicts these protagonists as relatively small, insignificant physical entities from which other people, and indeed any animate beings, can easily avert their gazes. "[T]o almost everybody she was a fine and picturesque country girl, and no more," Hardy's narrator says of Tess after an extensive passage describing her seemingly exceptional qualities.[35] In another chapter, his narrator describes how "Tess stood still upon the hemmed expanse of verdant flatness, like a fly on a billiard table of indefinite length, and of no more consequence to the surroundings than that fly. The sole effect of her presence upon the placid valley so far had been to excite the mind of a solitary heron, which, after descending to the ground not far from her path, stood with neck erect, looking at her."[36] In *Jude the Obscure*, when Jude finally passes the city limits of Christminster, the streetlamps "winked their yellow eyes at him dubiously, and as if, though they had been awaiting him all these years in disappointment at his tarrying, they did not much want him now."[37]

The effect of these passages is deepened as Hardy also shows how often Tess and Jude overestimate the attention that the personal qualities about which they are self-conscious—such as their loudness, or their eccentricity—actually garner from their

35. Hardy, *Tess of the D'Urbervilles*, 52.
36. Hardy, *Tess of the D'Urbervilles*, 159.
37. Hardy, *Jude the Obscure*, 83.

environments. Jude is so preoccupied with the exceptionality of his drive for knowledge that he fails to realize that the villagers who disapprove of this habit only do so occasionally and half-heartedly. Only once does it happen that "a private resident of an adjoining place informed the local policeman that the baker's boy should not be allowed to read while driving, and insisted that it was the constable's duty to catch him in the act."[38] The constable cautions Jude, and Jude becomes so suspicious after this one warning that he begins to watchfully await, and prepare himself for, this constable's reappearance. He fails to realize that the policeman soon afterward ceases to pay him any mind whatsoever; and that, in fact, "often on seeing the white tilt [of Jude's cart] over the hedges he would move in another direction."[39]

In more sophisticated fashion—dependent less on telling, and more on showing—Hardy uses Tess's voice to remind his readers of how small a community recognizes her existence. Hardy depicts Tess's voice as louder than the voices of the other women around her in a way that highlights both how difficult it is for her to feel connected to her community, and how trivial a distinction or nuisance Tess's loudness amounts to:

> The laughter rang louder; they clung to the gate, to the posts, rested on their staves, in the weakness engendered by their convulsions at the spectacle of Car. Our heroine, who had hitherto held her peace, at this wild moment could not help joining in with the rest.
>
> It was a misfortune—in more ways than one. No sooner did the dark queen hear the soberer richer note of Tess among those of the other work-people than a long smouldering sense

38. Hardy, *Jude the Obscure,* 35.
39. Hardy, *Jude the Obscure,* 35.

of rivalry inflamed her to madness. She sprang to her feet and closely faced the object of her dislike.

"How darest th' laugh at me, hussy!" she cried.

"I couldn't really help it when t'others did," apologized Tess, still tittering.[40]

There is something insistently pastoral about exchanges such as this one; as means of asserting Tess's individuality and rebelliousness, they are comically modest. As David James observes, such inter-actions test the narrow span of represented time and space these sounds can reliably cross.[41] After all of the narrator's talk about Tess's exceptionality, the one thing that empirically distinguishes her from other women—in a way that only a small group notices, and only occasionally—is the slightly deeper timbre of her laughter.[42]

This impression that his characters do not have a good sense of the impact they might have on their surrounding world increases when Tess and Jude attempt to travel. When Tess leaves her village, she continues to fear that she might encounter people she knows in neighboring ones. She also appears to assume, more generally, that all of Wessex is gossiping about her—as if this entire region were the equivalent of the tiny village in which she spent her childhood. To the extent that news of her past life does occasionally follow her elsewhere, many fewer people care about it—or know the details of

---

40. Hardy, *Tess of the D'Urbervilles*, 66–67. Such scenes of recognition through voice abound throughout Hardy's novels. In *Far from the Madding Crowd*, Fanny's lover Troy instantly identifies her when she speaks to him even though her figure is completely obscured by a snowstorm. In *Jude the Obscure*, Jude's first wife comes up to his window one evening. Her shape is barely discernible in the dimly lit street. Yet we know who she is as soon as she calls out "in a voice that was unmistakably Arabella's" (*Jude the Obscure*, 263).

41. David James, "Hearing Hardy: Soundscapes and the Profitable Reader," *Journal of Narrative Theory* 40, no. 2 (2010): 146.

42. Daniel Williams well describes the illusions of grandeur produced by these comically mini-mal social movements of Tess's in Williams, "Rumor, Reputation, and Sensation," 96–97.

it—than Tess anxiously estimates. Indeed, a great part of what she is blindsided by, when trying to hide her past from Angel, is how imprecise and easily dismissible the distant rumors that he hears about her are.[43] Jude, who wants to think of himself as a worldly person, also never leaves the circumference of a few towns and cities that surround the one he was born in. Within this small circumference, he is unable to expand his range of acquaintances beyond the two or three people whom he got to know when he was young. In a way that is as striking as it is comic, amid all the new towns he visits Jude fails to make even one new friend besides his former neighbor Arabella, his cousin Sue, and his primary school teacher Phillotson. Especially compared to Hardy's other characters in these novels—who travel as far as Brazil and Australia—both Tess and Jude are represented as unwittingly but inexorably provincial in their spatial movements and their relationships to the communities around them, however mobile and urbane they might seem to themselves.

Furthermore, in his descriptions of the acts of expression performed by these protagonists, Hardy singles out details that recall their narrow and easily circumscribed bodily limits. To show the progress of Tess's and Jude's relationships to the people they love, Hardy highlights their rapidly increasing degrees of physical closeness in a way that makes the boundaries of their bodies seem claustrophobic. In *Tess of the D'Urbervilles*, Alec seduces Tess in prosaically physical fashion. "D'Urberville began gathering specimens of the fruit for her, handing them back to her as he stooped; and, presently, selecting a specially fine product of the 'British Queen' variety, he stood up and held it by the stem to her mouth." Tess tries to stop him: " 'No—no!' she said quickly, putting her fingers between his hand and her lips. 'I would rather take it in my own hand.' 'Nonsense!' he insisted; and in a slight distress she

---

43. See also Daniel Williams, "Rumor, Reputation, and Sensation," 93–95.

parted her lips and took it in."[44] Much has been made of Tess as—variously—the embodiment of Christian or of pagan ideals, of society's oppression of women, or of the reading process itself as a form of voyeurism or exploitation.[45] Rather than reenact such larger social patterns or ideologies, Alec's imperatives draw attention to the small distances he needs to cross to become physically intimate with her.

In *Jude the Obscure*, this dynamic is repeated almost exactly—except it is the woman, and not the man, who quickly usurps control over the lover's body. "Take my arm," Jude says to Arabella. In response, "she took it, thoroughly, up to the shoulder. He felt the warmth of her body against his, and putting his stick under his other arm held with his right hand her right as it rested in its place."[46] Arabella takes Jude's arm in a way that feels "thorough," well beyond the effect he expected his request to have. In addition to emphasizing Arabella's sway over Jude, the description makes Jude's body seem small and easily accessible.

These protagonists' physical and mental finitude is further stressed by the air of detachment Hardy establishes between them and his narrators. As many critics have observed, there is something alienatingly distant about the diction with which Hardy's narrators describe his protagonists. In the conclusion of his *Thomas Hardy: Distance and Desire*, Miller proposes that the care Hardy's narrators devote to their disconnected, lonely central characters is even somewhat malevolent. "Far from granting his characters the oblivion they desire, his writing cooperates with the impersonal mind of the Void by keeping their fugitive moments of experience alive in the new form his words give them. His writing gives his people that immortality they flee."[47] It seems too simple to say that Hardy's characters merely

44. Hardy, *Tess of the D'Urbervilles*, 42.
45. Oliver Lovesey gives an extensive bibliography of these readings in "Reconstructing Tess."
46. Hardy, *Jude the Obscure*, 47.
47. Miller, *Thomas Hardy: Distance and Desire*, 239.

wish to avoid the limelight. But Miller is right that the vocabulary Hardy's narrators use to describe his protagonists is often aggressively general. "Thus the Durbeyfields, once D'Urbervilles saw descending upon them the destiny which, no doubt when they were among the Olympians of the county, they had caused to descend many a time, and severely enough, upon the heads of such landless ones as they themselves were now," Hardy's narrator says in commenting on Tess's and her family's reduction to abject poverty. "So do flux and reflux— the rhythm of change—alternate and persist in everything under the sky," this narrator continues with almost comic abstraction.[48] Of Jude entering Christminster, the narrator says that "he was a species of Dick Whittington whose spirit was touched to finer issues than mere material gain. He went along the outlying streets with the cautious tread of an explorer."[49]

The irony of such passages is multifaceted. On the one hand, these allusions build on the exaggerations created by these characters' own attempts to describe themselves through cultural tropes. On the other hand, these narrators' apparently more objective, erudite style also gestures toward the wealth of references that Tess and Jude not only could not persuasively embody, but do not even know about. Dick Whittington, flux, reflux, Olympian nobility—these are all bits of cultural capital of the kind that Tess and Jude strive, in their more ignorant ways, to relate to their lives.[50] The narrator's displays of erudition—which rephrase these characters' wishes and urges with a generality that is considerably beyond their reach—are another way of drawing attention to the paucity of inspirations these characters have for the abstractions to which they aspire. These

---

48. Hardy, *Tess of the D'Urbervilles*, 434.

49. Hardy, *Jude the Obscure*, 83.

50. Such passages also complicate accounts of this novel by psychoanalytic critics such as Kaja Silverman, who see Tess as constructed by, and responsive to, the male gaze of the implied narrator. Kaja Silverman, "History, Figuration, and Female Subjectivity in *Tess of the d'Urbervilles*," *NOVEL: A Forum on Fiction* 18, no. 1 (1984): 5–28. That is not to say Tess

characters are restricted, in their self-expression, to nothing more than vague attempts at generalizing from the immediate environment at hand.[51]

Hardy's secondary characters also contribute to this sense of isolation and excessive self-regard enveloping his protagonists. These secondary characters reinforce this impression not through their difference from, but in their surprising similarity to, the partial solipsism of the protagonists. If, for Alex Woloch, every minor character is a potential protagonist in the sense of standing in for an implicitly rich, complex human being, most of Hardy's secondary characters seem like potential flat protagonists: they tend toward an equally surprising sense of finitude. To linger with these secondary characters even for a while is to notice how narrow their viewpoints are, how exaggeratedly they center their self-understanding around a few concepts and gestures, and how difficult it is for anyone to add to these viewpoints or to change them.

is not frequently sexualized by those who see her; but it is to suggest that part of what Hardy questions is any person's capacity to stand in for any such broader abstraction, however much her viewer (or, in other cases, she herself) might desire her to do so.

51. Miller describes the social histories and conventions Hardy represents as sets of overlapping but never "wholly unified" smaller or larger spheres of reference. "Just outside each man are the people immediately around him. Beyond them is the whole community of which he is a part, with all its ties to other communities and to history. Beyond other people is the natural world which is the scene of their actions, intervening at every point to limit what they can do. The individual, other people, physical nature—these form a complex spatial and temporal continuum, overlapping and interacting in many ways without ever becoming wholly unified." Miller's comments underplay the fact that this sense of incomplete connectedness does not come (as might conventionally be assumed) from these characters' greater richness and complexity that would make any trope imposed upon her seem stereotypical. Instead, their particular minds and bodies seem to be too small and undramatic to embody these tropes adequately without making them seem like florid exaggerations, and without emphasizing these characters' ignorance of them. To fall in step with the generalities Jude and Tess try to inhabit, Hardy suggests, is to lose oneself in a world that only dreams of being expansive or abstract, in a world whose reliability and transposability into a more interactive and expansive sphere of relations can only seem credible as a trick of the eye. Miller, *Thomas Hardy: Distance and Desire*, 78.

One instance of such secondary character construction occurs early on in *Jude the Obscure*, when Hardy starts to introduce Sue. The sense of self-enclosure in which Hardy envelops her comes from the comic, anticlimactic proximity Sue establishes to the physical embodiments of her ideals—a proximity that indirectly suggests how distant any more abstract forms of these ideals are from her self-understanding. When she moves into a new apartment, Sue wants to decorate it with objects that will emphasize her unconventionality. She looks with disdain upon the devotional saint figures sold at most of the local market stalls. Styling herself as a Hellenic intellectual in the mold of Matthew Arnold, she buys two statues of naked Greek gods: "'How much are these two?' she said, touching with her finger the Venus and the Apollo—the largest figures on the tray."[52] But only two paragraphs later, Sue's courageous self-assessment begins to wobble:

> When they were paid for, and the man had gone, she began to be concerned as to what she should do with them. They seemed so very large now that they were in her possession, and so very naked. Being of a nervous temperament she trembled at her enterprise. When she handled them the white pipeclay came off on her gloves and jacket. After carrying them along a little way openly an idea came to her, and, pulling some huge burdock leaves, parsley, and other rank growths from the hedge, she wrapped up her burden as well as she could in these, so that what she carried appeared to be an enormous armful of green stuff gathered by a zealous lover of nature.[53]

Clumsily trying to hide the statues she has just congratulated herself on buying, Sue covers them with the grotesque exaggeration of a

52. Hardy, *Jude the Obscure*, 94.
53. Hardy, *Jude the Obscure*, 94.

fig leaf. The whiteness of the statues, which initially made them seem pure, begins to taint her clothes. In a moment, Sue moves from being proud of her liberality to seeming soiled and intensely self-conscious, as naked as the figures whose bodies she has just fastidiously covered.[54] The appearances of Sue and the statues she is carrying are reversed. Sue has been painted over with a layer of their scandalous white brilliance. Apollo and Venus have been wrapped up in a semblance of the propriety she is trying to shed.[55] Instead of elaborating on her Greek ideals in the context of her new environment, Sue clings to them as—literally—stiff, plaster types whose dusty whiteness she also starts to physically share.

This scene highlights, with comically excessive directness, the quality of Greek culture that will remain most important and pressing to Sue. It also makes an oversimplified comment about the more traditional Victorian values that constantly come into conflict with these Greek ideals in Sue's mind: Sue seems to want from Greek culture not only the freedom that she claims to assert here, but also a veneer of purity and inflexibility. When, later in the novel, she continues to invoke the Greeks—"I feel that we have returned to Greek joyousness, and have blinded ourselves to sickness and sorrow," she says to Jude at one point—these statements reiterate not only her values, but also the expectation that these values can make her immune to the world around her. They are supposed to allow her to exist in this world as if "blinded" to the more humbling or vulnerable aspects of what a human body might go through.[56] The ease with which the

54. In a way that, as Patrick O'Malley has noted, has not only classicist but also Gothic undertones. Patrick R. O'Malley, "Oxford's Ghosts: *Jude the Obscure* and the End of Gothic," *Modern Fiction Studies* 46, no. 3 (2000): 664.

55. John R. Doheny suggests that Sue is similarly trying to both imitate and distance herself from the cluster of personal characteristics embodied by Arabella: John R. Doheny, "Characterization in Hardy's *Jude the Obscure*: The Function of Arabella," in *Reading Thomas Hardy*, ed. Charles P.C. Pettit (London: Macmillan Press, 1998), 57–82.

56. Hardy, *Jude the Obscure*, 312.

plaster these statues are made of blends into Sue's clothing belies the distance that separates her from the complex social contexts and sets of beliefs these statues might be taken to stand for. It ironically showcases both Sue's eagerness to belong to these larger spheres of reference, and the naïveté of her belief that she might become part of the world these statues—or, more precisely, their marble originals— came from.

In *Tess of the D'Urbervilles*, Angel's attitude toward Tess—and toward romantic love in general—is represented as the reiteration of a single gesture: carrying a woman over a river. In the scene where this gesture is introduced, Angel takes Tess into his arms after he had just done the same with her fellow milkmaids Izz, Retty, and Marian. In the three prior cases, he proceeds "methodically"[57] and with marked detachment. The women's weight and the desires awakened in them by Angel's touch are described in unflattering, scientific detail, as if these women were troublesome farm animals. One is even objectified as a "sack of meal."[58] Though Angel's gestures and touches change in quality when he finally returns to also carry Tess over the river, they are part of what begins as a pattern of repetitive objectifications.

The second iteration of this gesture of lifting and carrying occurs considerably later in the novel. Angel goes into a fitful sleep after hearing Tess's confession and spurning her. In the middle of the night, he starts sleepwalking. He then takes Tess in his arms and begins to carry her toward the river, just as he did at the dairy farm a few months prior. "Clare came closer and bent over her. 'Dead, dead, dead!' he murmured. After fixedly regarding her for some moments with the same gaze of unmeasurable woe," the narrator continues, "he bent lower, enclosed her in his arms, and rolled her in the sheet as in a shroud. Then lifting her from the bed with as much respect

57. Hardy, *Tess of the D'Urbervilles*, 144.
58. Hardy, *Tess of the D'Urbervilles*, 144.

as one would show to a dead body, he carried her across the room, murmuring—'My poor, poor Tess—my dearest, darling Tess! So sweet, so good, so true!'"[59]

In this succession of episodes, Angel is not only ever more repetitive, but also ever less conscious. In the final scene he apparently has no awareness of his surroundings at all. Angel's repeated gesture showcases the persistence with which he seems unable to escape the first gesture through which he wooed Tess. It also deepens the suggestion that what he might want from Tess is not her particular story and person but some vague "sweet," "good," and "true" woman to hold and to carry.[60] Hardy creates a sense of narrative surprise by showing how little this character seems to change in order to adapt to his new settings. Angel's gesture is expressive of little beyond his obstinacy in trying to curb his world around a pattern that he recognizes and make this pattern into an ever more sweeping tool of managing his social bonds.[61] Hardy's successive descriptions decrease any impression of these gestures as responsive to or showing an awareness of any particularly wide and rich social and cultural environment. Instead, his narrative strategies contour out and follow a person who becomes ever more ensconced within himself, to the point of literal somnambulism.

In a way that further deepens their structural similarity to Hardy's protagonists, his secondary characters are also remarkably oblivious of the performative potential of their self-expression. Inversely mirroring Tess's and Jude's apparent belief that everyone's words and

59. Hardy, *Tess of the D'Urbervilles*, 247.
60. In early drafts, Hardy in fact experimented with giving Tess a more conceptual name—such as "Beauty"—that reflects the sense of failed abstraction conveyed here. I thank Daniel Williams for this observation.
61. Law and Linda Austin have read similar scenes across Hardy's fiction as palimpsests that let his characters gradually accumulate ever richer historical and social meanings. Law, "Sleeping Figures," 233–234; Linda M. Austin, "Hardy's Laodicean Narrative," *Modern Fiction Studies* 35, no. 2 (1989): 212.

gestures are addressed specifically to them, these secondary characters often are unaware of the possibility that anyone could understand
the things they say differently than they themselves do.[62] Between
their penchant for limited, obsessive attachments to small tropes
and phrases, and this general sense of insouciance, these characters
inadvertently push each other into sequences of misconceptions that
become extremely hard to eradicate. In *Tess*, one prime example of
this pattern is the exchange between Tess's father and the local parson with which the novel begins. Tess's father, Jack Durbeyfield,
asks the parson why he has recently taken to addressing him as "*Sir
John.*"[63] The parson is abashed. "It was only my whim," he says.[64] "It
was on account of a discovery I made some little time ago, whilst I
was hunting up pedigrees for the new county history. . . . Don't you
really know, Durbeyfield, that you are the linear representative of

---

62. This sense of oblivion is especially striking since, in Hardy's represented worlds, hardly a
statement is uttered without having at least some performative effect on its surroundings.
At least one conventional performative speech act is present in every one of Hardy's novels.
All fourteen novels include at least one marriage. In his most famous novels, these marriages (or first attempts at a marriage) occur before the novels' emotional climaxes. This is
the case in *Tess of the D'Urbervilles, The Woodlanders, The Mayor of Casterbridge, The Return
of the Native, Far from the Madding Crowd, Two on a Tower, A Pair of Blue Eyes, The Hand of
Ethelberta,* and *Jude the Obscure.* In other ones—*A Laodicean, Under the Greenwood Tree, The
Trumpet-Major, The Well-Beloved,* and *Desperate Remedies*—marriages mark the final move-
ment of the novel's denouement. A significant number of Hardy's novels also contain other
formally binding speech acts. Among these are business contracts, such as the selling of
Henchard's wife in *The Mayor of Casterbridge,* the rent agreement and the organ donation
agreement in *The Woodlanders,* and the castle renovation contract in *A Laodicean.* Another
frequent performative is the secret marriage engagement, such as the fidelity vow made by
Elfride to her lover in *A Pair of Blue Eyes* or the promise of remarriage made by Swithin to
Lady Constantine in *Two on a Tower.*

Hardy's novels stage escalating tensions between these conventional performative
speech acts and the unexpected performative effects of any more casual words these characters utter. In Hardy's represented worlds, marriages and other official contracts are not
just retroactively frustrating to most characters, but also strikingly brittle. Their importance
is usually nullified not by other conventional speech acts—a divorce or a juridical verdict—
but by commonplace statements one would not normally expect to be of consequence.

63. Hardy, *Tess of the D'Urbervilles,* 43.

64. Hardy, *Tess of the D'Urbervilles,* 43.

the ancient and knightly family of the d'Urbervilles?"[65] The parson admonishes Jack that he should do "nothing, nothing" about this—his heritage is only of antiquarian interest. Of course, that is not what happens. That night, Jack Durbeyfield has himself driven home in a cart and addressed as "Sir John" by the local villagers. Soon, he and his wife persuade Tess to seek out their "relatives," Alec D'Urberville and his mother; this decision ends up having a dramatic influence on Tess's life. Hardy's characters miscommunicate in great part because neither of them appreciates the other's potential stakes and interest in this piece of information. Jack Durbeyfield does not see how no one else besides himself might see this discovery of his lineage as particularly important or urgent; meanwhile, the parson does not assume that Durbeyfield could possibly take it as personally as he does, as a new means of defining himself.

In *Jude the Obscure*, Jude and Arabella's son, whom Jude calls Little Father Time, sees in everything he encounters premonitions of the premature death of a young living creature. It is toward this image that all his thoughts and feelings tend. As a result of this narrowness of focus—a narrowness that apparently escapes Jude and Sue's awareness—Sue's nervous avowal that she is overwhelmed with the number of children she has pushes Little Father Time to kill himself and his siblings. "Father went away to give us children room, didn't he?" the boy asks Sue. "Partly," she replies. Little Father Time pushes her further. "It would be better to be out o' the world than in it, wouldn't it?" "It would almost, dear."[66] Sue confirms the boy's assertion with the slight hesitation of an "almost," without making a direct connection between the child's aphorism and the overcrowded state of the family. Suddenly convinced that his guardians' worries are due—not "partly" but primarily—to

65. Hardy, *Tess of the D'Urbervilles*, 44.
66. Hardy, *Jude the Obscure*, 333.

the burden of having too many children, Little Father Time hangs his siblings and himself. Miller sees in the unpredictable performativity of these speech acts a representation of the fragmentation and failure of language.[67] But what Hardy represents here is, more precisely, a failure of mutual awareness.[68] Aaron Matz rightly compares this plot turn to Jonathan Swift's "Modest Proposal."[69] Despite his philosophical air, Little Father Time is only able to understand his existence through one, tragicomically limited physical experience or phenomenon with which no one except him is similarly obsessed. The only way he can try to make sense of his life is by invoking or enacting these associations at the slightest incentive. Sue, meanwhile, is blind to the ways in which her words might affect her child.

The way in which Tess and Jude—on whom Hardy's narratives focus most insistently—are caught between the unreachably abstract knowledge of their narrators, and the narrow, only contingently and unpredictably changeable preoccupations of the people around them, makes it seem ever more impossible for their lives to relate to, or stand in for, anything larger than their own particular selves. Addressing audiences that are not there to listen, through generalizations that are much less sharable and sustainable than they realize, Hardy's characters exist in fantasies of performance and communication whose limits they can neither transcend nor even quite appreciate.[70]

67. J. Hillis Miller, "Speech Acts, Decisions, and Community in *The Mayor of Casterbridge*," in *Thomas Hardy and Contemporary Literary Studies*, ed. Tim Dolin and Peter Widdowson (New York: Palgrave, 2004), 36–53.

68. Jane Lilienfeld describes these characters as "consuming" each other in a blurry disregard for boundaries of persons and objects that chimes with my own reading. Jane Lilienfeld, *Reading Alcoholisms: Theorizing Character and Narrative in Selected Novels of Thomas Hardy, James Joyce, and Virginia Woolf* (New York: St. Martin's Press, 1999).

69. Aaron Matz, "Terminal Satire and Jude the Obscure," *ELH* 73, no. 2 (2006): 532–533.

70. Lawrence Jay Dessner suggests that, in letting his characters trigger and be pulled into such coincidences, Hardy opens up his novels to a sense of time and space that is more capacious

The cumulative effect of these narrative strategies makes itself keenly felt toward the end of both novels, when Tess's and Jude's lives definitively fall into crisis. In the climaxes of both plots, the two protagonists reach for measures of self-expression that are extreme and, even conventionally speaking, very noticeable. Tess murders a man, is hunted down by police, and is publicly executed. More histrionically, Jude is brought to the point of feverishly howling biblical verses toward an open window. In such times of crisis, as in the scene with which I began, Tess and Jude try to defend or comfort themselves by sharing their views with others more openly, and more urgently, than they had before—revealing both the narrow simplicity of these views, and the vulnerable sense of isolation to which they are reduced in the face of the surrounding world, the vast majority of which does not even stoop to contradicting them. Even causing or incurring death does not suffice to make these characters seem remarkable to others. Instead, it turns their social irrelevance into an ever darker and ever more explicit joke.

At the end of the novel, Tess kills Alec after Angel finally returns to her; she is then arrested and sentenced to death. Speaking to Angel and to her sister Liza-Lu shortly before her execution, Tess claims to recognize herself in Liza-Lu and asks Angel to marry her:

> "She is so good and simple and pure. O, Angel—I wish you would marry her if you lose me, as you will do shortly. O, if you would!"
>
> "If I lose you I lose all! And she is my sister-in-law."

than that of a conventional, probability-bound realist novel. But rather than make his characters' world seem larger and richer, as Dessner proposes, Hardy paradoxically contracts it. His characters seem to be unaware of how they might come across to others despite the urgency with which they try to enclose their words and gestures in abstract norms and generalizations. Lawrence Jay Dessner, "Space, Time, and Coincidence in Hardy," *Studies in the Novel* 24, no. 2 (1992): 168.

"That's nothing, dearest. People marry sister-in-laws continually about Marlott; and 'Liza-Lu is so gentle and sweet, and she
is growing so beautiful. O, I could share you with her willingly
when we are spirits! If you would train her and teach her, Angel,
and bring her up for your own self! . . . She had all the best of me
without the bad of me; and if she were to become yours it would
almost seem as if death had not divided us."[71]

Even though, as Kathleen Blake has argued, this is an instance of
Tess's apparent boundarilessness, there is little about this loss of
boundaries that might make Tess seem like the nexus of a pantheistic
or naturalist worldview.[72] Tess claims that her younger sister has all
of her best qualities. She tells Angel that he can find with Liza-Lu
the happiness he had hoped to enjoy with her. Throughout the novel,
Liza-Lu is described merely as a set of beautiful, innocent features.
For Tess to reduce herself to a pretty face suggests that she has still
not found a way to describe herself and her own worth in a way that
goes beyond an aura of bodily innocence. The scene is doubtlessly
ironic. Still, it is ironic not through some greater depth or sophistication it reveals in Tess, but through the obstinacy with which Tess
clings to this oversimplified vision of her best self even as all of her life
has proven it to be shallow. This obstinacy makes Tess seem fiercely
self-sufficient, but also strikingly isolated from her husband and sister, who are taken aback by this suggestion.[73] In this final attempt to
tie her life to something larger than herself—and to articulate what

71. Hardy, *Tess of the D'Urbervilles*, 394.
72. Kathleen Blake, "Pure Tess: Hardy on Knowing a Woman," *Studies in English Literature, 1500–1900* 22, no. 4 (1982): 693.
73. Uttara Natarajan has argued that much of Hardy's fiction could be seen as adopting Walter Pater's notions of beauty but whittling them down to fit a much smaller scale of experience. That may be true—but the comparison obscures the striking ways in which Hardy's repre-sented worlds also keep changing tone and scale internally. In the mouths of his characters, Hardy readily allows even his most dramatic plotlines to become comic and stereotypically flat. Uttara Natarajan, "Pater and the Genealogy of Hardy's Modernity," *Studies in English Literature 1500–1900* 46, no. 4 (2006): 858–859.

values she has tried to represent—Tess once again inadvertently highlights the inadequacy of the terms she uses to make such connections. As Angel and Liza-Lu walk away together from Tess's hanging, their physical freedom serves as another reminder of how great a difference separates their fates from Tess's, to the extent that to think of them as embodying her qualities would be impossible. Hardy stresses how little of her suffering and death they are taking with them, even if—indeed, *especially* if—they were to take Tess up on her suggestion and get married.

In *Jude the Obscure*, perhaps the clearest equivalents of this final scene are Sue's many fights with Jude, which are eventually followed by Jude's death. In the first set of these crises, Sue accuses Jude of being too narrow-minded to be a good partner for her. "I did want and long to ennoble some man to higher aims; and when I saw you, and knew you wanted to be my comrade, I—shall I confess it?—thought that man might be you. But you take so much tradition on trust that I don't know what to say."[74] Jude replies by openly invoking the sense of limitation that the novel has been imposing on him from the start. "Well, dear;" he says, "I suppose one must take some things on trust. Life isn't long enough to work out everything in Euclid problems before you believe it. I take Christianity."[75]

This scene highlights Jude's awareness of his limitations, but also shows that coming to this awareness does not in itself allow Jude to transcend them, or to satisfy Sue. "We could wish ourselves to be wholly perspicacious beings," Butler says in *Giving an Account of Oneself*. For Butler, this wish is unattainable because it would require us "to disavow infancy, dependency, relationality, primary impressionability; it would be the wish to eradicate all the active and structuring traces of our psychological formations."[76] In Hardy's novels,

---

74. Hardy, *Jude the Obscure*, 161.
75. Hardy, *Jude the Obscure*, 161.
76. Butler, *Giving an Account of Oneself*, 102.

characters' perspicacity is challenged not by the unknowable complexity of their own origins, but by the readiness with which they believe in, and embrace, any narrative of these origins available to them. The kind of self-awareness Hardy models for his readers does not concern merely, as Butler puts it, the fact that any attention other people give to us is "a gift"—and, "being a gift, it carries the insuperable quality of gratuitousness."[77] It also concerns the limits to how much any person can offer in response to such an act of attention; to how much anyone can learn, either about a particular person's uniqueness or about the broader ideals she might embody, by attending to her as closely as possible.

This sense of limitedness becomes perhaps most poignant in the course of Jude's death. Jude has been hallucinating, and is not fully conscious. He calls out, now for Sue, and now for Arabella, but neither woman is actually there to help him. Sue has long abandoned him and returned to her husband Phillotson. Arabella, who has been taking care of him in his illness, has gone out to a fair. In her absence, Jude begins to recite passages from Job in as loud a voice as he can muster. "*Let the day perish wherein I was born, and the night in which it was said, There is a man child conceived,*" he cries out. "*Let that day be darkness; let not God regard it from above, neither let the light shine upon it. Lo let that night be solitary, let no joyful voice come therein.*"[78] As he recites these verses, they are repeatedly punctuated by voices from the crowd who are enjoying the fair outside Jude's window. "Hurrah!" this crowd keeps shouting. Hardy's narrator continues to interrupt Jude's speech by inserting these shouts into his recitation in parentheses.[79]

Jude's monologue is insistently communicative. Indeed, the parenthetical asides with which Hardy interweaves Jude's voice

77. Butler, *Giving an Account of Oneself*, 102.
78. Hardy, *Jude the Obscure*, 425.
79. Hardy, *Jude the Obscure*, 425.

ironically echo the famous scene in *Madame Bovary* where Rodolphe Boulanger seduces Emma Bovary to the accompaniment of a town council meeting. But this monologue also finds Jude at his loneliest, and his insistence that he is addressing someone—or that others should listen to him—is sadly presumptuous. There is no way Jude can prove to others that he is Job; indeed, in spite of what he might believe in his delirium, nobody is around to hear what he says. At this extreme, Hardy reduces his flat protagonists' monologues to unselfconscious speech in which they lose any awareness of how much, or how little, they might be attended to or overheard; speech whose major metatextual purpose seems to be to remind the reader of how narrow a scope of the world this protagonist's self-assessment encompasses or reaches. In such reflexive terms, this ending also marks Hardy's insistence that the apparently tragic figure he has created is not, in fact, another Job, or an equally generalizable figure of suffering. Indeed, it suggests that the kind of realism his novel pursues can only be achieved by persistently mocking, and undoing, its protagonists' claims to such generality. *Jude the Obscure* highlights that falling outside social norms puts one at risk of not being able to get back into them quickly or capably enough for one's particular plight to seem intelligible or interesting to others.[80] In Hardy's novels, to stake one's sense of self on other people's responses is to discover, first and foremost, how rare and cursory these responses are and how uncommon it is for one's particularity to be taken by others as a serious counterexample to broad social norms. It is to find out, further— or ironically *not* find out—that one almost certainly misses the social

---

80. As Virginia Woolf puts it in *The Common Reader*, "[Hardy's] light does not fall directly on the human heart. It passes over it and out on to the darkness of the heath and upon the trees swaying in the storm. When we look back into the room the group by the fireside is dispersed. Each man or woman is battling with the storm, alone." Virginia Woolf, "The Novels of Thomas Hardy," in *Hardy: The Tragic Novels*, ed. R.P. Draper (London: Macmillan, 1975), 75.

cues that actually might be significant for one's sense of self, or that might help one get beyond one's overwhelming self-regard.

Butler values narratives because they make us aware of how often our words and gestures contradict the norms we claim to follow, and how much such subversively imperfect performances might trouble or even change the world in which we live.[81] By contrast, the mode of critique toward which Hardy's character construction tends encourages his readers to consider how often such an attentive, easily troubled surrounding world is only a dream. If, for Butler, novels are valuable models of personal experience because they record its richness and difficulty of expression more finely than we can usually perceive it in real life, Hardy's novels show that one can also value the novel for exposing the expectation that others should recognize our lives as intrinsically rich and difficult as a hope that can, perhaps, only be fulfilled within the artifice of fictional representation. This mode of character construction is not merely dismissive of or misanthropic about personal experience. Hardy shows how much we can learn about ourselves by trying to better understand the various forms this fantasy of being attended to can take, and to uncover the bodily and mental limitations it might initially obscure. His character construction highlights that we might fail to notice many of the difficulties and contingencies of our acts of social performance if we take for granted that someone is always there to listen to us. His flat protagonists thus also help one see reasons why these experiences of finitude and indifference ought to occupy a more crucial

---

81. "I would suggest," she says further, "that the structure of address is not a feature of narrative, one of its many and variable attributes, but an interruption of narrative. The moment the story is addressed to someone, it assumes a rhetorical dimension that is not reducible to a narrative function. It presumes that someone, and it seeks to recruit and act upon that someone." This sense of sudden self-consciousness—and awareness of one's incomplete ability to express oneself—brings home the fact that, as Butler puts it, "the very possibility of linguistic agency is derived from the situation in which one finds oneself addressed by a language one never chose." Butler, *Giving an Account of Oneself*, 63, 53.

place in considerations of social performativity and of novels as depictions of it.

Marcel Proust, to whose *In Search of Lost Time* I turn in the following chapter, takes these reflections about each person's bodily and mental finitude one step further. His narrator Marcel tries to perform the near-impossible task of becoming aware of the indifference others feel toward him. What might I seem like to someone who does not care about me? Marcel asks himself. Incorporating some answer to this question into the story of his life is, for Proust's narrator, a constant challenge as well as a redemptive aesthetic opportunity.

4

The Solipsist

Marcel Proust's *In Search of Lost Time*

"Miss Albertine, . . . she is gone," says Françoise, the nurse of Marcel Proust's narrator, in the last pages of volume five of *In Search of Lost Time*.[1] Proust's narrator Marcel is distraught. He has been fighting with his lover Albertine for days on end; he even threatened to leave her earlier that week. But Albertine's capacity to simply depart one morning blindsides him. Albertine's supposed occasional lovers are much easier for this narrator to imagine than her capacity to not treat him as the center of her world, as she is his. The physical shock into which her departure throws him makes Marcel realize that he would never have been capable of an analogous gesture.

In Search of Lost Time has frequently been described as a sequence of Marcel's obsessions with other characters: Albertine, Gilberte, Bergotte, Elstir, the duchess of Guermantes, and many others. But the *Search* could also be seen, from an inverse perspective, as an extended study of the relative indifference that the objects of the narrator's care show toward him. Marcel is famously preoccupied with his easily

---

1. My translation. Montcrieff and Kilmartin translate this passage as "off she went." Marcel Proust, *In Search of Lost Time*, trans. C. K. Scott Moncrieff and Terence Kilmartin (New York: Modern Library, 1992), V.422. The original French has it as "Mlle Albertine . . . elle est partie." *A la recherche du temps perdu* (Paris: Folio, 1992), V.399.

overwhelmed sensitivity. But he is equally fascinated with what his mind and body seem like to people who do not respond to him as intensely as he experiences them: people for whom his presence, and the intense webs of perceptions that he weaves together, are marginal or irrelevant to how they perceive their world and themselves.

The Oxford English Dictionary defines solipsism as an "excessive regard for oneself and one's own interests, to the exclusion of others," or "in [a] neutral sense: isolation, solitude." Proust's narrator is a solipsist in both these senses, in a way that he struggles to come to terms with as an inescapable condition of the kind of art he might be able to create. Proust represents Marcel's limiting, intense self-regard as something that is not merely chosen but physiological: as an extreme instance of the corollaries of inhabiting a human body. Noticing and coming to terms with the narrow and idiosyncratic scope of his capacity for attention and care—and the consequently narrow overlap between his fascinations and the interests of other people around him—is the main existential and aesthetic challenge Proust's narrator faces as he tries to make sense of his life and write about it. This challenge makes Marcel a flat protagonist in a way that, as in Graffigny's *Letters of a Peruvian Woman*, collapses the distinction between this protagonist and the narrator commenting on his fate. Combining these perspectives is all the more difficult, in Proust, since the measure of his protagonist's flatness is not only his limited influence on his outward surroundings (as it is for Graffigny's Zilia), but, just as importantly, the felt finitude of his inner life.

Proust's novel is written at a point of heightened cultural interest in first-person experience, and of renewed belief in the value of its representation. "Humanity is immense and reality has a myriad forms," Henry James writes in *The Art of Fiction* shortly before Proust begins drafting his novel. "Experience is never limited, and it is never complete; it is an immense sensibility, a kind of huge spider-web of the finest silken threads suspended in the chamber of consciousness, and catching every airborne particle in its tissue."[2] For James and many other authors writing around this period, literature is valuable to the extent that it is able to awe its reader with depictions of this "immense sensibility," and to convey it with as much depth and commitment as possible.

In Proust's *Search*, the generalized interest of first-person experience is not simply affirmed; it is, instead, constantly interrogated.[3] Rather than just asserting the value of his attachments, and of the acts of imagination that he builds around them, Proust's narrator seeks to understand how the seemingly rich, totalizing worlds of feelings and sensations in which he immerses himself might only be confined to his own mind and body—and, as such, they might be uninteresting to anyone else.

To bring out the larger critical stakes of such a reading of *In Search of Lost Time*, I engage with Elaine Scarry's accounts of beauty as a means of making ourselves more open to our environments. For Scarry, beauty is an experience that "decenters" our sense of ourselves and helps us see the world from a more selfless, expansive perspective. It thereby also lets us engage with this world more objectively

2. Henry James, *The Art of Fiction and Other Essays* (New York: Oxford University Press, 1948), 10. Commenting on this turn in novelistic representation, Percy Lubbock describes it as the discovery of the true richness of subjective experience: "It is clear," he says, "that if we wish to see an abundance and multitude of life we shall find it more readily and more summarily by looking for an hour into a memory, a consciousness, than by merely watching the present events about an hour, however crowded." Percy Lubbock, *The Craft of Fiction* (New York: The Viking Press, 1964), 118.

3. In *Proust entre deux siècles*, Antoine Compagnon describes Marcel Proust as stranded among late Victorian organicism, Bergsonian vitalism, and fin-de-siècle decadence. For Compagnon the main purpose and motivation of *In Search of Lost Time* is to map out these conflicting notions of the world and gradually resolve them. "La décadence que condamne Bourget, le vitalisme ou l'organicisme qu'exalte Séailles, voilà donc les deux côtés entre lesquels Proust se débat. Peut-on imaginer, comme entre Méséglise et Combray, qu'il y ait une façon de les rejoindre?" [The decadence condemned by Bourget, the vitalism or organicism exalted by Séailles, are the two sides between which Proust tries to choose. Is it possible to imagine a way to bridge them, as one imagines bridging the gap between Méséglise and Combray?] Antoine Compagnon, *Proust entre deux siècles* (Paris: Seuil, 1989), 42.

and more broadly. "The concern demanded by the perfect vase or god or poem," she asserts in one of her examples,

> introduced me to a standard of care that I then began to extend to more ordinary objects (perhaps I began to notice and worry, for the first time, about my neglect for the ordinary object and, inspecting it more closely, may now even discover that it is not ordinary). Far from subtracting or robbing fragility from the ordinary vase, the extraordinary vase *involuntarily* introduced me to the recognition that vases are fragile, and I then *voluntarily* extended the consequences of that recognition to other objects in the same category.[4]

Scarry argues that Proust's novel instantiates this approach to beauty. The *Search*, she claims, enacts and reflects upon these intensifying and broadening effects that aesthetic experiences can have on a person's relationship to her world—so that even desire is experienced by Proust's narrator as ultimately (or, at least, most valuably) aesthetic in nature.[5]

Scarry accurately captures the prominent role that aesthetic experiences play, for Marcel, as inspirations for his self-expression and benchmarks for its potential larger value. Proust's narrator insistently reframes both his carnal and his abstract desires as revelations

---

4. Elaine Scarry, *On Beauty and Being Just* (Princeton, NJ: Princeton University Press, 1999), 66–67.

5. As she describes this process, here referring in particular to another writer, "like the coat-maker, the poet is working not to make the artifact (which is just the midpoint in the total action), but to remake human sentience; by means of the poem, he or she enters into and in some way alters the alive percipience of other persons." Elaine Scarry, *The Body in Pain* (Oxford and New York: Oxford University Press, 1987), 307. See also a similar argument made by Lynn Hunt and Steven Pinker in historical, rather than purely aesthetic, terms: Lynn Hunt, *Inventing Human Rights* (New York: Norton, 2008); Steven Pinker, *The Better Angels of Our Nature: Why Violence Has Declined* (New York: Viking, 2011). Scarry takes up Hunt's and Pinker's historical arguments in her writings for *Boston Review*.

of another person's beauty and of the beneficial, eye-opening effects that this beauty has on him. It is as such aesthetic revelations that his urges seem most satisfying and valuable to him. But, I argue, Proust as an author—and the aging, death-bound narrator who implicitly writes the *Search*—are ultimately less interested in this potential larger promise of aesthetic experiences than in the fact that these experiences usually fail to fulfill Marcel's expectations. As Proust's novel progresses, it stages ever more explicit realizations about how little even a very beautiful object can do to expand the narrow perspectives a person casts on the surrounding world. For Marcel, beauty becomes a limit point of discovering how little interest he actually has in other people or in the world he lives in, and how little interest he can expect others to have in him. Aesthetic experiences prove this point to him precisely because he treats them as his most intense and compelling instances of openness and expansiveness of vision; because they do most to foster his hopes that the way he sees the world, and the things that he notices about it, could turn out to be generally insightful, and unquestionably shared by others.

When he is struck by a person's beauty, Marcel initially believes that this experience helps him see his whole world better, by expanding the range of environments and social patterns of which he is aware and to which he might speak. Through his acts of aesthetic reflection and expression, he also believes himself to become ever more finely attuned and responsive to the people he loves. But it is just as important for Proust's narrator, and for the novel Proust writes, to recognize that the expansiveness and generosity of Marcel's aesthetic experiences is often dramatically insufficient to provide him with the kind of openness that he hopes for.[6] Experiences of beauty ultimately lead

---

6. In this emphasis on the narrator's bodily finitude, my reading of the *Search* is related to, but ultimately distinct from, what Martin Hägglund and Samuel Beckett have variously described as Proust's obsession with mortality and bodily weakness. "Proust had a bad memory," Samuel Beckett says in *Proust*—"as he had an inefficient habit, *because* he had an inefficient habit. The

him to discover not—as Scarry would have it—a more generous way of engaging with his environment, but the necessary limits to how far he can push such generosity: limits that make him, in my terms, a flat protagonist.[7] The culminating intellectual revelation of the *Search* comes when this narrator realizes that his rapturous experiences were ultimately much more instrumental to creating his own felt experience of his life—a felt experience that only he truly cares about and is able to notice—than in allowing him to connect to, or become aware of, the real-life others among whom he has led his existence. Proust treats this reversal not as a failure of art and of aesthetic experience, but as a means of mining them for insights into the finitude and social forgettability of the attachments by which his narrator is most deeply defined.

In early sections of Proust's novel, the youthful narrator is amazed by all the things he is made to care about by each person he loves.

man with a good memory does not remember anything because he does not forget anything." Hägglund makes a point similar to Beckett's when he says that Proust's narrator is preoccupied with his temporal limitations. This narrator, Hägglund says, gradually comes to recognize that his survival from one moment to another depends on continually, irreversibly shedding some parts of himself. As Hägglund puts it, *"pain and loss are part of what we desire,* pain and loss being integral to what makes anything desirable in the first place." Proust's narrator does represent the *Search* as a near-insurmountable mental and bodily effort that this narrator will not be able to complete before his death. But Beckett and Hägglund ultimately see the *Search* as a sincere expression of dread at the mortality and fallibility of an otherwise extremely complex, admirable individual—an individual whose sensitivity seems precious and unambiguously worth preserving. It is this acquiescent egotism that my argument questions. Samuel Beckett, *Proust* and *Three Dialogues* (London: Calder, 1965), 29; Martin Hägglund, *Dying for Time* (Cambridge, MA: Harvard University Press, 2012), 152.

7. "We stand in relation to Marcel," Scarry says in *Dreaming by the Book*, "in somewhat the same way that an earth station would stand to persons in a spaceship: we on the ground have some forms of sensory experience that are close to being in the spaceship (seeing visual images on a screen, hearing the astronauts' voices) and others for which we need to rely on the astronauts' reports." Elaine Scarry, *Dreaming by the Book* (New York: FSG, 1999), 25. Her cosmic metaphor captures the intense near-solipsism of any person's thoughts and sensations, and underlines the significance of any means one might find of transcending this sense of enclosure—which is what, she suggests, Marcel's evocative prose allows him to do. I would argue that, to the many other people represented in this novel, this narrator frequently seems like a space oddity, in Scarry's sense, because the referents around which his sense of himself and others is constructed seem as alien and incomprehensible as if they existed on a different planet.

His longings for other people trigger in him what seems like a relentless curiosity about the social discourses, norms, and histories with which these people's lives are intertwined. The feelings that he has for some particular acquaintance lead him to seek out echoes of her presence in the environments around him. These feelings also inspire him to derive from his immediate experiences more universal statements about society, aesthetics, and love. In these early episodes, Marcel usually loses track of the ways in which his rapturous preoccupations with others and the grandiose conclusions he draws from them are not shared by everyone around him, and especially not by the objects of his attention. He does not realize that—as the older version of himself retroactively points out—what he conceives of as acts of affective generosity and communion are often anything but.

To love Gilberte is thus, for the young narrator, to discover in how vast an array of sites, activities, and communities he appears to find evidence of her presence and her personal history. He is fascinated with the Champs-Elysées because that is where he is able to meet her. He also becomes passionate about letter writing because that is their means of daily communication. Marcel carefully observes Gilberte's parents because they know aspects of her life he cannot yet access; he loves visiting her house because it embodies her taste and upbringing. In this early passage, Gilberte metaphorically expands onto her surroundings, making him notice and appreciate her parents just as intensely: "I waited for [Madame Swann] to go past, as thrilled as though she were Gilberte, whose parents, impregnated, like everything that surrounded her, with her own special charm, excited in me as keen a passion as she did herself, indeed a still more painful agitation (since their point of contact with her was that intimate, that internal part of her life from which I was excluded)."[8]

8. Proust, *In Search of Lost Time*, I.594. "J'attendais qu'elle passât [Mme Swann], ému comme si c'avait été Gilberte, dont les parents, imprégnés comme tout ce qui l'entourait, de son

The array of bodies and objects that Gilberte's personality and habits lead Marcel to appreciate makes her seem like a cipher that can bestow new clarity and meaning onto ever greater parts of his lived environment. The narrator's love for Gilberte seems to let him discover new qualities of bedrooms and living rooms, new meanings and pleasures of an afternoon tea, new reasons for the fondness he now also feels for her family. It seems to help him understand, and be curious about, not only her particular words and appearance, but a widening material and social sphere. In his intense attentiveness, Marcel begins to treat Gilberte as a gateway to ever vaster and more mysterious social and philosophical truths.[9] On the face of it, these representations of the narrator's heightened sensitivity embody what Scarry describes as the open-mindedness and perceptiveness generated by beauty: as a result of becoming enthralled with a particular person, this narrator is suddenly more responsive to everything else around him. Searching in his entire environment for further signs or echoes of the young woman he loves, and seeking to replicate or return to her image in whatever way he can, he seems to notice this whole environment more acutely.

But Proust rapidly undercuts this youthful narrator's fascinations. He emphasizes, with much irony, that his narrator's obsessions are still confined to a singular human being. Furthermore, only Marcel, and nobody around him, treats this one person as the center of a broader understanding of the world. The depths and details he finds in this person consequently cannot help him understand even the intentions and wishes of the very being whom he adores. To lose

charme, excitaient en moi autant d'amour qu'elle et même un trouble plus douloureux (parce que leur point de contact avec elle était cette partie intestine de sa vie qui m'était interdite)" (*A la recherche du temps perdu*, I.411–412). All passages from Proust are henceforth cited in-text, with the English quoted directly and the French appended in footnotes.

9. His interest in her becomes what Kristeva calls a "cult" in which any small aspect of her behavior seems like a key to potentially endless insights. Julia Kristeva, *Proust and the Sense of Time* (London: Faber and Faber, 1993), 98.

oneself in such an intense regard for someone, Proust suggests, is easy. But the aesthetic sense of richness and expansiveness to which such longings give rise do not open Marcel up to a vision of his world that is less tightly circumscribed by his desires. Nor do they help him appreciate that, even if the full scope of his obsessions and of the forms of curiosity they give rise to were made visible to others, these other people would probably not fall in step with them.

This undercurrent of irony pervades the older narrator's descriptions of the loves and fascinations of his younger self; it is distinguishable in the over-generalizations for which the narrator shows his younger self to rapidly reach. For instance, after he becomes fascinated with the princess of Guermantes, the young narrator attends a performance by the famous actress Berma just in order to see the princess there. As soon as he is seated at the opera house, he starts turning around to look at the princess's balcony loge. In a long, luxurious description, he marvels at how favorably her appearance, dress, and ease of manners compare to his and those of everyone around him. It seems to him that the beautiful, dignified pose the princess strikes among her entourage defines beyond dispute why anyone in the audience should admire her. "When they caught sight of the Princess," he says, "all those who were looking round to see who was in the audience felt the rightful throne of beauty rise up in their hearts." Marcel also begins to feel that the beauty of this entire opera hall is an extended expression of the princess's charm. It seems to him that her appearance explains and ties together everything around her. "[L]ike certain artists who, instead of the letters of their names, set at the foot of their canvasses a figure that is beautiful in itself, a butterfly, a lizard, a flower, so it was the figure of a delicious face and body that the Princess affixed at the corner of her box, thereby showing that beauty can be the noblest of signatures."[10] She is poised within her

10. Proust, III.39–40. "Et cependant, en reconnaissant la princesse, tous ceux qui cherchaient à savoir qui était dans la salle sentaient se relever dans leur cœur le trône légitime

loge the way an artist's autograph hovers in the corner of a painting he made.

Earnest as they are, these generalizations become ever more implausible. Soon the narrator does not merely treat the princess as the center of this whole opera house, but also speculates that she might participate in some additional, hidden realms of social knowledge and experience. "Certainly," he says, "I was very far from concluding that she and her guests were mere human beings like the rest of the audience. I understood that what they were doing there was only a game, and that as a prelude to the acts of their real life (of which, presumably, this was not where they lived the most important part) they had arranged, in obedience to a ritual unknown to me, to pretend to offer and to decline sweets, a gesture robbed of ordinary significance and regulated beforehand like the steps of a dancer who alternately raises herself on her toes and circles around a scarf." "For all I knew," the narrator continues, "perhaps at the moment of offering him her sweets, the goddess was saying, with that note of irony in her voice (for I saw her smile): 'Will you have a sweet?' "[11] Out of these putative secret lives he weaves a vast mythology that turns this opera house into the underwater palaces of Neptune. "Within the boundaries of their domain," he says, "the radiant daughters of the

---

de la beauté. . . . [C]omme certains artistes qui, au lieu des lettres de leur nom, mettent au bas de leur toile une forme belle par elle-même, un papillon, un lézard, une fleur, de même c'était la forme d'un corps et d'un visage délicieux que la princesse apposait à l'angle de sa loge, montrant par là que la beauté peut être la plus noble des signatures" (III.35).

11. Proust, III. 40–41. "Certes j'étais bien loin d'en conclure qu'elle et ses invités fussent des êtres pareils aux autres. Je comprenais bien que ce qu'ils faisaient là n'était qu'un jeu, et que pour préluder aux actes de leur vie véritable (dont sans doute ce n'est pas ici qu'ils vivaient la partie importante) ils convenaient en vertu des rites ignorés de moi, ils feignaient d'offrir et de refuser des bonbons, geste dépouillé de sa signification et réglé d'avance comme le pas d'une danseuse qui tour à tour s'élève sur sa pointe et tourne autour d'une écharpe. Qui sait? Peut-être au moment où elle offrait ses bonbons, la Déesse disait-elle sur ce ton d'ironie (car je la voyais sourire): 'voulez-vous des bonbons?' " (III.35–36).

sea were constantly turning round to smile up at the bearded tritons who clung to the anfractuosities of the cliff, or towards some aquatic demi-god whose skull was a polished stone on to which the tide had washed a smooth covering of seaweed, and his gaze a disc of rock crystal."[12]

To follow Marcel in these associations is, of course, to appreciate how vivid and immediately compelling they are. But as René Girard puts it, the narrator dreams up, rather than just discovers, the "enchanted gardens" into which those he loves lead him.[13] Beautiful as his visions are, their capacity to actually explain his environments is slight. Indeed, when Marcel is finally introduced to the princess, he discovers that her glib superficiality and detachment, behind which he currently divines such mysteries, are in themselves her main source of charm. And once his passionate interest in her wanes, the princess's shallowness becomes the thing he most enjoys about her company.

In *On Beauty and Being Just*, Scarry argues that "something beautiful fills the mind yet invites the search for something beyond itself, something larger or something of the same scale with which it needs to be brought into relation."[14] The *Search* shows how little this expanded form of vision ultimately amounts to. As the novel progresses, Marcel begins to look for ways of perceiving himself and others that enhance his awareness of how limited his range of interest in his surrounding world remains even when this interest is at its most generous and expansive. He also starts to notice how contingent and

12. Proust, III.36. "De la limite de leur domaine, les radieuses filles de la mer se retournaient à tout moment en souriant vers des tritons barbus pendus aux anfractuosités de l'abîme, ou vers quelque demi-dieu aquatique ayant pour crâne un galet poli sur lequel le flot avait ramené une algue lisse et pour regard un disque en cristal de roche" (III.34).
13. René Girard, "Introduction," in *Proust: A Collection of Critical Essays*, ed. René Girard (Englewood Cliffs, NJ: Prentice-Hall, 1962), 4.
14. Scarry, *On Beauty and Being Just*, 29.

unreliable is other people's capacity and willingness to include his imagined worlds, or even his person, in the small scope of their own preoccupations.

Proust's narrator first begins to consider the finitude of his own perceptions and interests by looking out onto the people around him. In the characters he befriends in early volumes of the *Search*, Marcel finds mirrors of his own aesthetic enchantments, as well as parallax views of the incompatibility of these enchantments with the world as it is seen by others. Like the story of Swann's obsessive love for Odette that the narrator recounts before he has the self-awareness to apply its conclusions to his own love life, the narrator's early depictions of characters like Saint-Loup or Charlus obliquely reflect some of the insights into his own solipsism that he eventually develops and embraces.

Charlus and Saint-Loup are usually oblivious to how their behavior might be responded to by anyone except for a few people they already care about. Marcel is fascinated by these characters' initial capacity to treat him with perfect indifference, as well as by the intensity with which they eventually befriend him to the exclusion of almost everyone else. To the young Saint-Loup, people whom he does not already know and care about do not seem to exist at all. Here, the narrator describes a first impression of him: "He seemed not to hear that a person's name was being announced to him; not a muscle of his face moved; his eyes, in which there shone not the faintest gleam of human sympathy, showed merely, in the insensibility, in the inanity of their gaze an exaggeration failing which there would have been nothing to distinguish them from lifeless mirrors."[15] Strolling around

---

15. Proust, II.359. "Il sembla ne pas entendre qu'on lui nommait quelqu'un, aucun muscle de son visage ne bougea; ses yeux ou ne brilla pas la plus faible lueur de sympathie humaine, montrèrent simplement dans l'insensibilité, dans l'inanité du regard, une exagération à défaut de laquelle rien ne les eût différenciés de miroirs sans vie" (II.298–299). As Germaine Brée puts it, in passages such as this one Saint-Loup is transformed from a person into a sort of gloriously indifferent, monstrous deity. "The young sun-god, who is to

Balbec, Saint-Loup acts as if none of the people around him could move him to as much as smile. The way in which Marcel conveys this indifference makes it seem inborn and immutable. This renders even greater his surprise when, upon being introduced to the narrator by Madame de Villeparisis, Saint-Loup rapidly becomes charming toward him. Proust's narrator is struck by this transition—which is as instantaneous as a phase shift—between the way Saint-Loup treats him before, and after, the narrator has been accepted into his small friend group. Saint-Loup's capacity for such indifference toward anybody to whom he does not already feel drawn or beholden seems seductive and miraculous to the young Marcel in ways he does not at that point fully explain to himself.

A few summers later, a slightly older narrator describes his fascination with Saint-Loup's extreme selectiveness of focus more overtly, and at greater length. While they are at a restaurant, Saint-Loup performs a feat of nonchalance toward the other guests assembled there in order to join the narrator at their table more quickly:

> Between the tables and the wall electric wires were stretched at a certain height; without the slightest hesitation Saint-Loup jumped nimbly over them like a steeplechaser taking a fence; embarrassed that it should be done wholly for my benefit and to save me the trouble of a very minor disturbance, I was at the same time amazed at the precision with which my friend performed this feat of acrobatics; and in this I was not alone; for although they would probably have been only moderately appreciative of a similar display on the part of a more humbly

become an intimate and devoted friend, is rapidly transformed into a monster of 'innate hardness' and 'insolence' when he passes the narrator without greeting him, 'his slender body just as inflexibly straight' as when seen before, 'his head just as high, his glance indifferent.'" Germaine Brée, "The Inhuman World of Pleasure," in *Proust: A Collection of Critical Essays*, ed. René Girard (Englewood Cliffs, NJ: Prentice-Hall, 1962), 77.

born and less generous client, the proprietor and his staff stood
fascinated, like race-goers in the enclosure. . . . and when Saint-
Loup, having to get past his friends, climbed on to the back of
the bench behind them and ran along it, balancing himself like
a tight-rope walker, discreet applause broke from the body of
the room.[16]

Marcel emphasizes that Saint-Loup instantly becomes an almost
universal spectacle—drawing the eyes and the applause of everyone
around him—even though Saint-Loup's own attention is directed
merely at the immediate obstacles that separate him from rejoining
his friends. The young aristocrat's eye easily glides over the onlookers in whom he incites great interest. He seems to forget even that
these people are there, let alone that he might owe them a more cir-
cumspect way of navigating the restaurant. To the young narrator,
this selective oblivion provides moving proof of Saint-Loup's affection for him. Only through the ironic exaggerations with which the
narrator's older self retroactively recounts this episode does Proust
suggest that Saint-Loup's careful elegance might hinge on a narrowness of vision that is less an immediate choice than a permanent
character trait.

As the two men's friendship continues, these contradictions
become increasingly explicit. Such experiences of being selected by
Saint-Loup amid the sea of this young aristocrat's general indifference

16. Proust, III.475. "Entre les tables, des fils électriques étaient tendus à une certaine hauteur;
sans s'y embarrasser Saint-Loup les sauta adroitement comme un cheval de course un
obstacle; confus qu'elle s'exerçât uniquement pour moi et dans le but de m'éviter un mouvement bien simple, j'étais en même temps émerveillé de cette sûreté avec laquelle mon ami
accomplissait cet exercice de voltage; et je n'étais pas le seul; car encore qu'ils l'eussent sans
doute médiocrement goûté de la part d'un moins aristocratique et moins généreux client,
le patron et les garçons restaient fascinés, comme des connaisseurs au pesage . . . quand
Saint-Loup, ayant à passer derrière ses amis, grimpa sur le rebord du dossier et s'y avança
en équilibre, des applaudissements discrets éclatèrent dans le fond de la salle" (III.399).

are soon complicated, in the narrator's mind, by moments when he realizes that his and Saint-Loup's spheres of care do not completely overlap. At first, the narrator notices only that Saint-Loup matches and reciprocates his own intense interest in him. Eventually, Proust's narrator also discovers that, despite this sense of reciprocity, he and Saint-Loup are generally moved by, and organize their lives around, considerably different people and sensations. He is unable to see much interest in preoccupations that Saint-Loup finds overwhelmingly rich and fascinating. These affective and intellectual gaps cause him embarrassment and stupefaction. This happens, for example, when he realizes that a woman he knew merely as a prostitute is Saint-Loup's adored lover Rachel:

> In this woman who was for him the epitome of love, of all the sweet things of life, whose personality, mysteriously enshrined as in a tabernacle, was the object that occupied incessantly his toiling imagination, whom he felt that he would never really know, as to whom he asked herself what could be her secret self, behind the veil of eyes and flesh—in this woman I recognized instantaneously "Rachel when from the Lord," she who, but a few years since (women change their situation so rapidly in that world, when they do change) used to say to the procuress: "Tomorrow evening, then, if you want me for someone, you'll send round for me, won't you?"[17]

17. Proust, III.176. "Cette femme qui était pour lui tout l'amour, toutes les douceurs possibles de la vie, dont la personnalité, mystérieusement enfermée dans un corps comme dans un Tabernacle, était l'objet encore sur lequel travaillait sans cesse l'imagination de mon ami, qu'il sentait qu'il ne connaîtrait jamais, dont il se demandait perpétuellement ce qu'elle était en elle-même, derrière le voile des regards et de la chair, dans cette femme je reconnus à l'instant 'Rachel quand du Seigneur,' celle qui, il y a quelques années—les femmes changent si vite de situation dans ce monde-là, quand elles en changent—disait à la maquerelle: 'Alors, demain soir, si vous avez besoin de moi pour quelqu'un, vous me ferez chercher'" (III.150).

Proust's narrator has slept with this woman many times. But it would never have occurred to him that this person could become centrally important to anybody's life. Marcel marvels both at the wealth of nuance and of insight that Saint-Loup draws out about this person, and at how little these nuances and insights move him as he listens to his friend. He is struck by how little he himself cares to test Saint-Loup's praises of Rachel, even ones that—like Saint-Loup's intuitions of her talent—do eventually prove to have some foundation in reality. Rather than see his and Saint-Loup's interests as forming part of one, generalizable, shared sensitivity, the narrator begins to catch glimpses of their mutual perspectives as two circumferences of attention that overlap much less completely than he might have expected—implicitly also revealing the short radius that each of them might encompass in the first place.[18]

At other times, Marcel is much more casual in noting the presence of such opaque, idiosyncratic networks of associations to which he has no access. He gets a hint of an implied series of resonances between a person's word or gesture and a larger history of this person's loves and obsessions—resonances that are often considerably more plausible and promising than the ones that lead him on long jealous quests when they issue from his lovers—but then he does not feel inclined to pursue this series of potentially rich associations any further. The narrator experiences such indifference during a long walk he takes with Charlus. In a way that echoes his description of Saint-Loup in the restaurant, he is initially struck by how appealing

18. Katja Hautstein helpfully describes such scenes as follows: "What I find in *A la recherche* is not only holistic emotionality, but its advancing displacement by the rapid increase in what I propose be called 'emotional cavities.' These are zones where there is no longer any interaction or closeness, no emotional contact or correspondence between the narrator and the world he perceives, but rather emotional distance and difference, zones where the narrator is left alone, standing before the frame." Katja Haustein, "Proust's Emotional Cavities: Vision and Affect in *A la recherche du temps perdu*," *French Studies: A Quarterly Review* 63, no. 2 (2009): 162.

and noticeable Charlus is to others. The baron is irresistibly visible. His appearance is so commanding that he captivates not only Marcel but also passing cab drivers. It seems that everyone in the street is interested in and responsive to him, and the narrator feels flattered to be walking by his side.

A few moments into their conversation, Charlus jestingly uses the word "truqueur," an obscure slang term for a male prostitute. The narrator comments on this slip as follows: "Society people always like talking slang, and people who may be suspected of certain things like to show that they are not afraid to mention them. A proof of innocence in their eyes. But they have lost their sense of proportion," he continues, "they are no longer capable of realizing the point beyond which a certain pleasantry will become too technical, too flagrant, will be a proof rather of corruption than of ingenuousness."[19] The baron invokes a vulgar expression in order to show that he himself is childlike in these matters, so completely detached from the obscenities the word suggests that he does not realize how inappropriate it is. Yet the word "truqueur" is "too specific" a "pleasantry." It veers so far from decorous speech, and from common sexual knowledge in the narrator's circles, that it is hard to believe a truly naïve person would pick it up and use it by accident.

In the midst of his dramatic visibility, Charlus commits a flagrant indiscretion. To use Gilles Deleuze's phrasing, he "betrays" himself.[20]

19. Proust, III.339. "Les gens du monde aiment volontiers à parler argot, et les gens à qui on peut reprocher certaines choses, à montrer qu'ils ne craignent pas de parler d'elles. Preuve d'innocence à leurs yeux. Mais ils ont perdu l'échelle, ne se rendent plus compte du degré à partir duquel une certaine plaisanterie deviendra trop spéciale, trop choquante, sera plutôt une preuve de corruption que de naïveté" (III.285).

20. Gilles Deleuze, *Proust and Signs* (Minneapolis: University of Minnesota Press, 2000), 26–27. As Deleuze says some pages later, "Charlus presents himself as an enormous flashing indicator, a huge optical and vocal vessel: anyone who listens to Charlus or who meets his gaze finds himself confronting a secret, a mystery to be penetrated, to be interpreted, which he presents from the start as likely to proceed to the point of madness" (Deleuze, *Proust and Signs*, 172). Maurois finds Charlus's inability to hide this socially unacceptable part of his

But even though Marcel notices this revelation, he does not pursue it further, despite the nearly universal, intense interest that, as he claims, Charlus inspires in everyone around him. The narrator's subsequent discoveries of Charlus' secrets also proceed as a series of what appear to be purely accidental encounters and unveilings: as when he sees Charlus and Jupien together at the beginning of volume four, or when he runs into Charlus at a BDSM venue in the novel's last volume. Even though the rest of the world is watching Charlus closely, he himself does not think much about Charlus's secrets until he literally walks into them.

Such shows of indifference to Charlus's private life are, of course, easily read as signs of the narrator's repression. As many critics have observed, they reveal the narrator's unwillingness to admit that his own sexual desires might not be dissimilar to the baron's.[21] But on a much more immediate level, these scenes highlight how much is going on around Marcel that he not only has limited knowledge of but also is in no rush to uncover. They serve as indirect reminders of how small a part of his world he ever decides to probe, and how arbitrarily disconnected his foci of interest might be even from concerns that, perhaps, ought to be more central to him, and are already significant to many people he knows.

In ways that are at first similarly oblique, Marcel begins to understand his own body as a complementary physical reminder that the sites and inspirations of his intensely aesthetic experiences might be surprisingly restricted and unshared by other people. Here, he reacts to the good news of his upcoming trip to Venice by becoming physically ill. "I felt myself undergoing a miraculous disincarnation,"

---

life to be so striking and so blatant that he describes him as a monster. André Maurois, *A la recherche de Marcel Proust* (Paris: Hachette, 1949), 260.

21. See, for example, Michael Lucey, "Proust's Queer Metalepses," *MLN* 116, no. 4 (2001): 795–815; Eve Kosofsky Sedgwick, *Epistemology of the Closet* (Berkeley: University of California Press, 1990).

Marcel says, "which was at once accompanied by that vague desire to vomit which one feels when one has developed a very sore throat; and I had to be put to bed with a fever so persistent that the doctor declared not only that a visit now to Florence and Venice was absolutely out of the question, but that, even when I had completely recovered, I must for at least a year give up all idea of traveling and be kept from anything that was liable to excite me."[22]

It turns out that the narrator's mind and body can hardly take not only Venice, but the mere thought of Venice. Even the mention of visiting it throws him into such rapture that he has to be bedridden for weeks. Comically enough, the unknown aesthetic pleasures he desires are unavailable to him not because of some universalized epistemic gap or social obstacle, but because his body cannot handle them. As the passage first promises and then withholds an unprecedented, vast expansion of the novel's represented world, it makes this world as it is now seem small and flimsy by comparison. For several more hundreds of pages, the Venice that Marcel longs for will exist in his mind and in the environments he represents as nothing more than a few photographs, sketches, and names.[23]

Fragments such as these dramatize Marcel's receptiveness. He can apparently have overpowering reactions to Venice even when just a meager metonymy of this city is present before him. But these episodes also highlight that the intense experiences he undergoes are more indicative of his bodily finitude than of the expansive ranges of his fascinations

---

22. Proust, I.559. "Je sentis s'opérer en moi une miraculeuse désincarnation; elle se doubla aussitôt de la vague envie de vomir qu'on éprouve quand on vient de prendre un gros mal de gorge, et on dût me mettre au lit avec une fièvre si tenace, que le docteur déclara qu'il fallait renoncer non seulement à me laisser partir maintenant à Florence et à Venise mais, même quand je serais entièrement rétabli, m'éviter d'ici au moins un an, tout projet de voyage et toute cause d'agitation" (I.386).

23. Sara Danius describes similar reactions that Proust's narrator has to early automobiles in "The Aesthetics of the Windshield: Proust and the Modernist Rhetoric of Speed," *Modernism/modernity* 8, no. 1 (2001): 99–126.

and raptures. Such passages also begin to reframe his inability to take note of anything more than small slivers of his surrounding environments, as a necessary condition of his experience.[24] Rather than break open his sense of solipsism, these episodes reveal that there is something physically inescapable about the immediacy and narrowness of what he cares about, and about the limits to how much he can take in at any given moment. Moments of aesthetic enthusiasm prove this point most powerfully precisely because, as Scarry aptly remarks, they mark the instances when this narrator strains to become as generously open as he can to his world and what this world might lead him to consider.

In a similar sequence of comic realizations, while visiting Gilberte the narrator notices how often the intensity of his preoccupation with her is not measured directly by her personal qualities but by the amount of coffee or tea that he imbibes while thinking about or being with her:

> Meanwhile Gilberte was making "my" tea. I would go on drinking it indefinitely, although a single cup would keep me awake for twenty-four hours. As a consequence of which my mother always used to say: "What a nuisance it is; this child can never go to the Swanns' without coming home ill."[25]

> Because of the violence of my heart-beats, my doses of caffeine were reduced; the palpitations ceased. Whereupon I asked myself whether it was not to some extent the drug that had been

24. This gives a comic dimension to Eve Sedgwick's otherwise serious claim, in *The Weather in Proust*, that like the philosopher Plotinus Proust's narrator sees his environments and his interior self as inseparable from each other. See Eve Sedgwick, *The Weather in Proust* (Durham, NC: Duke University Press, 2012).

25. Proust, II.91. "En attendant, Gilberte me faisait 'mon thé.' J'en buvais indéfiniment, alors qu'une seule tasse m'empêchait de dormir pour vingt-quatre heures. Aussi ma mère avait-elle l'habitude de dire: 'C'est ennuyeux, cet enfant ne peut aller chez les Swann sans rentrer malade'" (II.77–78).

responsible for the anguish I had felt when I had fallen out with Gilberte, an anguish which I had attributed, whenever it recurred, to the pain of not seeing her any more or of running the risk of seeing her only when she was a prey to the same ill-humor.[26]

Leo Bersani argues that, in the absence of a secure connection to those he loves, Marcel feels that he also does not know himself: "he has lost his sense of himself; he is nothing more than a beating heart and an [anxious] attention."[27] Yet paradoxically, such moments when the narrator finds himself reduced to "a beating heart" in an over-caffeinated body are not only signs of self-loss but also paths toward an increasingly acute self-awareness. In both fragments, Proust's emphasis is on how absorbing as well as on how flattening Marcel's relationship to the triggers of his sensations is. His body fuses together the many affective and physiological stimuli by which he feels assaulted and overwhelmed. The intense, obsessive attentiveness and rapture created by such experiences is—the narrator comes to realize—an indication of his inward confusion much more directly than it is a precise measure of or response to any person or object beyond him.

Such realizations about the solipsism of the narrator's curiosity and aesthetic rapture are further reinforced by passages where Marcel is made to understand how pathetic and uninteresting his inward experiences frequently are to others. His sensitivity to a loved person often registers merely as a nuisance. As his mother admonishes him midway through the novel, after his family moves in next door

26. Proust, II.251. "A cause de la violence de mes battements de cœur on me fit diminuer la caféine, ils cessèrent. Alors je me demandai si ce n'était pas un peu à elle qu'était due cette angoisse que j'avais éprouvée quand je m'étais à peu près brouillé avec Gilberte, et que j'avais attribuée, chaque fois qu'elle se renouvelait, à la souffrance de ne plus voir mon amie, ou de risquer de ne la voir qu'en proie à la même mauvaise humeur" (II.178).

27. Leo Bersani, *Marcel Proust: The Fictions of Life and of Art* (New York: Oxford University Press, 1965), 26.

to one of the Guermantes' family mansions: "You really must stop
hanging about trying to meet Mme de Guermantes. You're becoming a laughing-stock. Besides, look how ill your grandmother is, you
really have something more serious to think about than waylaying a
woman who doesn't care a straw about you." The effect of this revelation on the narrator's mind is quick and dramatic. As he puts it,
"instantaneously—like a hypnotist who brings you back from the
distant country in which you imagined yourself to be, and opens your
eyes for you, or like the doctor who, by recalling you to a sense of
duty and reality, cures you of an imaginary disease in which you had
been wallowing—[my mother] had awakened me from an unduly
protracted dream."[28]

Marcel describes his mother as a doctor or a hypnotizer. With
her one word and gesture, his intense focus on the princess breaks.
He is stunned both by how easily this spell is broken, and by how
tightly it held him while it lasted. His infatuation was much more visible than he had realized. To the princess it was also only a spectacle
of his awkwardness and undesirability, to which she responded with
the same kind of indifference that he himself shows when confronted
with Charlus's and Saint-Loup's lovers. As in the passage from *Swann
in Love* with which I began my introduction, what seems to be most
shocking for the narrator is not the princess's inability to recognize
his fascination with her, but the fact that she can become aware of
it without taking much interest in its existence. His intense admiration for her—an admiration about which he can barely stop thinking,

---

28. Proust, III.428. " 'Ne continue pas tes sorties pour rencontrer Mme de Guermantes, tu es
la fable de la maison. D'ailleurs, vois comme ta grand-mère est souffrante, tu as vraiment
des choses plus sérieuses que de te poster sur le chemin d'une femme qui se moque de toi,'
d'un seul coup, comme un hypnotiseur, qui vous fait revenir du lointain pays où vous vous
imaginiez être, et vous rouvre les yeux, ou comme le médecin qui, vous rappelant au sentiment du devoir et de la réalité, vous guérit d'un mal imaginaire dont vous vous complaisiez,
ma mère m'avait réveillé d'un trop long songe" (III.360).

even for a minute—registers as merely another annoying episode within her busy social life.

Realizations such as these are eventually driven home by a series of crises in which Marcel feels estranged even from people who are closest to him. The first such crisis comes with the death of his grandmother. This grandmother is a figure whose doting attention to her grandson seems infinite. She shows constant concern for his health and well-being, and showers him with gifts. In an episode to which Marcel frequently returns, his grandmother comforts him during their stay in Balbec by coming over to his bedside whenever he knocks on the wall between her room and his. To the young narrator, the act of knocking on this wall and seeing her appear almost immediately proves that the new, unknown landscape of Balbec is not entirely hostile toward him. He can still find, within this new environment, some anchors of support that are constant and unquestionable, and whose care for him unwaveringly matches the intensity of his own impulses and needs.

Midway through the *Search*, this grandmother dies of an illness that her family initially dismisses as hypochondria. A great part of the shock Marcel experiences during this period comes from his realization that, in her pain and bewilderment, his grandmother can no longer pay attention to him. In a flash, her body becomes entirely overwhelmed with nothing else but its own illness, abandoning its ties to anything besides itself. The first stroke that precipitates her sickness takes place during her walk with Marcel around Paris. She and the narrator have been strolling together, arm in arm, when she brusquely asks to sit down. The narrator turns his eyes toward her. "I looked at her more closely and was struck by the disjointedness of her gait," says the narrator. "Her hat was crooked, her cloak stained; she had the disheveled and disgruntled appearance, the flushed, slightly dazed look of a person who has just been knocked down by a carriage or pulled out of a ditch." The narrator discovers that his grandmother's condition may be more serious than he initially thought. He studies her appearance. Its details come together into a shocking image of a deep, violent crisis, as evident and frightening as injury in a traffic accident. The sphere of what she cares about is suddenly confined merely to a desperate, ineffective attentiveness to her own bodily coordination. As they sit there, Marcel hopes that his grandmother's weakness might pass. "I was afraid you were feeling sick, Grandmamma," he says; "are you feeling better now?"[29] But when they go see a doctor later that day, he confirms that she has just undergone a serious stroke, and is not likely to survive much longer.

As Marcel's grandmother's illness progresses, the intensity of her pain is measured by how difficult it becomes for her to attend to anything except the moment-by-moment coherence and sustainability of her own bodily movements. In *The Body in Pain*, Scarry describes the experience of suffering as an extreme discovery of our non-negotiable personal investment in our individual existence.[30] For Proust, witnessing another person's pain is, similarly, a revelation of the qualitative difference between this person's contingent attentiveness to her surroundings and her immersion in her own physical experience. The grandmother's attempts to mimic her prior concern about him and his mother expose ever more strongly how constrained her world has become and how little strength she now has to venture out of her suffering. "Ah! my dear," his grandmother says to his mother, "it's dreadful to have to stay in bed on a beautiful sunny

---

29. Proust, III.357. "Je la regardai mieux et fus frappé de sa démarche saccadée. Son chapeau était de travers, son manteau sale, elle avait l'aspect désordonné et mécontent, la figure rouge et préoccupée d'une personne qui vient d'être bousculée par une voiture ou qu'on a retirée d'un fossé. —J'ai eu peur que tu n'aies eu une nausée, grand'mère; te sens-tu mieux?" (III.311).

30. Scarry, *The Body in Pain*, 55. She also argues that the intense presence of a person's pain confers an analogously great sense of presence on the agents by whom this pain is caused. "The physical pain is so incontestably real that it seems to confer its quality of 'incontestable reality' on that power that has brought it into being." Scarry, *The Body in Pain*, 27.

day like this when one wants to be out in the fresh air—I've been weeping with rage against your instructions." "I'm not in pain," she continues, "I'm complaining because I'm not lying very comfortably, I feel my hair is untidy, I feel sick, I knocked my head against the wall." "But," the narrator notes in the midst of this description, "she could not get rid of the anguish in her eyes, the sweat on her forehead, the convulsive start, checked at once, of her limbs."[31] In these accounts of his grandmother as a body seeking some semblance of comfort, Proust shows how unable she is to hide the small scope of the comfort she seeks. His grandmother is caught in a futile effort to pretend to herself and to her daughter and grandson that the pain she feels is not caused merely by her body, but by a much wider network of this body's ties to the outer world. She tries to make her family believe that the causal chain creating this pain is larger and more malleable than they fear. As the grandmother's illness progresses, Marcel realizes that noting these narrow circumferences of his grandmother's immediate concerns—circumferences within which he himself is no longer included—is the only means he still has of understanding what is happening to her.

After his grandmother's death, Marcel transfers his intense, crisis-inducing modes of attention—and hopes of being cared for—onto his lover Albertine. Marcel wants to be the only person in Albertine's life. He wants to know everything about her past and present; he also treats her, as he previously treated Gilberte and Madame de Guermantes, as a supposed entry point into social and existential mysteries much greater than her individual self. This conviction starts to seem increasingly, comically misguided. Equally comic is

31. Proust, III.371. "'Ah! Ma fille, c'est affreux, rester couchée par ce beau soleil quand on voudrait aller se promener, je pleure de rage contre vos prescriptions.' Mais elle ne pouvait pas empêcher le gémissement de ses regards, la sueur de son front, le sursaut convulsif, aussitôt réprimé, de ses membres. 'Je n'ai pas mal, je me plains parce que je suis mal couchée, je me sens les cheveux en désordre, j'ai mal au cœur, je me suis cognée contre le mur'" (III.313).

the narrator's inability to see that Albertine does not reciprocate the intensity of his interest in her—in a way that makes her more cognizant than he is about the fragility of their relationship and its effective isolation from the world around them. As Marcel persists in aestheticizing his longings for Albertine through metaphors of starlight, truth, and infinity, Proust shows ever more forcefully how little what Marcel conceives of as expansive and open-ended experiences of her charm and beauty have to do with an actual broadening of his perspectives. Indeed, the ardor with which this narrator responds to her as an object of his admiration reveals itself to be an obstacle to his engagement with anything except his own bodily and mental states.

Here, in an early description of Albertine, Marcel turns every detail of her appearance into a source of insight, and a supposed means of expanding his relationship to her onto an ever broader social context: "In speaking, Albertine kept her head motionless and her nostrils pinched, and scarcely moved her lips. The result of this was a drawling, nasal sound, into the composition of which there entered perhaps a provincial heredity, a juvenile affectation of British phlegm, the teaching of a foreign governess and a congestive hypertrophy of the mucus of the nose." "Whenever I had gone for several days without seeing her," he continues, "I would refresh my spirit by repeating to myself: 'We don't ever see you playing golf,' with the nasal intonation in which she had uttered the words, point blank, without moving a muscle of her face. And I thought then that there was no one in the world so desirable."[32] As Compagnon puts it, in passages such as these the narrator's sensitivity is like a "telescope" that

32. Proust, II.528. "En parlant, Albertine gardait la tête immobile, les narines serrées, ne faisait remuer que le bout des lèvres. Il en résultait ainsi un son traînard et nasal dans la composition duquel entraient peut-être des hérédités provinciales, une affectation juvénile de flegme britannique, les leçons d'une institutrice étrangère et une hypertrophie congestive de la muqueuse du nez. . . . Chaque fois que j'étais quelques jours sans la rencontrer, je m'exaltais en me répétant: 'On ne vous voit jamais au golf,' avec le ton nasal sur lequel elle

hones in on a small portion of reality as if it were a large and complex world.[33] In the narrator's eyes, each small feature of Albertine's tone and demeanor becomes a window onto her life and social circle that needs to be reproduced and reconsidered ad infinitum.

The more involved the narrator's relationship to Albertine becomes, the broader a world of past histories and relations he deduces from her statements and gestures. He grows concerned not only with her immediate presence beside him but with enlarging narratives of how and with whom she spends her free time, by whom she might also be loved, what she might really think about him and about other people. Their love affair triggers in him a flurry of investigative activity. He pours out page after page, and lies awake night after night, speculating about what she did on a particular day when they did not see each other. During their interactions, the narrator is unable to take any single account she gives him of her life as final. He expects to find beyond each of her answers an ever greater, hidden wealth of knowledge that might tie her to huge networks of other men and women.

These investigations soon become myopic. Marcel locks himself in an echo chamber of his fears precisely because of the relentless inquisitiveness with which he pursues their purported objects:

> "She asked me all of a sudden whether I was fond of women."
> (But if she only "seemed to remember" that Gilberte had taken
> her home, how could she say with such precision that Gilberte
> had asked her this odd question?) "In fact, I don't know what
> weird idea came into my head to fool her, but I told her that
> I was." (It was as though Albertine was afraid that Gilberte had

l'avait dit, toute droite, sans bouger la tête. Et je pensais alors qu'il n'existait pas de personne plus désirable" (II.477).

33. Compagnon, *Proust entre deux siècles*, 49.

told me this and did not want me to see that she was lying to me.) "But we did nothing at all." (It was strange, if they had exchanged these confidences, that they should have done nothing, especially as, before this, they had kissed, according to Albertine.)[34]

In this passage, the narrator follows every phrase uttered by Albertine with a parenthetical hypothesis that tries to connect her story to an increasing number of other stories she has already told him, or to what he has found out about her from others. His close readings of Albertine's statements take up more room than these statements do in themselves. They also continue to interrupt the flow of her monologue as he retells it to his implied reader. The networks of hypotheses he constructs exist within a mental space apart from the physical world they share, a space into which he keeps imaginatively backtracking. His thoughts and feelings are not in synergy with their actual interactions, but in constant competition with them, adding up to an alternative parenthetical world of their own. Proust mocks his narrator's belief in the expansiveness and richness of his attentiveness to Albertine as an increasingly obvious blind spot in this narrator's field of vision. Indeed, it seems that the narrator's unawareness about the myopia of his acts of curiosity is a major reason why he cannot understand his detached, increasingly frustrated lover.[35]

34. Proust, V.429–430. "Elle me demanda tout d'un coup si j'aimais les femmes." (Mais si elle ne faisait que croire se rappeler que Gilberte l'avait ramenée, comment pouvait-elle dire avec autant de précision que Gilberte lui avait posé cette question bizarre?) "Même, je ne sais quelle idée baroque me prit de la mystifier, je lui répondis que oui." (On aurait dit qu'Albertine craignait que Gilberte m'eût raconté cela et qu'elle ne voulait pas que je constatasse qu'elle me mentait.) "Mais nous ne fîmes rien du tout." (C'était étrange, si elles avaient échangé ces confidences, qu'elles n'eussent rien fait, surtout qu'avant cela même, elles s'étaient embrassées dans la voiture, au dire d'Albertine) (V.362).
35. In the course of her descriptions of the value of experiencing beauty, Scarry speaks back to an imagined critic who argues that to attend to one beautiful object is to lose from sight the many others to which we could be attending. That is not true, Scarry contends, even if we do always, by necessity, only attend to one beautiful object at a time. This is because the

As his preoccupation with Albertine's unknowable past life deepens, Marcel begins to describe her in increasingly aestheticized, grandiose terms. He sees his admiration for her as the pinnacle and fulfillment of many prior moments of aesthetic rapture by which, as he believes, his understanding of his environments and of the people around him has gradually been expanded and deepened. In the course of such rhapsodizing, he compares caressing Albertine to touching a "stone." The "interior" he wants to touch, the "salt" and "starlight" of her true being, are always beyond his reach. Marcel's anguish about Albertine's unreachable worlds of experience is all the more tragicomic since Albertine lets him do anything he pleases with her body, and also lets him ask her any questions he wants: "I could, if I chose, take Albertine on my knee, hold her head in my hands, I could caress her, run my hands slowly over her, but, just as if I had been handling a stone which encloses the salt of immemorial oceans or the light of a star, I felt that I was touching no more than the sealed envelope of a person who inwardly reached to infinity."[36] Marcel's inability to understand what it might be like to actually communicate with Albertine is embodied in this passage with particular force since, as he examines her body and claims to have these profound revelations about it, Albertine herself is sleeping. As he tries to imagine the intricate multitude and depth of her social ties, the narrator consistently

experience of beauty increases our standards for what it means to attend to others, and to care about them. Proust does not subvert this perspective by suggesting—as Scarry implies one might—that the gaze that we turn to beauty is inherently objectifying. Instead, Proust's narrative begins to show that the intensely responsive regard we learn to pay to people and objects we care about—and that we might extend from them to other objects and people— is never quite as relevant to or insightful about the larger world as we might fantasize it to be in our preoccupation with it. Scarry, *On Beauty and Being Just*, 66–67.

36. Proust, V.441. "Je pouvais bien prendre Albertine sur mes genoux, tenir sa tête dans mes mains, je pouvais la caresser, passer longuement mes mains sur elle, mais, comme si j'eusse manié une pierre qui enferme la salure des océans immémoriaux ou le rayon d'une étoile, je sentais que je touchais seulement l'enveloppe close d'un être qui par l'intérieur accédait à l'infini" (V.372).

underestimates the ease with which she is able to let go of, or forget about, any of them, including her ties to himself.[37] When she finally leaves him, in the passage I describe in the opening of this chapter, Marcel is all the more dumbstruck since his intense, supposedly aesthetic preoccupation with her has apparently caused him to forget that she might exist apart from his fantasies—and do something that the branching world of his speculations has not predicted.

In the course of this sequence of disillusionments, Marcel begins to study the limits of the imagined worlds that his aesthetic raptures forge. His recurrent experiences of being overwhelmed by the few objects of his admiration eventually ground his understanding of the purpose of the novel he is composing. Bersani argues that, through writing, Proust's narrator is eventually able "to create a world where imaginative fantasy is no longer a sign of helplessness, but rather an instrument of ideal control and possession."[38] I agree with Bersani to a point: as the *Search* progresses, processes of reduction and simplification that at first seem merely confused and comic are recuperated as forms of self-awareness. But I also stress that these moments of fantasy are not "ideal": they do not allow Proust's narrator to transcend his material limitations, or make this narrator less ensconced within himself. Instead, Proust's narrator redescribes the small circumferences and narrow broader relevance of his loves and cares as a necessary measure of what, as he represents it, his experience effectively amounts to.[39]

---

37. As Deleuze has observed, these early failed obsessions begin to ground what will become the narrator's generally pessimistic view of interpersonal communication and connectedness: "friendship never establishes anything but false communications, based on misunderstandings, and frames only false windows. This is why love, more lucid, makes it a principle to renounce all communication." Deleuze, *Proust and Signs*, 42.

38. Bersani, *Marcel Proust*, 93.

39. John Lurz describes the narrator's efforts at understanding himself, and the art that comes out of them, as existing "'in between' the material and the immaterial." But the narrator's mimetic efforts instead appear to document how closely even his grandest philosophies

Before Marcel embraces this sense of finitude as an inspiration for his writing, he merely fears it. He is most fearful of the flatness and vagueness of the represented worlds to which the limitedness of his experiences gives rise.[40] Marcel first experiences this concern when Norpois, a friend of his father's, reproaches him with shallowness and self-indulgence upon reading his adolescent writing:

> I can now understand more easily, when I bear in mind your altogether excessive regard for Begotte, the few lines that you showed me just now, which it would be ungracious of me not to overlook, since you yourself told me in all simplicity that they were merely a childish scribble. (I had indeed said so, but I did not mean a word of it.) . . . But one can see in what you showed me the unfortunate influence of Bergotte. You will not, of course, be surprised when I say that it had none of his qualities, since he is a past-master in the art—entirely superficial by the by—of handling a certain style of which, at your age, you cannot have acquired even the rudiments.[41]

are anchored to small slivers of the material world. The narrator stresses with increasing force that he cannot and should not hope to exit this immediate world or to transcend it, if he wants to do justice to the process by which his thoughts and feelings appear to shape and command his attention. John Lurz, "Sleeping with Proust: Reading, Sensation, and the Books of the *Recherche*," *NLH* 42, no. 1 (2011): 131.

40. Describing the narrator's fascination with the painter Elstir—one of the artists whom he wants to emulate—Sara Danius rightly suggests that he finds in the constraint and darkness of Elstir's studio an invitation to artistic freedom: "The dark room turns into a metaphor for the artist's power to recreate the world as he pleases." Danius, "Aesthetics of the Windshield," 102.

41. Proust, II.52. "Je comprends mieux maintenant, en me reportant à votre admiration tout à fait exagérée pour Bergotte, les quelques lignes que vous m'avez montrées tout à l'heure et sur lesquelles j'aurais mauvais grâce à ne pas passer l'éponge, puisque vous avez dit vous-même en toute simplicité, que ce n'était qu'un griffonnage d'enfant (je l'avais dit, en effet, mais je n'en pensais pas un mot). . . . Mais on voit dans ce que vous m'avez montré la mauvaise influence de Bergotte. Evidemment, je ne vous étonnerai pas en vous disant qu'il n'y avait là aucune de ses qualités, puisqu'il est passé maître dans l'art tout superficiel du reste, d'un certain style dont à votre âge vous ne pouvez posséder même le rudiment" (II.45).

Norpois is dining with the narrator's parents and offers to read some of their son's essays. He initially does not comment on the piece the narrator hands him. When Marcel confesses that he loves the contemporary author Bergotte, Norpois criticizes his writing doubly. First, says Norpois, Bergotte is not a good writer to model oneself on. Second, even though he now sees that the narrator tried to imitate Bergotte, Norpois believes that he has not succeeded.

The experience the narrator describes in the short essay he gives to Norpois is one of his most moving aesthetic revelations to date. He composes early versions of it in a carriage while crossing the Combray countryside and hearing the bells of the neighboring Martinville. To the young narrator, this combination of sights and sounds seemed like a discovery of natural and human beauty; in the brief passage Norpois reads, he tries to convey both the intensity of this experience and its great significance to him. But to Norpois, the description is thin and trivial. The narrator's attempt at recreating his intense exhilaration does not succeed even in making these experiences basically credible to this outside reader.

In the larger context of Proust's novel, Norpois is not a reliable judge of writing. But the ease with which he altogether refuses to engage with the narrator's description highlights that Marcel's easily overwhelmed sensitivity is a potential weakness. The narrator's habit of drawing meaning out of what is always a very limited number of immediate objects of attention does not lead him to social or philosophical generalizations others will necessarily find valuable. Paradoxically, Marcel deals with this sense of solipsism by turning such moments of disenchantment into the main objects of his novel's mimetic attention. Proust's narrator shows ever more self-consciously that, despite their apparent open-endedness, his mental efforts are tethered to a small number of places, objects, and people, and his particular relations to them are not generally shared by or compelling to others. For the aging narrator, the writing process becomes a means of representing this narrow circumference of his experience, and of sustaining an awareness that this experience—even at its most urgent and expansive to him—might not matter to anyone except himself.

The progress of the *Search* is thus marked by the increasing confidence with which its narrator abandons his initial efforts to extract some broader networks of connection from the objects and persons immediately before him. Instead, Marcel highlights the smallness and flimsiness of the perceptions to which his body and mind attend at each instance. Many of the narrator's self-affirming aphorisms soon begin to describe the extent to which any object or person to which he becomes attached will always take him by surprise. He will inevitably be blindsided by things and people he finds beautiful because they resist his attempts to turn his experiences of them into broader, usable forms of knowledge. Here, the narrator describes the sudden surge of joy he feels upon being offered milk by a beautiful local woman on a train to Balbec: "I felt on seeing her," he says, "that desire to live which is reborn in us whenever we become conscious anew of beauty and of happiness." As he tries to explain to himself why this encounter is so surprising to him, he emphasizes how difficult it is to keep in mind the radical particularity of any object of his admiration. "We invariably forget that these are individual qualities," he comments, "and, mentally substituting for them a conventional type at which we arrive by striking a sort of mean among the different faces that have taken our fancy, among the pleasures we have known, we are left with mere abstract images which are lifeless and insipid because they lack precisely that element of novelty, different from anything we have known, that element which is peculiar to beauty and to happiness." To re-encounter beauty after such a descent into "insipid" abstractions forces one to see how little these abstractions, and the real people and objects they are meant to synthesize, have to do with each other. As he puts it, "we deliver on life a pessimistic judgment which we suppose to be accurate, for we believed that we were taking happiness and beauty into account, whereas in fact we left them out and replaced them by syntheses in which there is not a single atom of either."[42]

This passage is striking both in its joyful precision and in its sense of defeat. Marcel struggles to articulate general rules of how and when he finds something beautiful. He finds that he can only do so by acknowledging that an experience of beauty is never removable from a particular, tightly circumscribed occasion. The woman he describes awakens in him not only a sensation of beauty, but also the recognition that he is powerless to carry or to generalize this beauty any further—even though, as Scarry observes in commenting on this fragment, he very much wants to do so.[43]

42. Proust, II.269. "Je ressentis devant elle ce désir de vivre qui renaît en nous chaque fois que nous prenons de nouveau conscience de la beauté et du bonheur. Nous oublions toujours qu'ils sont individuels et, leur substituant dans notre esprit un type de convention que nous formons en faisant une sorte de moyenne entre les différents visages qui nous ont plu, entre les plaisirs que nous avons connus, nous n'avons que des images abstraites qui sont languissantes et fades parce qu'il leur manque précisément ce caractère d'une chose nouvelle, différente de ce que nous avons connu, ce caractère qui est propre à la beauté et au bonheur. Et nous portons sur la vie un jugement pessimiste et que nous supposons juste, car nous avons cru y faire entrer en ligne de compte le bonheur et la beauté, quand nous les avons omis et remplacés par des synthèses où d'eux il n'y a pas un seul atome" (II.224).

43. "Proust wishes her to remain forever in his perceptual field and will alter his own location to bring that about," she says. "This willingness to continually revise one's own location in order to place oneself in the path of beauty is the basic impulse underlying education." Scarry, *On Beauty and Being Just*, 7. Commenting on moments of such sudden surprise, Deleuze suggests that patterns and regularities only become visible in this narrator's life after he has already enacted them unconsciously: "Not causing us to know anything, the law teaches us what it is only by marking our flesh, by already applying punishment to us." These statements well capture the narrator's recurrent, sometimes humiliated sense of shock at the small help his thoughts and feelings can give him in navigating his real social and material worlds. But to call these experiences of surprise retroactive discoveries of universal laws is to belie the extent to which the narrator ties the potential value of his sensitivity precisely to its capacity to thus be blindsided by the world around him, to suddenly doubt that any universal patterns could possibly have shaped or predicted a particular person he sees. To the extent that they might help one see the world anew, they do so not by reminding one of its larger circumferences, but by recalling how little relation one's life bears to these larger circumferences in the first place. Deleuze, *Proust and Signs*, 132.

This sense of limitedness finally also shapes Marcel's experiences of involuntary memory, which many critics rightly describe as the cornerstone of his understanding both of art and of his life. On the one hand, in the course of involuntary memories, the narrator recognizes how much greater than he had recalled are the spans of time and space that his body has traversed throughout his lifetime.[44] The spells of involuntary memory that bookend Proust's novel—his first flash of reminiscences caused by the madeleine, and the series of such flashes that precede the party he attends in the last volume—inspire this narrator to a feeling of personal independence and aesthetic self-possession. The narrator feels free both from the hold the immediate present has on him, and from the passage of time that has gradually made his past seem irretrievable. In the first volume, he describes the piece of madeleine he eats as a kind of sacramental communion. In the last volume, he spends many pages deriving from his experiences of a cracked pavement and of the sound of bells larger truths about his lifelong relationship to time.

On the other hand, these episodes highlight the triviality and idiosyncrasy of the sensations that allow Marcel to arrive at the revelations that he finds so satisfying. The kinds of objects within which his particular presence waits to be recognized are not landscapes or houses, or great public artworks, but small imperfections in the pavement, or individual bites of cookies. They offer him bits of sensation on which even he himself can only focus when he is completely alone,

---

44. As Poulet puts it, "Between this regained sensation and the present sensation there is established a relationship of the same nature as that between the faith of the child and the object of his belief; and from this metaphoric relationship between two impressions there has finally surged up the self; not a present self, without content, at the disposal of time and death; and not a past self, lost, and hardly retrievable; but an essential self, liberated from time and contingency, a primal and perpetual being, the creator of itself, the author of an 'eternal song immediately recognized.'" Georges Poulet, "Proust and Human Time," in *Proust: A Collection of Critical Essays*, ed. René Girard (Englewood Cliffs, NJ: Prentice-Hall, 1962), 171.

and that—once he has noticed them—almost immediately threaten to disappear from view. These memories do not simply sweep him up, and immerse him in the past, as effortlessly as critical accounts of these scenes often make it seem. Instead, Marcel needs to exert a considerable effort to keep these ephemeral sensations in view. "I shut out every obstacle, every extraneous idea, I stop my ears and screen my attention from the sounds of the next room," says the narrator as soon as he begins to discern the memories toward which the madeleine could be leading him.[45] He soon needs even to stop drinking his tea and eating more of his cookie, lest repetitions of his initial sensation might dilute it. After another wave of memories comes flooding back to him at the end of the volume, he shuts himself in his host's library to make sure none of the other guests will distract him from his meditations. Soon after leaving this party, he also suffers a small stroke that effectively prevents him from being able ever to relive a similar moment of reminiscence for the rest of his life. "Since the day of the staircase" where he has this stroke, Marcel says, "nothing in the world, no happiness, whether it came from friendship or the progress of my book or the hope of fame, reached me except as a sunshine unclouded but so pale that it no longer had the virtue to warm me, to make me live, to instill in me any desire; and yet, faint though it was, it was still too dazzling for my eyes, I closed them and turned my face to the wall."[46]

In this sense, involuntary memories are eerily appropriate as Marcel's defining aesthetic and existential revelations not simply

---

45. Proust, I.61. "[J]'écarte tout obstacle, toute idée étrangère, j'abrite mes oreilles et mon attention contre les bruits de la chambre voisine" (I.44).
46. Proust, VII.522. "Depuis le jour de l'escalier, rien du monde, aucun bonheur, qu'il vînt de l'amitié des gens, des progrès de mon œuvre, de l'espérance de la gloire, ne parvenait plus à moi que comme un si pâle grand soleil, qu'il n'avait plus la vertu de me réchauffer, de me faire vivre, de me donner un désir quelconque, et encore était-il trop brillant, si blême qu'il fût, pour mes yeux qui préféraient se fermer, et je me retournais du côté du mur" (VII.347).

in light of the vivid sensory recollections they provoke, but also because the conditions of these recollections mirror and amplify what the narrator has come to see as the necessary finitude and restricted interest of his immediate experience. The sensory experiences that move him to intense flashes of memory are ones that would have been easy to forget about, and that have always existed in the periphery even of his own awareness. They are also particular to his mind and body: he could hardly expect any of his surviving friends or lovers to respond to these quotidian sensations with anything like his excitement and nostalgia, and he does not even for a moment entertain the idea of sharing these experiences with the other people immediately around him. In this sense, despite the abstract terms in which this narrator often expresses himself in the course of these revelations, they are marked by a sense of self-enclosure that, unlike at many other points throughout this novel, he appears to merely acknowledge and accept as a necessary condition of making his life seem meaningful to himself.

As Marcel describes the means by which he wants to turn these recalled experiences into a novel, the metaphors he uses are reminiscent of the way in which, in *Oroonoko*, Aphra Behn justifies her narrator's interest in an otherwise unknown African prince. In her account of the themes and form of her narrative, Behn's narrator paradoxically describes her stories about Oroonoko as both too detailed and not detailed enough. On the one hand, she continually emphasizes how difficult it is to convey the full impact Oroonoko has on all of his observers, and how much grander a narrative he might deserve than she is able to provide given her limited knowledge of him and the confining conditions in which his life took place. On the other hand, Behn's narrator underlines that she is aware of the tedium her readers might feel upon being confronted with this unexpectedly detailed representation of a stranger's life. There are many parts of

Oroonoko's life that she has therefore, she says, omitted from her text out of respect for her readers.

The final pages of Proust's narrative are marked by a similar tension. On the one hand, Marcel says that he realizes how insignificant his account of his life will probably seem to anyone but himself. Reflecting on this sense of triviality, the narrator describes his experience of the madeleine as—in Hannah Freed-Thall's terms—a "conjuring trick" akin to the Japanese art of making small pieces of paper fold out to resemble recognizable objects when dipped in a bowl of water:[47]

And as in the game wherein the Japanese amuse themselves by filling a porcelain bowl with water and steeping in it little pieces of paper which until then are without character or form, but, the moment they become wet, stretch and twist and take on color and distinctive shape, become flowers or houses or people, solid and recognizable, so in that moment all the flowers in our garden and in M. Swann's park, and the water-lilies on the Vivonne and the good folk of the village and their little dwellings and the parish church and the whole of Combray and its surroundings, taking shape and solidity, sprang into being, town and gardens alike, from my cup of tea.[48]

47. Hannah Freed-Thall, "'Prestige of a Momentary Diamond': Economies of Distinction in Proust," *NLH* 43, no. 1 (2012): 162.
48. Proust, I.64. "Et comme dans ce jeu où les Japonais s'amusent à tremper dans un bol de porcelaine rempli d'eau, de petits morceaux de papier jusque-là indistincts qui, à peine y sont-ils plongés s'étirent, se contournent, se colorent, se différencient, deviennent des fleurs, des maisons, des personnages consistants et reconnaissables, de même maintenant toutes les fleurs de notre jardin et celles du parc de M. Swann, et les nymphéas de la Vivonne, et les bonnes gens du village et leurs petits logis et l'église et tout Combray et ses environs, tout cela qui prend forme et solidité, est sorti, ville et jardins, de ma tasse de thé" (I.47).

In metaphors such as these, Marcel self-consciously reenacts the imaginative leaps that, during his youth, make him see echoes of the woman he admires in an entire opera hall. He develops an apparently full, coherent universe out of a few small and ephemeral bits of matter. Voiced with the irony of this narrator's final retroactive perspective, this image dramatizes how private and idiosyncratic a spectacle the narrator has thus committed himself to forging. It highlights that much of what makes this spectacle seem precious to him might be easily lost in the larger world, for which it might only constitute an exoticized, refined pastime.

On the other hand, in the last sentence of the *Search*, Marcel also describes the process of writing his novel from the opposite angle. He represents it as the forced contraction and simplification of a world that he experiences as unspeakably rich in content. He suggests that if he tried to describe the people he recalls with the breadth and diversity of detail he ideally aims for—an effort for which he realizes he does not have the strength anyway—his representations of them would be bloated out of the kind of proportion his reader presumably expects:

> If I were given long enough to accomplish my work, I should not fail, even if the effect were to make them resemble monsters, to describe men as occupying so considerable a place, compared with the restricted place which is reserved for them in space, a place on the contrary prolonged past measure, for simultaneously, like giants plunged into the years, they touch the distant epochs through which they have lived, between which so many days have come to range themselves—in Time.[49]

49. Proust, VI.531–532. "Aussi, si elle [la force] m'était laissée assez longtemps pour accomplir mon œuvre, ne manquerais-je pas d'abord d'y décrire les hommes, cela dût-il les faire ressembler à des êtres monstrueux, comme occupant une place si considérable, à côté de celle si restreinte qui leur est réservée dans l'espace, une place au contraire prolongée sans

This last passage—which represents Time's full, unreachable plentitude—also turns this plentitude into something grotesque and hostile. As he imagines it, the outcome of capturing one's experience exhaustively would be a mass of impressions that do not coalesce into anything like the people the narrator attempted to evoke; a mass of impressions that reveals merely how incompatible the intense, accumulating focus of his interests and sensations might be with the larger world into which he now tries to reintroduce them.

As is the case in the analogous passages of *Oroonoko*, Proust's metaphors for his narrator's writing process might seem contradictory. This narrator represents his thoughts and feelings as, at once, too vivid and too flimsy, excessively robust and paper-thin. These seeming contradictions are resolved if one sees Marcel as an instance of the flat protagonist—and his development throughout the *Search* as marked by an effort to recognize this quality of "flatness" as a condition and consequence of his apparently inescapable solipsism. Marcel concedes that he is, simultaneously, too preoccupied with his immediate experience, and too restricted in his range of engagements with the world, to represent his life in a way that would not seem at once detached and intensely myopic; as disconnected from the larger world, as it would be full of conviction about the relevance of every grain of feelings, thoughts, and sensations that he is able to remember. In these concluding metaphors, Proust's narrator frames the process of acknowledging this tension as a central mimetic goal. It is only by lingering within it that he is able to capture and represent to himself the particular kind of care that he urgently felt toward the world in which he has lived and the experiences that he has had there.

mesure puisqu'ils touchent simultanément, comme des géants plongés dans les années à des époques, vécues par eux si distantes, entre lesquelles tant de jours sont venus se placer—dans le Temps" (VII.353).

Most critics read the ending of the *Search* as recuperative and optimistic. It is usually interpreted as a declaration that, in spite of all the isolation and incomprehension the narrator has suffered, and in spite of how much of his life he has lost or squandered, the novel that he now decides to write gives him means to recuperate these past losses and atone for them. As Richard Macksey puts it, time, "this destroyer of all external objects of desire becomes, in turn, a creative force: it allows recollection. Value resides only in past experience possessed and translated in the present. The artist's two means to achieve this vital simultaneity are memory and metaphor."[50] Bersani makes a similar point, attributing this salutary quality to the writing process that ties such memories and metaphors together: "Proust's narrative is constantly dramatic in the sense that it does not merely record the anxieties and disappointments of Marcel's life, but provides at every moment the instruments of combat that transform a discouragingly alien world into the substance of a self-affirmation. It is, therefore, the work we have been reading that reveals to the narrator and the reader how, exactly, the fiction of remembering can be a way to exploit the full creativity of fiction, that is, the possibilities it offers for self-creation."[51]

In response to these prior interpretations, I suggest that there is something ironic and purposefully self-limiting in Proust's final emphasis on what Deleuze calls the "material explanation" and basis of his imaginative efforts. These last memories do not "constitute the unity" of the *Search* in the sense of endowing it with an expansive breadth and depth that Marcel's successive aesthetic raptures kept turning out to not possess.[52] Instead, as the narrator reaches for these

---

50. Richard Macksey, "The Architecture of Time: Dialectics and Structure," in *Proust: A Collection of Critical Essays*, ed. René Girard (Englewood Cliffs, NJ: Prentice-Hall, 1962), 119.

51. Bersani, *Marcel Proust*, 245. See also Lucey, "Proust's Queer Metalepses," 810.

52. Deleuze, *Proust and Signs*, 3; quoting Proust, III.375.

small sensations, he realizes how difficult it is for him to maintain or justify his centrality even within his own narrative. They serve him as extreme embodiments of the kind of mental and physical confinement in which all of his life and thinking was led.

"Beauty always takes place in the particular," says Scarry, "and if there are no particulars, the chances of seeing it go down."[53] Within the context of Proust's novel, this notion of particularity takes on a very different meaning than Scarry intends. By trying to represent his own preoccupations the way that other people's preoccupations frequently seem to him—as unwarranted, excessive, and inexplicable—Proust's narrator highlights the sense of isolation to which he is reduced even when his feelings and thoughts are sweeping and overwhelming. Proust models the process of writing about oneself as an attempt to perceive how self-enclosed each person is within her intense regard for a few centers of attention; as an attempt to understand oneself not only from within, but also from beyond, these experiences, by always reminding oneself of a world in which they might not matter at all. Circumscribing the finitude of his thoughts and perceptions—however all-important they also always seem to him—is, for Marcel, what ultimately makes his project of writing about himself satisfying and worthwhile. It is also the means by which this narrator pictures to himself, and prepares himself for, his impending death.

53. Scarry, *On Beauty and Being Just*, 18.

Conclusion

"Their stupidity is mine and it is sinking me," Gustave Flaubert writes to Edma Roger des Genettes while drafting *Bouvard and Pécuchet.* "I have probably damaged my brain quite seriously."[1] Bouvard and Pécuchet, the characters about whom he is complaining, are copy clerks who have come into money and use their wealth to educate themselves. Over hundreds of pages, Flaubert mocks the platitudes and over-generalizations into which this pursuit of knowledge leads them.

Flaubert—for whom the simplifications a novel commits are its main weakness—might have feared that many of the characters described here would have a similar "softening" effect on the reader's mind.[2] I see flat protagonists as revealing, rather than inducing, a dimension of their readers' subjective self-regard that a harsh critic might describe as narrow-minded or "stupid." The novels I examine help their reader articulate a sense of wonder about why we would ever expect others to consistently attach much importance to our thoughts and feelings. They also give us means of turning this sense of wonder into a springboard for inquiries into our immediate and interpersonal experiences. As they fruitlessly repeat the same words

1. Gustave Flaubert, Letter to Edma Roger des Genettes, April 1875. Collected in Gustave Flaubert, *Selected Letters,* trans. Geoffrey Wall (London: Penguin, 1992), 391.
2. Flaubert, *Selected Letters,* 391.

and gestures, Tess and Jude challenge their readers to test whether their own inner lives are not similarly, humblingly finite. While Graffigny's and Charrière's protagonists wait for someone to respond to their letters, their narratives suggest that these characters' disappointed hopefulness is an experience in which many of us might unknowingly share.

One often hears novels being praised for their representations of deep, complex individuals. They are seen to thereby enhance our appreciation of how complicated and meaningful any particular person's experience might be. By contrast, the works examined here—which focus more on the person seeking connectedness and attention than on the one bestowing it—highlight how hard it is to compel those around one to choose one's personal experience over the many other foci to which they could be attending. These novels stress the finitude of our bodies and minds as objects of other people's concern. They bring out the relative paucity of ways in which any person's self-expression enriches or even just surprises the world around her. The more fully and comprehensively we convey ourselves to others, these novels suggest, the more clearly this act of expression is limited, in its range and insights, by the limits of our singular existence.

Flat Protagonists aims to place these displays of bodily and mental finitude more firmly at the center of what novels can, and are perhaps uniquely positioned to, teach their readers. I redescribe the necessarily narrow mimetic bounds of their genre not as wishful metonymies of the much larger world our lives relate to, but as extreme reminders of how small a segment of reality we might be willing to mistake for all of it, and how much else there is in the world around us that we never come to know or care about. The novels I examine suggest that some of their genre's most important insights lie in its capacity to confront us with the vastness of the indifference that we inevitably bear toward most of the world and that most of this world bears toward us.

Flat Protagonists thus turns what has conventionally been seen as a weakness of the novel—its necessary confinement to a small number of words on a few hundred pages, and to reduced representations of human beings—into an unexpected critical strength. Marcel's obsessiveness, or Oroonoko's disappointed idealism, are—by the light of these books' representation of them—objects not just of mockery, but of reflection on how easy such forms of self-aggrandizement are to fall into, and how difficult the generalizations to which they give rise are to escape. By negatively gesturing toward a world much broader than any particular person's networks of experiences and cares, these novels help us imagine what it might be like to take this indifferent, unknown and unknowable world beyond us, rather than the immediate spheres of our cares, as a baseline for what our philosophies and art ought to be able to grasp. They also show why this aspirational or utopian aesthetics of finitude and indifference might not be stupid, and might indeed turn out to be urgently necessary. By the light of their flat protagonists, each gesture of putting away a novel we are reading is a gesture of hope that the suddenly alienating disconnectedness and indifference of the surrounding real world, and the minuteness of our particular place within it, will become, if only for a while, more acutely present to us.

BIBLIOGRAPHY

Ablow, Rachel. *The Marriage of Minds: Reading Sympathy in the Victorian Marriage Plot*. Stanford, CA: Stanford University Press, 2007.

———. "Tortured Sympathies: Victorian Literature and the Ticking Time-Bomb Scenario." *ELH* 80, no. 4 (Winter 2013): 1145–1171.

Ahmed, Sara. "Willful Parts." *NLH* 42, no. 2 (2011): 231–253.

Allison, Jenene J. *Revealing Difference: The Fiction of Isabelle de Charrière*. Newark: University of Delaware Press, 1995.

Anderson, Amanda. "Character and Ideology." *NLH* 42, no. 2 (2011): 209–229.

Andrade, Susan. "White Skin, Black Masks: Colonialism and the Sexual Politics of *Oroonoko*." *Cultural Critique* 27 (1994): 189–214.

Anger, Suzy. *Victorian Interpretation*. Ithaca, NY: Cornell University Press, 2005.

Armstrong, Nancy. *Desire and Domestic Fiction*. New York: Oxford University Press, 1987.

———. *Fiction in the Age of Photography*. Cambridge, MA: Harvard University Press, 1999.

———. "The Fiction of Bourgeois Morality and the Paradox of Individualism." In *The Novel*, edited by Franco Moretti, vol. 2, 349–388. Princeton, NJ: Princeton University Press, 2006.

———. *How Novels Think: The Limits of British Individualism from 1719–1900*. New York: Columbia University Press, 2005.

Asquith, Mark. *Thomas Hardy, Metaphysics, and Music*. New York: Palgrave, 2005.

Austin, Linda M. "Hardy's Laodicean Narrative." *Modern Fiction Studies* 35, no. 2 (1989): 211–222.

Auyoung, Elaine. "The Sense of Something More in Art and Experience." *Style* 44, no. 4 (2010): 547–565.

Bakhtin, Mikhail. *The Dialogic Imagination*. Austin: University of Texas Press, 1982.

———. *Speech Genres and Other Late Essays*. Translated by Vern McGee. Austin: University of Texas Press, 1986.

Ballaster, Ros. "Fiction Feigning Femininity: False Counts and Pageant Kings in Aphra Behn's Popish Plot Writings." In *Aphra Behn Studies*, edited by Janet Todd, 50–65. New York: Cambridge University Press, 1996.

Barthes, Roland. "The Reality Effect." In *The Rustle of Language*, translated by Richard Howard, 141–148. Berkeley: University of California Press, 1989.

Beckett, Samuel. *Proust* and *Three Dialogues*. London: Calder, 1965.

Beckman, Richard. "A Character Typology for Hardy's Novels." *ELH* 30, no. 1 (1963): 70–87.

Behn, Aphra. Oroonoko *and Other Writings*. New York: Oxford University Press, 2009.

Benjamin, Walter. "The Storyteller." In *Illuminations*, translated by Harry Zohn, 83–110. New York: Schocken, 1969.

Berger, Sheila. *Thomas Hardy and Visual Structures: Framing, Disruption, Process*. New York: New York University Press, 1990.

Bersani, Leo. *Marcel Proust: The Fictions of Life and of Art*. New York: Oxford University Press, 1965.

Bertrand-Jennings, Chantal. "Nathalie Sarraute: Genèse d'une écriture." *The French Review* 83, no. 1 (2009): 78–89.

Best, Stephen, and Sharon Marcus. "Surface Reading: An Introduction." *Representations* 108, no. 1 (2009): 1–21.

Blake, Kathleen. "Pure Tess: Hardy on Knowing a Woman." *Studies in English Literature, 1500–1900* 22, no. 4 (1982): 689–705.

Blondel, Charles. *La Psychographie de Marcel Proust*. Paris: Librairie Philosophique J. Vrin, 1932.

Booth, Wayne. *The Rhetoric of Fiction*. Chicago: Chicago University Press, 1961.

Bostic, Heidi. "Graffigny's Self, Graffigny's Friend: Intimate Sharing in the Correspondence 1750–52." *Studies in Eighteenth Century Culture* 42, no. 1 (2013): 215–236.

Boué, Rachel. "Lieux et figures de la sensation dans l'oeuvre de Nathalie Sarraute." *Littérature* 89 (1993): 58–67.

Brée, Germaine. "The Inhuman World of Pleasure." In *Proust: A Collection of Critical Essays*, edited by René Girard, 69–87. Englewood Cliffs, NJ: Prentice-Hall, 1962.

Brooks, Peter. *Reading for the Plot: Design and Intention in Narrative*. Cambridge, MA: Harvard University Press, 1992.

Brouard-Arends, Isabelle. "De l'allégeance à la contestation: la représentation de l'intimité dans l'univers Romanesque d'Isabelle de Charrière." In *Une Européenne: Isabelle de Charrière en son siècle*, edited by Doris Jakobec and Jean-Daniel Candaux, 149–158. Neuchâtel: Editions Gilles Attinger, 1994.

Buell, Lawrence. "Introduction: In Pursuit of Ethics." *PMLA* 114, no. 1 (1999): 7–19.

Butler, Judith. *Bodies that Matter*. New York: Routledge, 1993.

———. *Giving an Account of Oneself*. New York: Fordham University Press, 2005.

———. *The Psychic Life of Power*. Stanford, CA: Stanford University Press, 1997.

———. "Values of Difficulty." In *Just Being Difficult? Academic Writing in the Public Arena*, edited by Jonathan Culler and Kevin Lamb, 199–215. Palo Alto, CA: Stanford University Press, 2003.

Carnell, Rachel. "Subverting Tragic Conventions: Aphra Behn's Turn to the Novel." *Studies in the Novel* 31, no. 2 (1999): 133–151.

Cazenobe, Colette. "Les lumières au pouvoir: la 'philosophie' d'Isabelle de Charrière à l'épreuve de la Révolution." In *Une Européenne: Isabelle de Charrière en son siècle*, edited by Doris Jakobec and Jean-Daniel Candaux, 87–121. Neuchâtel: Editions Gilles Attinger, 1994.

———. "La temporalité vécue chez Madame de Charrière." *Revue d'Histoire littéraire de la France* 100, no. 6 (2000): 1505–1510.

Charrière, Isabelle de. *Letters of Mistress Henley, Published by Her Friend*. Translated by Philip Stewart and Jean Vache. New York: MLA, 1993.

———. *Lettres de Mistriss Henley, publiées par son amie*. New York: MLA, 1993.

———. *The Nobleman and Other Romances*. New York: Penguin, 2012.

Chibka, Robert L. "Oh! Do Not Fear a Woman's Invention: Truth, Falsehood, and Fiction in Aphra Behn's *Oroonoko*." *Texas Studies in Literature and Language* 30, no. 4 (1988): 510–537.

Christoff, Alicia. "Alone with Tess." *NOVEL: A Forum on Fiction* 48, no. 1 (2015): 18–44.

Citton, Yves. "L'économie du bon ménage: Chagrins domestiques et soucis éthiques autour d'Isabelle de Charrière." In *Romancières des XVIIIe et XIXe siècles*, edited by Catherine Mariette and Damien Zanone. Grenoble, forthcoming.

Cohn, Dorrit. *Transparent Minds: Narrative Modes for Presenting Consciousness in Fiction*. Princeton, NJ: Princeton University Press, 1984.

Cohn, Ruby. "Nathalie Sarraute's Sub-Consciousversations." *MLN* 78, no. 3 (1963): 261–270.

Compagnon, Antoine. *Proust entre deux siècles*. Paris: Seuil, 1989.

Cossy, Valerie. "Isabelle de Charrière, Frances Burney et le métier d'écrivain." In *Une Européenne: Isabelle de Charrière en son siècle*, edited by Doris Jakobec and Jean-Daniel Candaux, 125–140. Neuchâtel: Editions Gilles Attinger, 1994.

Courtney, Cecil P. "Bovarysme et réalisme dans la correspondance de Belle de Zuylen." In *Isabelle de Charrière (Belle de Zuylen): De la correspondance au roman épistolaire*, edited by Yvette Went-Daoust, 15–22. Amsterdam and Atlanta, GA: CRIN, 1995.

Culler, Jonathan, and Kevin Lamb, eds. *Just Being Difficult? Academic Writing in the Public Arena*. Palo Alto, CA: Stanford University Press, 2003.

Danius, Sara. "The Aesthetics of the Windshield: Proust and the Modernist Rhetoric of Speed." *Modernism/modernity* 8, no. 1 (2001): 99–126.

DeJean, Joan. *Tender Geographies: Women and the Origin of the Novel in France.* New York: Columbia University Press, 1991.

Deleuze, Gilles. *Proust and Signs.* Minneapolis: University of Minnesota Press, 2000.

Deleuze, Gilles, and Claire Parnet. *Dialogues.* Translated by Hugh Tomlinson and Barbara Habberjam. New York: Columbia University Press, 1987.

Dessner, Lawrence Jay. "Space, Time, and Coincidence in Hardy." *Studies in the Novel* 24, no. 2 (1992): 154–172.

Dickson, Vernon Guy. "Truth, Wonder, and Exemplarity in Aphra Behn's *Oroonoko.*" *Studies in English Literature 1500–1900* 47, no. 3 (2007): 573–594.

Dobie, Madeleine. "The Subject of Writing: Language, Epistemology, and Identity in the *Lettres d'une Péruvienne.*" *The Eighteenth Century* 38, no. 2 (1997): 99–117.

Doheny, John R. "Characterization in Hardy's *Jude the Obscure*: The Function of Arabella." In *Reading Thomas Hardy,* edited by Charles P. C. Pettit, 57–82. London: Macmillan Press, 1998.

Dolin, Tim, and Peter Widdowson, eds. *Thomas Hardy and Contemporary Literary Studies.* New York: Palgrave, 2004.

Draper, R. P., ed. *Hardy: The Tragic Novels.* London: Macmillan, 1975.

Dubois, Pierre H. "Le scepticisme d'Isabelle de Charrière." In *Une Européenne: Isabelle de Charrière en son siècle,* edited by Doris Jakobec and Jean-Daniel Candaux, 37–44. Neuchâtel: Editions Gilles Attinger, 1994.

Eagle, Christopher. "On 'This' and 'That' in Proust: Deixis and Typologies in *A la recherche du temps perdu.*" *MLN* 121, no. 4 (2006): 989–1008.

Ferguson, Moira. "*Oroonoko*: Birth of a Paradigm." *NLH* 23, no. 2 (1992): 339–359.

Fisch, Gina. "Charrière's Untimely Realism: Aesthetic Representation and Literary Pedagogy in *Lettres de Lausanne* and *La Princesse de Clèves.*" *MLN* 119, no. 5 (2004): 1058–1082.

Flaubert, Gustave. *L'Education sentimentale.* Paris: Folio, 1965.

———. *Selected Letters.* Translated by Geoffrey Wall. London: Penguin, 1992.

———. *A Sentimental Education.* Translated by Douglas Parmée. New York: Oxford University Press, 2008.

Forster, E. M. *Aspects of the Novel.* London: Mariner Books, 1956.

Fowler, Elizabeth. *Literary Character: The Human Figure in Early English Writing.* Ithaca, NY: Cornell University Press, 2003.

Freed-Thall, Hannah. "'Prestige of a Momentary Diamond': Economies of Distinction in Proust." *NLH* 43, no. 1 (2012): 159–178.

Frohock, Richard. "Violence and Awe: The Foundations of Government in Aphra Behn's New World Settings." *Eighteenth-Century Fiction* 8, no. 4 (1996): 437–452.

Gallagher, Catherine. "Introduction: Cultural and Historical Background." In *Oroonoko; or, The Royal Slave,* by Aphra Behn, edited by Catherine Gallagher, 3–25. Boston: Bedford, 2000.

———. "*Oroonoko's* Blackness." In *Aphra Behn Studies,* edited by Janet Todd, 235–258. New York: Cambridge University Press, 1996.

————. "The Rise of Fictionality." In *The Novel*, edited by Franco Moretti, vol. 1, 336–363. Princeton, NJ: Princeton University Press, 2006.

Gerrig, Richard. *Experiencing Narrative Worlds: On the Psychological Activities of Reading*. New Haven, CT: Yale University Press, 1993.

Gilot, Michel. "La voix d'Isabelle de Charrière." In *Une Européenne: Isabelle de Charrière en son siècle*, edited by Doris Jakobec and Jean-Daniel Candaux, 25–36. Neuchâtel: Editions Gilles Attinger, 1994.

Girard, René. *Deceit, Desire, and the Novel: Self and Other in Literary Structure*. Baltimore: Johns Hopkins University Press, 1976.

————. "Introduction." In *Proust: A Collection of Critical Essays*, edited by René Girard, 1–12. Englewood Cliffs, NJ: Prentice-Hall, 1962.

————, ed. *Proust: A Collection of Critical Essays*. Englewood Cliffs, NJ: Prentice-Hall, 1962.

Gleize, Jean-Marie. "L'un et l'autre." *Littérature* 118 (2000): 71–77.

Goode, John. "Hardy and Marxism." In *Critical Essays on Thomas Hardy: The Novels*, edited by Dale Kramer, 21–37. Boston: G.K. Hall, 1990.

————. *Thomas Hardy*. Oxford: Blackwell, 1988.

Graffigny, Françoise de. *Letters from a Peruvian Woman*. Translated by David Kornacker. New York: MLA, 1993.

————. *Lettres d'une Péruvienne*. New York: MLA, 1992.

Greiner, Rae. *Sympathetic Realism in Nineteenth-Century British Fiction*. Baltimore: Johns Hopkins University Press, 2012.

Gustafson, Daniel. "Cultural Memory and the Royalist Political Aesthetic in Aphra Behn's Later Works." *Restoration: Studies in English Literary Culture, 1660–1700* 36, no. 2 (2012): 1–22.

Hägglund, Martin. *Dying for Time*. Cambridge, MA: Harvard University Press, 2012.

Hardy, Barbara. "Passion in Context." In *Critical Essays on Thomas Hardy: The Novels*, edited by Dale Kramer, 73–85. Boston: G.K. Hall, 1990.

Hardy, Thomas. *Jude the Obscure*. New York: Penguin, 1998.

————. *Tess of the D'Urbervilles*. New York: Penguin, 2003.

Harol, Corrinne. "The Passion of Oroonoko: Passive Obedience, the Royal Slave, and Aphra Behn's Baroque Realism." *ELH* 79, no. 2 (2012): 447–475.

Haustein, Katja. "Proust's Emotional Cavities: Vision and Affect in *A la recherche du temps perdu*." *French Studies: A Quarterly Review* 63, no. 2 (2009): 161–173.

Henchman, Anna. "Hardy's Stargazers and the Astronomy of Other Minds." *Victorian Studies* 51, no. 1 (2008): 37–64.

Hilger, Stephanie. "Comment peut-on être Péruvienne? Françoise de Graffigny, a Strategic *Femme de Lettres*." *College Literature* 32, no. 2 (2005): 62–82.

Hollander, Rachel. "Daniel Deronda and the Ethics of Alterity." *Literature, Interpretation, Theory* 16 (2005): 75–99.

————. "Novel Ethics: Alterity and Form in *Jacob's Room*." *Twentieth-Century Literature* 53 (2007): 40–66.

Holmesland, Oddvar. "Aphra Behn's *Oroonoko*: Cultural Dialectics and the Novel." *ELH* 68, no. 1 (2001): 57–79.

Hughes, Derek, and Janet Todd, eds. *The Cambridge Companion to Aphra Behn*. New York: Cambridge University Press, 2005.

Hunt, Lynn. *Inventing Human Rights*. New York: Norton, 2008.

Hutner, Heidi, ed. *Rereading Aphra Behn: History, Theory, and Criticism*. Charlottesville: University Press of Virginia, 1993.

Ingarden, Roman. *Cognition of the Literary Work of Art*. Translated by Ruth Ann Crowley and Kenneth R. Olson. Evanston, IL: Northwestern University Press, 1973.

Irwin, Michael. *Reading Thomas Hardy's Landscapes*. New York: St. Martin's Press, 2000.

Iser, Wolfgang. *The Act of Reading: A Theory of Aesthetic Response*. Baltimore: Johns Hopkins University Press, 1978.

Isikoff, Erin. "The Temple, the Château, and the Female Space: Nancy Miller's Overreading of Graffigny's *Lettres d'une Péruvienne*." *Dalhousie French Studies* 33 (1995): 15–26.

Iwanishniw, Susan B. "Behn's Novel Investment in *Oroonoko*: Kingship, Slavery and Tobacco in English Colonialism." *South Atlantic Review* 63, no. 2 (1998): 75–98.

Jacobus, Mary. "Hardy's Magian Retrospect." In *Critical Essays on Thomas Hardy: The Novels*, edited by Dale Kramer, 38–53. Boston: G.K. Hall, 1990.

Jaeger, Kathleen M. *Male and Female Roles in the Eighteenth Century: The Challenge to Replacement and Displacement in the Novels of Isabelle de Charrière*. New York: Peter Lang, 1994.

Jaffe, Audrey. *Scenes of Sympathy: Identity and Representation in Victorian Fiction*. Ithaca, NY: Cornell University Press, 2000.

Jakobec, Doris, and Jean-Daniel Candaux, eds. *Une Européenne: Isabelle de Charrière en son siècle*. Neuchâtel: Editions Gilles Attinger, 1994.

James, David. "Hearing Hardy: Soundscapes and the Profitable Reader." *Journal of Narrative Theory* 40, no. 2 (2010): 131–155.

James, Henry. *The Art of Fiction and Other Essays*. New York: Oxford University Press, 1948.

———. *The Letters of Henry James*. Edited by Percy Lubbock. 2 vols. New York: Scribner, 1920.

Jaquier, Claire. "Le damier, la harpe, la robe salie: médiations et symboles du désir dans l'œuvre Romanesque d'Isabelle de Charrière." In *Une Européenne: Isabelle de Charrière en son siècle*, edited by Doris Jakobec and Jean-Daniel Candaux, 177–186. Neuchâtel: Editions Gilles Attinger, 1994.

Johnson, Lionel. *The Art of Thomas Hardy*. New York: Haskell, 1973.

Keen, Suzanne. *Empathy and the Novel*. New York: Oxford University Press, 2007.

Kornbluh, Anna. "Obscure Forms: The Letter, the Law, and the Line in Hardy's Social Geometry." *NOVEL: A Forum on Fiction* 48, no. 1 (2015): 1–17.

Kristeva, Julia. *Proust and the Sense of Time*. London: Faber and Faber, 1993.

Laden, Marie-Paule. "'Quel aimable et cruel petit livre': Mme de Charrière's *Mistriss Henley*." *French Forum* (1986): 289–299.

———. "*Trois femmes*: Isabelle de Charrière et la réappropriation." *French Forum* 28, no. 3 (2003): 25–39.

Lanser, Susan. "Courting Death: *Roman, romantisme,* and *Mistriss Henley*'s Narrative Practices." *Eighteenth Century Life* 13, no. 1 (1989): 49–59.

Law, Jules David. "Sleeping Figures: Hardy, History, and the Gendered Body." *ELH* 65, no. 1 (1998): 223–257.

Lawrence, D. H. "The Real Tragedy" (1914). In *The Tragic Novels*, edited by R. P. Draper, 64–72. London: Macmillan, 1975.

Levine, George. "Thomas Hardy's *The Mayor of Casterbridge*: Reversing the Real." In *Critical Essays on Thomas Hardy: The Novels*, edited by Dale Kramer, 169–189. Boston: G.K. Hall, 1990.

Lilienfeld, Jane. *Reading Alcoholisms: Theorizing Character and Narrative in Selected Novels of Thomas Hardy, James Joyce, and Virginia Woolf*. New York: St. Martin's Press, 1999.

Lipking, Joanna. "Confusing Matters: Searching the Backgrounds of *Oroonoko*." In *Aphra Behn Studies*, edited by Janet Todd, 259–281. New York: Cambridge University Press, 1996.

———. "'Others,' Slaves, and Colonists in *Oroonoko*." In *The Cambridge Companion to Aphra Behn*, edited by Derek Hughes and Janet Todd, 166–187. New York: Cambridge University Press, 2005.

Lovesey, Oliver. "Reconstructing Tess." *Studies in English Literature, 1500–1900* 43, no. 4 (2003): 913–938.

Lubbock, Percy. *The Craft of Fiction*. New York: The Viking Press, 1964.

Lucey, Michael. "Proust's Queer Metalepses." *MLN* 116, no. 4 (2001): 795–815.

Lukacs, Georg. *The Theory of the Novel*. Translated by Anna Bostock. Cambridge, MA: MIT Press, 1971.

Lurz, John. "Sleeping with Proust: Reading, Sensation, and the Books of the *Recherche*." *NLH* 42, no. 1 (2011): 129–146.

Lynch, Deidre. *The Economy of Character: Novels, Market Culture, and the Business of Inner Meaning*. Chicago and London: University of Chicago Press, 1998.

Macey, J. David, Jr. "Eden Revisited: Re-visions of the Garden in Astell's *Serious Proposal*, Scott's *Millenium Hall*, and Graffigny's *Lettres d'une Péruvienne*." *Eighteenth-Century Fiction* 9, no. 2 (1997): 161–182.

Macksey, Richard. "The Architecture of Time: Dialectics and Structure." In *Proust: A Collection of Critical Essays*, edited by René Girard, 104–121. Englewood Cliffs, NJ: Prentice-Hall, 1962.

Mallipeddi, Ramesh. "Spectacle, Spectatorship, and Sympathy in Aphra Behn's *Oroonoko*." *Eighteenth-Century Studies* 45, no. 4 (2012): 475–496.

Mariette, Catherine, and Damien Zanone, eds. *Romancières des XVIIIe et XIXe siècles.* Grenoble, forthcoming.

———. "Terminal Satire and *Jude the Obscure.*" *ELH* 73, no. 2 (2006): 519–547.

Matz, Aaron. *Satire in the Age of Realism.* Cambridge, UK: Cambridge University Press, 2010.

Maurois, André. *A la recherche de Marcel Proust.* Paris: Hachette, 1949.

McKeon, Michael. *The Origins of the English Novel, 1600–1740.* Baltimore: Johns Hopkins University Press, 1987.

Meadowsong, Zena. "Thomas Hardy and the Machine: The Mechanical Deformation of Narrative Realism in *Tess of the d'Urbervilles.*" *Nineteenth-Century Literature* 64 (2009): 225–248.

Miller, D. A. *The Novel and the Police.* Berkeley: University of California Press, 1988.

Miller, J. Hillis. "Speech Acts, Decisions, and Community in *The Mayor of Casterbridge.*" In *Thomas Hardy and Contemporary Literary Studies,* edited by Tim Dolin and Peter Widdowson, 36–53. New York: Palgrave, 2004.

———. *Thomas Hardy: Distance and Desire.* Cambridge, MA: Harvard University Press, 1970.

Miller, Nancy K. "Men's Reading, Women's Writing: Gender and the Rise of the Novel." *Yale French Studies* 75 (1988): 40–55.

Moore, Kevin Z. *The Descent of the Imagination: Postromantic Culture in the Later Novels of Thomas Hardy.* New York: New York University Press, 1990.

Moretti, Franco, ed. *The Novel.* Princeton, NJ: Princeton University Press, 2006.

———. "Serious Century." In *The Novel,* edited by Franco Moretti, vol. 1, 364–400. Princeton, NJ: Princeton University Press, 2006.

———. *The Way of the World: The Bildungsroman in European Culture.* New York: Verso, 2000.

Moser-Verrey, Monique. "Isabelle de Charrière en quête d'une meilleure entente." *Stanford French Review* 11, no. 1 (1987): 63–76.

Moyn, Samuel. "On the Genealogy of Morals." *The Nation,* March 29, 2007, online at www.thenation.com/article/genealogy-morals/.

———. "Torture and Taboo: On Elaine Scarry." *The Nation,* February 5, 2013, online at www.thenation.com/article/torture-and-taboo-elaine-scarry/.

Natarajan, Uttara. "Pater and the Genealogy of Hardy's Modernity." *Studies in English Literature 1500–1900* 46, no. 4 (2006): 849–861.

Nussbaum, Martha. "Fictions of the Soul." *Philosophy and Literature* 7, no. 2 (1983): 145–161.

———. *Love's Knowledge.* New York: Oxford University Press, 1992.

———. *Political Emotions: Why Love Matters for Justice.* Cambridge, MA: Harvard University Press, 2013.

O'Malley, Patrick R. "Oxford's Ghosts: *Jude the Obscure* and the End of Gothic." *Modern Fiction Studies* 46, no. 3 (2000): 646–671.

Pavel, Thomas G. *Fictional Worlds.* Cambridge, MA: Harvard University Press, 1986.

BIBLIOGRAPHY

Pearson, Jacqueline. "Gender and Narrative in the Fiction of Aphra Behn." *The Review of English Studies* 42, no. 165 (1991): 40–56.

———. "Slave Princes and Lady Monsters: Gender and Ethnic Difference in the Work of Aphra Behn." In *Aphra Behn Studies*, edited by Janet Todd, 219–234. New York: Cambridge University Press, 1996.

Pettit, Charles P. C., ed. *Reading Thomas Hardy*. London: Macmillan Press, 1998.

Phelan, James. *Reading People, Reading Plots*. Chicago: University of Chicago Press, 1989.

Pinch, Adela. *Thinking about Other People in Nineteenth-Century British Writing*. Cambridge, UK: Cambridge University Press, 2010.

Pinker, Steven. *The Better Angels of Our Nature: Why Violence Has Declined*. New York: Viking, 2011.

Potolsky, Matthew. "Hardy, Shaftesbury, and Aesthetic Education." *SEL Studies in English Literature 1500–1900* 46, no. 4 (2006): 863–878.

Poulet, Georges. "Proust and Human Time." In *Proust: A Collection of Critical Essays*, edited by René Girard, 150–178. Englewood Cliffs, NJ: Prentice-Hall, 1962.

Prendegast, Christopher. *The Order of Mimesis*. Cambridge, UK: Cambridge University Press, 1986.

Proust, Marcel. *A la recherche du temps perdu*. Paris: Folio, 1992.

———. *In Search of Lost Time*. Translated by C. K. Scott Moncrieff and Terence Kilmartin. New York: Modern Library, 1992.

Pyle, Forest. "Demands of History: Narrative Crisis in *Jude the Obscure*." *NLH* 26, no. 2 (1995): 359–378.

Rimmer, Mary. "Hardy, Victorian Culture and Provinciality." In *Palgrave Advances in Thomas Hardy Studies*, edited by Philip Mallett, 135–155. London: Palgrave, 2004.

Rivero, Albert J. "Aphra Behn's *Oroonoko* and the 'Blank Spaces' of Colonial Fictions." *Studies in English Literature 1500–1900* 39, no. 3 (1999): 443–462.

Robbe-Grillet, Alain. *For a New Novel*. Translated by Richard Howard. Evanston, IL: Northwestern University Press, 1992.

———. *La Jalousie*. Paris: Editions de minuit, 1957.

———. *Projet pour une révolution à New York*. Paris: Editions de minuit, 1970.

Robson, Catherine. "'Where Heaves the Turf': Thomas Hardy and the Boundaries of the Earth." *Victorian Literature and Culture* 32, no. 2 (2004): 495–503.

Ronen, Ruth. "Completing the Incompleteness of Fictional Entities." *Poetics Today* 9 (1988): 497–514.

Rooksby, Emma. "Moral Theory in the Fiction of Isabelle de Charrière: The Case of *Three Women*." *Hypatia* 20, no. 1 (2005): 1–20.

Rosenthal, Laura J. "*Oroonoko*: Reception, Ideology, and Narrative Strategy." In *The Cambridge Companion to Aphra Behn*, edited by Derek Hughes and Janet Todd, 151–165. New York: Cambridge University Press, 2005.

Rosset, François. "Les nœuds du langage dans les *Lettres d'une Péruvienne*." *Revue d'Histoire littéraire de la France* 96, no. 6 (1996): 1106–1127.

Roulston, Christine. "No Simple Correspondence: Mme de Graffigny as 'Epistolière' and as Epistolary Novelist." *L'Esprit Créateur* 40, no. 4 (2000): 31–37.

———. "Seeing the Other in Mme de Graffigny's *Lettres d'une Péruvienne*." *Eighteenth-Century Fiction* 9, no. 3 (1997): 309–326.

Samson, Guillemette. "De Neuchâtel à la Martinique: espace et mouvement chez Mme de Charrière." *Eighteenth-Century Fiction* 12, no. 1 (1999): 61–73.

Sarraute, Nathalie. *Do You Hear Them?* Translated by Maria Jolas. Milner, IL: Dalkey Archive Press, 2004.

———. *L'ère du soupçon*. Paris: Gallimard, 1956.

———. *L'Usage de la parole*. Paris: Gallimard, 1980.

———. *Vous les entendez?* Paris: Gallimard, 1972.

Sartre, Jean-Paul. "The Anti-Novel of Nathalie Sarraute." Translated by Beth Brombert. *Yale French Studies* 16 (1955): 40–44.

Scarry, Elaine. *The Body in Pain*. Oxford and New York: Oxford University Press, 1987.

———. *Dreaming by the Book*. New York: FSG, 1999.

———. *On Beauty and Being Just*. Princeton, NJ: Princeton University Press, 1999.

———. "Participial Acts: Working." In *Resisting Representation*, 49–90. New York: Oxford University Press, 1994.

———. "Poetry Changed the World." *Boston Review* 37, no. 4 (2012): 66–70.

Sedgwick, Eve Kosofsky. *Epistemology of the Closet*. Berkeley: University of California Press, 1990.

———. *The Weather in Proust*. Durham, NC: Duke University Press, 2012.

Showalter, English. "Mme de Graffigny, Reader of Fiction." *Eighteenth-Century Fiction* 13, no. 2–3 (2001): 461–476.

Siebenschuh, William R. "Hardy and the Imagery of Place." *Studies in English Literature 1500–1900* 39, no. 4 (1999): 773–789.

Sills, Adam. "Surveying 'The Map of Slavery' in Aphra Behn's *Oroonoko*." *Journal of Narrative Theory* 36, no. 3 (2006): 314–340.

Silverman, Kaja. "History, Figuration, and Female Subjectivity in *Tess of the d'Urbervilles*." *NOVEL: A Forum on Fiction* 18, no. 1 (1984): 5–28.

Simon, Julia. "On Collecting Culture in Graffigny: The Construction of an 'Authentic' *Péruvienne*." *The Eighteenth Century* 44, no. 1 (2003): 25–44.

Smith, Murray. *Engaging Characters: Fiction, Emotion, and the Cinema*. Oxford: Clarendon Press, 1995.

Smith, Paul J. "Madame de Charrière lectrice de La Fontaine." In *Une Européenne: Isabelle de Charrière en son siècle*, edited by Doris Jakobec and Jean-Daniel Candaux, 49–63. Neuchâtel: Editions Gilles Attinger, 1994.

Sorum, Eve. "Hardy's Geography of Narrative Empathy." *Studies in the Novel* 43, no. 2 (2011): 179–199.

Spacks, Patricia Meyer. *Privacy: Concealing the Eighteenth-Century Self.* Chicago: University of Chicago Press, 2003.

Spencer, Jane. *Aphra Behn's Afterlife.* New York: Oxford University Press, 2000.

Spengemann, William C. "The Earliest American Novel: Aphra Behn's *Oroonoko.*" *Nineteenth-Century Fiction* 38, no. 4 (1984): 384–414.

Spivak, Gayatri. "Ethics and Politics in Tagore, Coetzee, and Certain Scenes of Teaching." *Diacritics* 32, no. 3–4 (2002): 17–31.

Springer, Marlene. *Hardy's Use of Allusion.* Lawrence: University Press of Kansas, 1983.

Sprinker, Michael. *History and Ideology in Proust.* New York: Cambridge University Press, 1994.

Starobinski, Jean. "Belle en ses miroirs." Conférence prononcée le 15 juin 1990 à Genève lors de la rencontre de l'Association Belle de Zuylen—Isabelle de Charrière et de l'Association Suisse des Amis de Madame de Charrière.

Summer, Rosemary. *Thomas Hardy: Psychological Novelist.* London: Macmillan, 1981.

Sussman, Charlotte. "The Other Problem with Women: Reproduction and Slave Culture in Aphra Behn's *Oroonoko.*" In *Rereading Aphra Behn: History, Theory, and Criticism,* edited by Heidi Hutner, 212–233. Charlottesville: University Press of Virginia, 1993.

Thomas, Downing A. "Economy and Identity in Graffigny's *Lettres d'une Péruvienne.*" *South Central Review* 10, no. 4 (1993): 55–72.

Thorel-Cailleteau, Sylvie. "The Poetry of Mediocrity." In *The Novel,* edited by Franco Moretti, vol. 2, 64–94. Princeton, NJ: Princeton University Press, 2006.

Todd, Janet, ed. *Aphra Behn Studies.* New York: Cambridge University Press, 1996.

———. "Introduction." In *Aphra Behn Studies,* edited by Janet Todd, 1–12. New York: Cambridge University Press, 1996.

———. "Who is Silvia? What is She? Feminine Identity in Aphra Behn's *Love-Letters Between a Nobleman and His Sister.*" In *Aphra Behn Studies,* edited by Janet Todd, 199–218. New York: Cambridge University Press, 1996.

Undank, Jack. "Graffigny's Room of Her Own." *French Forum* 13, no. 3 (1988): 297–318.

Vanpée, Janie. "From Graffigny's *Lettres d'une Péruvienne* to Leila Sebbar's and Nancy Huston's *Lettres parisiennes*: Figuring Cultural Displacement." *Dalhousie French Studies* 61 (2002): 135–146.

Vermeule, Blakey. *Why Do We Care about Literary Characters?* Baltimore: Johns Hopkins University Press, 2011.

Vigar, Penelope. *The Novels of Thomas Hardy: Illusion and Reality.* London: Athlone Press, 1974.

Visconsi, Eliot. "A Degenerate Race: English Barbarism in Aphra Behn's *Oroonoko* and *The Widow Ranter.*" *ELH* 69, no. 3 (2002): 673–701.

Warner, Michael. *Publics and Counterpublics.* New York: Zone Books, 2005.

Watt, Ian. *The Rise of the Novel: Studies in Defoe, Richardson, and Fielding*. Berkeley: University of California Press, 1964.

Went-Daoust, Yvette, ed. *Isabelle de Charrière (Belle de Zuylen): De la correspondance au roman épistolaire*. Amsterdam and Atlanta, GA: CRIN, 1995.

Whatley, Janet. "The Eighteenth-Century Canon: Works Lost and Found." *French Review* 61 (1988): 414–420.

Wike, Jonathan. "The World as Text in Hardy's Fiction." *Nineteenth-Century Literature* 47, no. 4 (1993): 455–471.

Williams, Bernard. *Shame and Necessity*. Berkeley: University of California Press, 1993.

Williams, Daniel. "Rumor, Reputation, and Sensation in *Tess of the D'Urbervilles*." *NOVEL: A Forum on Fiction* 46, no. 1 (2013): 93–115.

Williams, Raymond. "The Educated Observer and the Passionate Participant." In *Hardy: The Tragic Novels*, edited by R. P. Draper, 94–105. London: Macmillan, 1975.

Woloch, Alex. *The One vs. the Many: Minor Characters and the Space of the Protagonist in the Novel*. Princeton, NJ: Princeton University Press, 2003.

Woolf, Virginia. *Mrs. Dalloway*. London: Harcourt, 1981 [1925].

———. "The Novels of Thomas Hardy." In *Hardy: The Tragic Novels*, edited by R. P. Draper, 73–79. London: Macmillan, 1975.

———. *The Waves*. New York: Harvest Books, 1978.

Yang, Chi-ming. "Asia Out of Place: The Aesthetics of Incorruptibility in Behn's *Oroonoko*." *Eighteenth-Century Studies* 42, no. 2 (2009): 235–253.

Yeazell, Ruth. "The Lighting Design of Hardy's Novels." *Nineteenth-Century Literature* 64, no. 1 (2009): 48–75.

Young, Elizabeth V. "Aphra Behn, Gender, and Pastoral." *Studies in English Literature, 1500–1900* 33, no. 3 (1993): 523–543.

Zunshine, Lisa. *Why We Read Fiction: Theory of Mind and the Novel*. Columbus: Ohio State University Press, 2006.

INDEX

adultery, 99
aesthetic enthusiasm, 147
aesthetic representation, 79
agency: letters and, 51; of Tess, 102
Albertine (fictional character),
 152–55, 156
Alec D'Urberville (fictional character), 106,
 121; child with, 101–2
Angel Clare (fictional character), 91–92, 99,
 102, 116, 121, 123
Aphra Behn's Afterlife (Spencer), 23n4
Arabella (fictional character), 104, 111,
 119, 124
aristocratic proto-novels, 53
Armstrong, Nancy, 8, 17, 83; aesthetic
 representation and, 79; Charrière
 and, 51; cultural development and,
 49; Graffigny and, 51; on letter-
 writing, 64; on literary history, 67;
 on *Pamela*, 50; writing as power
 and, 59
Arnold, Matthew, 114
The Art of Fiction (James), 12n14, 129
Austen, Jane, 6, 59, 75n39
Austin, Linda, 117n61
Australia, 110
awareness: interpersonal, 2, 7;
 mutual, 120
Aza (fictional character), 54–55, 56;
 infidelity of, 64

Ballaster, Ros, 26
Balzac, Honoré de, 88
beauty, 132, 160, 169; Hardy and, 122n73;
 of luxury items, 30; open-mindedness
 and, 135; Pater and, 122n73;
 perceptiveness and, 135; Scarry and,
 130, 131, 135; sharing experiences of,
 19; sites of, 8; of Zilia, 62
Beckett, Samuel, 132n6
Behn, Aphra, 1, 20, 53, 62n23, 88, 164;
 empiricism and, 16; material world and,
 88; narratives of, 17, 36, 40; romance and,
 16; social world and, 88. *See also Oroonoko*
Bergotte, 159
Bersani, Leo, 148, 157
Best, Stephen, 7n9
Bildung, 105
Bildungsroman, 7
Blake, Kathleen, 122
The Body in Pain (Scarry), 151
Booth, Wayne, 13
Bostic, Heidi, 53n6
Bouvard and Pécuchet (Flaubert), 170
Brazil, 110
Brontë, Charlotte, 88
Butler, Judith, 8, 97, 99, 123; bodies and,
 94, 94n7; embodied selfhood and, 93;
 Hardy and, 95, 95n10; narratives and,
 126; performativity and, 19, 93; self-
 expression and, 95n9

INDEX